Language Strategies for Bilingual Families

PARENTS' and TEACHERS' GUIDES
Series Editor: Professor Colin Baker, *University of Wales, Bangor, Wales, Great Britain*

The Care and Education of a Deaf Child: A Book for Parents
Pamela Knight and Ruth Swanwick
Dyslexia: A Parents' and Teachers' Guide
Trevor Payne and Elizabeth Turner
Guía para padres y maestros de niños bilingües
Alma Flor Ada and Colin Baker
Making Sense in Sign: A Lifeline for a Deaf Child
Jenny Froude
A Parents' and Teachers' Guide to Bilingualism
Colin Baker
Second Language Students in Mainstream Classrooms
Coreen Sears

Other Books of Interest
The Care and Education of Young Bilinguals: An Introduction to Professionals
Colin Baker
Encyclopedia of Bilingualism and Bilingual Education
Colin Baker and Sylvia Prys Jones
Understanding Deaf Culture: In Search of Deafhood
Paddy Ladd

Please contact us for the latest book information:
Multilingual Matters, Frankfurt Lodge, Clevedon Hall,
Victoria Road, Clevedon, BS21 7HH, England
http://www.multilingual-matters.com

PARENTS' AND TEACHERS' GUIDES 7
Series Editor: Colin Baker

Language Strategies for Bilingual Families

The One-Parent-One-Language Approach

Suzanne Barron-Hauwaert

MULTILINGUAL MATTERS LTD
Clevedon • Buffalo • Toronto

Library of Congress Cataloging in Publication Data
Barron-Hauwaert, Suzanne.
Language Strategies for Bilingual Families: The One-Parent-One-Language Approach
Suzanne Barron-Hauwaert, 1st ed.
Parents' and Teachers' Guides No. 7
Includes bibliographical references and index.
1. Bilingualism in children. 2. Family–Language. I. Title. II. Series.
P115.2.B37 2004
306.44'6–dc22   2003017736

British Library Cataloguing in Publication Data
A catalogue entry for this book is available from the British Library.

ISBN 1-85359-715-5 (hbk)
ISBN 1-85359-714-7 (pbk)

Multilingual Matters Ltd
UK: Frankfurt Lodge, Clevedon Hall, Victoria Road, Clevedon BS21 7HH.
USA: UTP, 2250 Military Road, Tonawanda, NY 14150, USA.
Canada: UTP, 5201 Dufferin Street, North York, Ontario M3H 5T8, Canada.

Typeset by Florence Production Ltd.
Printed and bound in Great Britain by the Cromwell Press Ltd.

Contents

Introduction

About the Book ix

The Organisation of the Book xi

The Study and Parents' Contribution to this Book xii

My Background xiv

Notes xv

1 The One-Parent-One-Language Approach. What is it?

Part One: The Origins of the OPOL Approach – Maurice Grammont
and his Advice to Ronjat 1

From Grammont to OPOL 3

Research Done on Child Bilingualism 5

What the Parents Think About OPOL 7

Part Two: Mixing and Code-Switching Within the OPOL Approach 10

Mixing and Code-Switching and Parental Acceptance 12

Parental Language Use With Their Children 15

What Do The Parents Think About Mixing . . . ? 17

Summary 22

**2 The First Three Years and Establishing the One-Parent-One-Language
Approach**

Part One: Very Young Children and Language Learning 23

Bonding and Talking to a New Baby in Two Languages –
Motherese and Fatherese 25

Consistent Language Use at Home 27

Getting Advice and Increasing Exposure to One Language 28

Part Two: Stages of Development and the Emerging Bilingual 30

Language Differentiation – 'Mummy says Milk, *Papa dit lait*' 31

Language Refusal and Reluctance to Talk in Young Children 33

The False Monolingual Strategy 36

Summary 40

3 Starting School and Becoming Bicultural – One-Culture-One-Person?

    Part One: The Parent's Choice of School 48
    Monolingual School Environment 50
    Parental Involvement 51
    Homework 52
    Foreign Language Classes in a Parental Language or a
        Third Language 53
    Gender Differences 54
    The Effect of the Peer Group 57
    Part Two: The Cultural Heritage of the Parents 59
    Importance of Culture for the Parents 61
    Bicultural Identity and Anomie 66
    How Our Children Reacted to Growing Up with Two (or More)
        Cultures 68
    Summary 69

4 Interaction Between Family Members and the One-Person-One-Language Approach

    Part One: Conversations With Both Parents and the Children 77
    Linguistic Ability of the Parents 82
    Part Two: Grandparents and their Support 83
    Grandparents and their Linguistic Role 85
    What Parents Said About Their Extended Family 87
    Part Three: Studies on Siblings 92
    Siblings and Their Use of Language Together 94
    Effect on Language Proficiency by Having a Sibling 96
    Cousins and Same-Age Friends 97
    Part Four: Communication With the Outside World and Visitors 99
    What the Parents Said About Group Language Use 100
    Summary 102

5 One-Parent-One-Language Families – Expectations and the Reality

    Part One: An Ideal World vs the Reality of the OPOL Family 109
    The Parents Beliefs About Bilingualism 111
    Advantages and Disadvantages 113
    Differences Between Mothers and Fathers 117
    The Prestige Value of One Language 120
    Part Two: Testing Times for the Bilingual Family 122
    Feeling Isolated and Excluded Within the Family 123
    One-Parent Families 127
    Speech Problems 129
    Summary 131

6 Living With Three or More Languages ... One-Parent-Two-Languages (or More)

Part One: Defining Trilingualism and Multilingualism 138
   Trilingual Family Case Studies 141
   Autobiographical Studies 144
   Parent's Viewpoints of Being Part of a Multilingual Family 145
   What Do the Parents Think About Trilingualism? 146
Part Two: 1999 Survey – Issues Surrounding Multilingual Families 149
   (a) Dominant Languages Within the Family: Country-Language
      vs Family-Language 151
   (b) Language Use Within the Home 152
   (c) Education of the Trilingual Child 153
   (d) Living With Three Cultures 154
   Conclusions: One-Parent-Two-Languages (or More ...) 155
Summary 156

7 Seven Strategies for Language Use Within the Family

Part One: The Parents' Options Within the Family 163
   (1) OPOL – ML (Majority-Language Strongest) 165
   (2) OPOL – mL (Minority-Language Supported By
      the Other Parent) 167
   (3) Minority-Language at Home (mL@H) 169
   (4) Trilingual Strategy 170
   (5) Mixed Strategy 172
   (6) Time and Place Strategy 175
   (7) The 'Artificial' or 'Non-Native' Strategy 177
Part Two: Changing Strategies To Suit the Circumstances 178
   The Parent's Choice of Strategy 180
   The Parent's Comments Regarding Changing Strategies 182
Summary 184

8 The One-Parent-One-Language Approach in the Twenty-First Century

From Grammont and OPOL – 100 Years On 192
Allow Some Mixing at Young Age and Encourage Later
Code-Switching 192
Consistent OPOL in the Early Years 193
The Possible Effects of School and Peer Pressure on
Language Use 193
Extended Family Involvement and Gaining Their Support 194
Trilingual and Multilingual Families 194
Parents as Role Models 194
Choose a Strategy to Support the Minority-Language 195
OPOL for the Twenty-First Century 195

Appendixes

Appendix 1: Studies on Bilingual Children 198
Appendix 2: The 2001 OPOL Questionaire 201
Appendix 3: Parent's Nationalities and Country of Residence 205
Appendix 4: Case Study Families List 207

Sources of Information for Bilingual Families 209
Glossary 211
References 215
Index 220

Introduction

About the Book

This book is a result of six years of being part of a bilingual family and a researcher into trilingualism and bilingualism. I first heard about the one-person-one-language approach from friends with bilingual children and from the children whom I taught English as a second language to. It was promoted as the 'best' parental strategy and was already lodged in my mind when our first child was born in 1997. I had seen it put into practice and truly believed that the *only* way to raise a child was with two languages. We quickly put it into practice, with a combination of natural language use and strict arrangement of language exposure, but as I watched our children develop I realised there were many unanswered questions.

This book, therefore, aims to look in depth at the issues surrounding the almost mythological approach and see if it really works. It is often claimed that the one-person-one-language or OPOL approach is a rather elitist strategy, chosen mainly by parents in a high socio-economic group. Often the parents both speak the majority-language of the community where they live. They are often well integrated in that community too, choosing a local school and encouraging friendships with local children. Therefore contact with the other language or minority-language is restricted, and needs extra effort to help the child acquire and maintain it. Over the last century parents have been confused by negative attitudes in society towards bilingualism and it's potential damaging effects. Even just a generation ago a person marrying and moving to his or her partner's country would be strongly encouraging to 'drop' their language for the children's benefit. Now we appear to have reached a more realistic appraisal – accepting there are some areas like mixing, language-delay and being at home in both cultures, which may take time to resolve. The benefits easily outweigh these, such as higher cognitive skills, an awareness of language and it's structure and sensitivity to other people's speech and culture.

I wanted to find out if one-person-one-language or any other specific language strategy is as important and relevant as the books and guidance for parents suggest. I researched previous studies done on families using the OPOL approach. I particularly wanted to discover whether any factors affect the success of the approach. The ten questions, which I decided to investigate more, were:

---

(1) Should the family follow a strict OPOL strategy or mix languages when talking to the child?
(2) Can the parents' linguistic ability affect the child's language use?
(3) Is the language of the country where the family live strongest for the child?
(4) Do siblings change language use within the family?
(5) Does it matter what language the parents speak together?
(6) What kind of school do parents choose for their bilingual children?
(7) Are the parent's attitudes to the other language and culture an important factor?
(8) What role does the extended family play in helping the child become bilingual?
(9) What kind of resources and language teaching should parents do to ensure a balanced input and active use of both languages?
(10) Is there a difference between very young bilinguals and older school-age children?

What kind of bilingual family am I referring to? A bilingual family is something we can never really pin down to a definition. It is a mixture of at least two languages or dialects and two or more cultures. The parents may be from widely differing backgrounds or have a lot in common. They may have from one to six children, with varying degrees of sibling success and failure in becoming bilingual. Their circumstances, country of residence and choice of school can change from year to year and some lead nomadic lives or are expatriates. In nearly all the families one parent is away from their home country and culture.

Important decisions on language policy and the strategy within the family are usually made along the way, with changes brought in when one language appears under-used or age-related issues may force a rethinking of how the languages are shared and valued. Children from bilingual families usually appear to be very adaptable, accepting and open to change. Contrary to many (mainly monocultural) opinions, they can live quite happily with two or more languages and benefit from this. They can also cope with two cultures and enjoy seeing two sides to life. They can manage bilingual schooling and are usually able to learn to become both articulate and literate in both languages. Most importantly children learn to have an emotional link with each language, which gives them the impetus to use that language and inspires them to learn and use each language as much as possible.

I believe that OPOL does have an important role to play in the bilingual family. However, several factors have to be taken into account before assuming that it will guarantee bilingual children. OPOL is not the only way to bring up children bilingually and it should be adapted to suit each family. It deserves closer examination and analysis of how it can be appropriate for each individual family. Throughout this book I use examples from families, data from a survey on over a 100 families and current research on bilingualism and multilingualism. The academic information is important as it often forms the basis of advice given to bilingual families and the field of bilingualism has recently made great progress in showing the interaction of children and parents using two or more languages.

The Organisation of the Book

I begin with a review of what OPOL actually is in Chapter 1. Where did the term come from? How has it evolved over the century? What does it mean for different academics and current researchers? The three early linguists credited with putting OPOL on the map in terms of bilingual parenting are Maurice Grammont, Louis Ronjat and Werner Leopold. They are discussed in detail and their legacy to dual-language families examined. I also look at other famous case studies such as George Saunders, Traute Taeschner and Susanne Dökpe alongside definitions of OPOL by current academics. Furthermore, in Chapter 1, I take a closer look at the mixing of languages and code-switching – the very thing that OPOL is supposed to prevent. We examine what the parents think OPOL actually is and how they perceive it within the family.

Chapter 2 deals with the first three years of a bilingual child's life and the emerging languages. The importance of the use of each language from the beginning is highlighted along with parental linguistic features such as motherese and fatherese. The issue of a young child's refusal to actually use a language, or passive language, are part of this chapter, along with some case studies showing how parents are dealing with some of the difficulties of having a young bilingual child. The strong link of parent to child is emphasised, particularly the mother in the beginning and later on, the father. Case studies tell us of parents just starting out and their hopes and plans for the future.

We then move onto the school-age children in Chapter 3, who are more influenced by their peer group than their parents. As they grow emotionally and physically their language needs change and the emphasis switches to a cultural input rather than a linguistic one. This age group can also refuse to use a language or become passive, depending on their motivation and exposure to a language. The way the parents in the study pass on their language through their culture is described. Some case studies in this chapter show a wide cultural gap, between for example a Japanese wife and an English husband and how they deal with that and form a bicultural identity.

The extended family is the main subject of Chapter 4. We examine the siblings, the grandparents and other family members such as aunts and cousins and their effect on language use. The parents' comments and case studies showing how grandparents and families have affected a child's bilingualism confirm the attitudes and support these extended family members bring. There are case studies about grandparents and families who were closely involved in helping the child.

I wanted to include the trilingual and multilingual families too, as they often follow a kind of OPOL approach and need advice too. Chapter 5 details the different types of multilingual families and looks at how they deal with three or more languages in the home. This chapter also includes a study I did in 1999 on ten trilingual families and their children. Case studies report the reality of a trilingual family and families reflect how different it is to a bilingual one.

In Chapter 6 we look at the often under-rated issue of parental attitudes and discuss the effect a positive outlook on the other parents' language and culture can have on a child's future bilingualism. In this section I also examine the effect of feminine and masculine role models and how they could affect language use. Some difficulties of being a bilingual family are discussed such as feelings of isolation and of being left out, children's speech problems and the bigger issues of family separation or divorce or death of a parent. I compare the 'ideal' family situation to a more typical family as a way to show that often our ideals are often higher that the real state of affairs in a family.

I describe types of parental strategies in Chapter 7. The OPOL approach itself can have different emphasis depending on country of residence or parents' language use and we look at these features. I also talk about other approaches such as Minority-Language at Home, Time and Place, Trilingual and Mixed Language strategies. Several case studies show these strategies in action with families using a third language between them for communication or separating languages according to location.

Chapter 8 gives a working model of OPOL for the twenty-first century. The needs of the parents, children and extended family can now be balanced along-side modern parenting practices and beliefs, which were not around 100 years ago when OPOL was first discussed. I think that it is vital to have some kind of strategy in place but with a flexibility and adaptation to suit each family member and age of the children. As we adapt our parenting styles to suit the age and cognitive level of the child, the language policy should also grow and evolve progressively with less emphasis on strict partition and more on an appropriate language usage to suit the circumstances of the global world we now live in.

There is a list of previous studies done on child bilingualism and multilingualism in Appendix 1: Studies on Bilingual Children, and a bibliography for those who want to research or read more about the subject. Further reading and related websites are at the end of the book too. Chapter 1 gives information on the most important case-studies written about bilingual children, and links to relevant journals and newsletters.

Finally, towards the end of the book there is a Glossary section. Readers are advised to consult this section for an explanation of any terms they may not be familiar with.

The Study and Parents' Contribution to this Book

This book is not only a review of academic research done on families living with two languages; it also includes real-life families bringing up their children bilingually and multilingually. In 2001 I contacted various families around the world through *The Bilingual Family Newsletter* and an Internet bilingual chat-list (*Biling-fam*) who were willing to complete a questionnaire about the OPOL approach. The actual questionnaire can be seen in Appendix 2: The 2001 OPOL Questionnaire. The questionnaire was available in a postal version or online and I asked specifically for both parents to complete their own part of the questionnaire so I could compare both maternal and paternal attitudes and strategies. There was no specific age range for children, but in general they ranged from one year-old up to adult age. The majority were in the pre-school age-group (aged two-and-a-half to five years) or primary school (age 5 to 11 years) age range (see Figure I.1).

The questionnaire was in English, which did restrict some parents who did not speak English. I had a wide range of over 30 nationalities and languages, with English being the majority-language, living in 21 different countries. The nationality of both parents and country of residence for all the families can be seen in Appendix 3: Parent's Nationalities and Country of Residence.

The final number of completed questionnaires was nearly 120. About 25 were disqualified from the data processing as they were only filled in by one parent. However, I have still used their comments in the book, as they are interesting and valid. Of the fully completed questionnaires with both mother and father filling in a part, I had a total of 93 couples and 156 children. These families and children were used for the statistical graphs and data tables that you see throughout the book.

Later on in 2002, I selected 30 families who I thought were a particular example of OPOL or other parental strategies. They encompassed a wide range of languages, nationalities and styles of family language parenting. I interviewed them either in person, mainly those living in England who were available to meet me, or by means of an informal email chat, where families were asked to tell me more about certain interesting comments they had made in the questionnaire. These case studies are linked to chapters, so there are families who have very young families, ones with school-age children, trilingual families, families where the grandparents or extended family play an important role or families who have experienced some difficulties

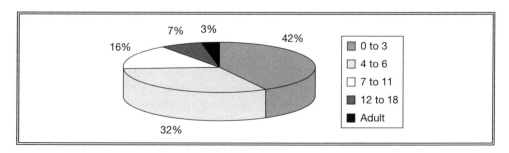

Figure I.1 Age range of children in the study

in bringing up their children bilingually. All together they form a fascinating snap-shot of a real bilingual's families worries, success stories and experience gained over time. The case studies are linked to a particular chapter but often overlap so they can be relevant to more than one area. Appendix 4: Case Study Families List lists all the families and the areas that they are relevant to, such as young families or trilingual families.

My Background

After taking my first degree in art and design in 1993 I retrained as a teacher of English as a foreign language. I wanted to travel and work at the same time and this seemed a good way to combine my creativity and interest in other cultures. I taught English to both adults and children in Japan, Poland and Budapest. One such job was supporting English as a second language with primary school chil-dren in an international school. Several children came from bilingual families and I was fascinated when I met the family in parent-teacher consultations as to how two languages would be used. There was often rapid code-switching, translation if necessary or both parents would speak excellent English to me. The children came to me for daily extra tuition but usually were up to standard after one or two school years. I noticed that they rapidly forgot their minority-language as the pressure to keep up with their English-speaking friends and please their teachers and parents motivated them to speak English.

I had not really considered my own potential bilingual family very much until our first-born son, Marc, arrived in 1997 in Budapest, Hungary. My French husband, Jacques and I had always spoken English because I lacked confidence in speaking French, although I understood it. We began as many couples do, each wanting the other one to keep their language and enjoying seeing the other partner using their own language with the new baby and forming a close bond. As new parents were just happy when he babbled and cooed at us and we both heard our own language in these early attempts at communication. We didn't really consider that the outside language might have any effect at this point. A few years on, after postings to Egypt and Switzerland, we had our second child, Nina, who was born in Zurich in 1999. Marc was a late talker and we began to wonder if our strategy was in fact the best way to help him become bilingual. I was studying for a Master's degree in education, by distance learning, as a way to combine motherhood with gaining more knowledge about teaching. The course included language and linguistics and I decided to write my final dissertation on language use within trilingual families, where each parent spoke a different language and then lived in a third language country as we were doing. This brought up many questions of parental language use, attitudes, choice of school language and living within two or more cultures. At home with the children I saw first-hand Marc's and Nina's verbal frustration, especially with the extended family, their delay in talking and confusion over what to do or say sometimes. Furthermore, my previously low-level French skills had improved as I heard Jacques speaking more French and I spent more time with my in-laws. Our language uses had changed over the years and we were mixing more and finding it harder to implement the OPOL approach strictly.

Chatting informally to other parents in similar situations I began to compile a list of unanswered questions about how to bring up our children bilingually. As a writer on bilingualism and member of the Editorial Board for *The Bilingual Family Newsletter* from 1999 onwards, I saw clearly the concerns and worries that parents had about how to best chose and implement a parental language strategy. Letters asking for advice on language mixing, speech problems, school issues and dealings with the extended family confirmed my hunch that parental strategies, especially the infamous OPOL one, needed more investigation. Finally, in 2001, I attended a conference on bilingualism in Bristol, south-west England and proposed my idea for a book for parents to the Multilingual Matters team. It would bring together previous studies, current research and questions parents ask and their own opinions and family stories. This is the result and I hope it goes some way to answering your questions and doubts about OPOL too.

Notes

1. When referring to each language I use the words 'majority-language' for the language of the community or country where the family live.
2. When referring to the 'minority-language' it is the one only used by one parent. There is no reference to a particular language having less prestige or value.
3. The one-person-one-language and one-parent-one-language approaches are frequently referred to as 'OPOL' throughout the book.
4. Bilingual family languages are listed as 'Mother/Father'. For example, in my case it would be English/French.
5. Trilingual languages are listed as 'Mother/Father/Community' language. For example, if we lived in Germany it would be English/French/German.

Chapter 1

The One-Parent-One-Language Approach. What is it?

In the first part of this chapter we look at the origins of the one-parent-one-language (OPOL) approach. Who first coined the phrase? How has it changed over the last century? Who were the early pioneers of child bilingualism? We hear about Jules Ronjat and Werner Leopold, and how their detailed notes on their children helped us see how a child becomes bilingual. Several decades later several linguists such as George Saunders, Traute Taeschner and Charlotte Hoffmann produced more case studies, giving us fascinating insights into a child's life with two or more languages. What do modern parents think OPOL is and how do they apply it within their families? We hear their comments and views on OPOL nowadays.

The second part of the chapter investigates mixing and code-switching in children, which can cause conflict within bilingual families. Should a child mix languages? Is code-switching acceptable or useful? When does language mixing become code-switching? We hear what parents think about their children's code-switching alongside some studies of this linguistic behaviour. Most important is the recent approach of looking at the whole family's interactions and how each parent or sibling can affect a child's choice of using one language or switching.

Part One: The Origins of the OPOL Approach – Maurice Grammont and his Advice to Ronjat

The original term came from a French linguist, Maurice Grammont, who published a book in 1902 titled *Observations sur le langage des enfants* (*Observations on Children's Language*), in which he introduced the idea of *une personne; une langue*. Literally translated from the French as one person; one language, Grammont theorised that by strictly separating the two languages from the beginning the child would subsequently learn both languages easily without too much confusion or mixing of languages. By associating each language with a specific person the chances of mixing languages are significantly reduced. Furthermore, by using his or her own language each parent gives an example of adult language use. They also have the opportunity to form a natural emotional relationship with the child through their language.

1

Several years later Grammont's friend and fellow linguist Jules Ronjat sought advice from him. Ronjat was married to a German national living in Paris and they had a son, Louis, born in 1908, whom they wished to bring up bilingually. Ronjat reports Grammont's advice (1913: 3):

> Nothing has to be taught to the child. You must simply speak to him, when there is something to be said, in one of the two languages that you want him to learn. But there is a key factor, and that is that each language must be represented by a different person, you, for example always speak French to him, his mother German. Never reverse these roles. In this way, when he begins to speak he will speak the two languages without being conscious of doing so and without having made any special effort to learn them. (Translated from French).

Ronjat went on to record and transcribe Louis' language development until he was four years and ten months old. He then published this linguistic biography in *Le Developpement du langage: observe chez un enfant bilingue* (*The Development of Language: Observations of a Bilingual Child*). Ronjat recommended what he called the *Grammont Formula* in his description of Louis' positive child bilingualism. He cited the continual use at home of two languages from birth as a major factor in achieving bilingualism and noted that Louis had acquired and mastered two languages in a similar phonological order to that of the average monolingual child. The child learnt German from both his mother and his German nanny, and French from the father and from the French-speaking community he grew up in. Ronjat also spoke German to his wife thus giving her linguistic support as the minority speaker. Louis rarely mixed languages and after age of three was clearly aware of the difference in his two languages and would change languages to adjust to the person he was talking to. We even have some information on Louis Ronjat as a teenager, aged 15; he apparently remained bilingual throughout preferring to read in German and take his school examinations in French.

In the 1920s and 1930s several laboratory studies showed bilingualism to be negative because it risked overloading a child's mental capacity. These studies have now been disqualified due to dubious research techniques and IQ testing in only one language, which was unsuitable and unfair for young children. The only other well-documented study of this period was by Pavlovitch, a Serbian linguist, living in Paris with his Serbian wife. He compiled a one-year study in 1920 on his own son, Dusan. He recorded data from the age of 13 months onwards on Dusan, who had previously only heard Serbian from his parents. They then employed a close family friend to speak only French to the child for several hours a day. The child subsequently spoke good French, although in this case it was quite a probable outcome as the family was living in Paris. Nonetheless it shows the effect that a close one-to-one relationship can have and how it can facilitate language learning.

Twenty years later the same parental strategy of *une personne; une langue* was successfully applied by another parent-linguist Werner Leopold, who was familiar with Ronjat's case study. Leopold himself was born in London to German parents, who moved back to Germany when he was three years old. After completing his schooling in German he moved to America and married a third-generation German-American. When their first daughter, Hildegard, was born in 1930 they decided to bring her up bilingually. Leopard spoke only German while his wife spoke English although she understood and could speak German. In fact, in comparison to the Ronjat family, there were several changes in parental language use within the Leopold house with Werner frequently using English and his wife using German when holidaying in Germany. Although Mrs Leopold understood German she preferred not to speak it in America, but nonetheless did use it when visiting family in Germany.

Leopold's diary study from age two months to age seven (with additional observations up to age 14) formed a famous four-volume series of books published from 1939–49 describing Hildegard's progress in the acquisition of two languages. Apart from a three-month visit to Germany when she was a year old, her father was the only source of German for Hildegard. Her father's dedication in supporting Hildegard's language learning paid off and like Louis Ronjat she acquired both English and German at similar levels to a child of her own age. She mixed languages briefly as a young child but soon grew out of it and by the age of about three was able to select the right language according to who she was talking to. When almost five she spent several months in Germany and had no problems to communicate with family and friends there.

We also have some information on Hildegard aged 15 too; by this point she was reluctant to use German and it had become the weaker language as factors such as friends, school and her life in America dominated her life. Her younger sister, Karla, six years younger than Hildegard, unfortunately did not achieve as much success as her sister and Leopold (1949b: 159) described her, aged five: '(Karla's) German is extremely limited. She scatters some German words over her English sentences when she speaks to me, as a sort of concession to my way of speaking.' However, at age 19, Karla went to Germany by herself and was perfectly able to converse with the locals. So all the effort had been worth it in the end and her passive German knowledge became active in the right linguistic environment.

Since Leopold's immense study there was a gap of about 30 years while linguists applied themselves to studying first language acquisition and language learning. Pioneers in the 1960s and 1970s, such as Roger Brown who pinpointed the stages of language acquisition in a child and Noam Chomsky who proposed an innate knowledge of grammar eclipsed the bilingual children research for a while. But around 1980 the interest resumed and several new interpretations of *une personne; une langue* became evident.

From Grammont to OPOL . . .

The anglicised version of the term became common within linguist circles and was in frequent use in books and articles by the 1980s as a way to describe a child being brought up as a simultaneous bilingual. Typically, this is a child learning both languages at the same time from parents using two different languages right from birth). Here are some examples from well-known researchers working in the fields of linguistics, sociolinguistics and child bilingualism, which show the evolution of the original term:

Variations on the Terms:

une-personne; une langue	Grammont (1902)
The Grammont Formula	Ronjat (1913)
Grammont Formula: one person; one language	Schmidt-Mackay (1971)
Ronjat's one parent, one language principle	Bain and Yu (1980)
one-parent-one-language principle	Döpke (1992a)
one-person-one-language system	Saunders (1982)
one-person/one-language principle	Taeschner (1983)
one-person/one-language procedure	Taeschner (1983)
one-person/one-language strategy	Arnberg (1987)
one-person-one-language method	Romaine (1995)
one-person-one-language approach	Lyon (1996)
one-person-one-language strategy	Lanza (1992)
one-person-one-language policy	Juan-Garau and Perez-Vidal (2001)
Grammont's one-parent-one-language rule	Hamers and Blanc (2000)
Grammont's Principle	Hamers and Blanc (2000)
OPOL	*The Bilingual Family Newsletter* (1996)
OPOL	Bilingual website (2000)

As we can see, along the way it has been adapted to suit the author. The terms that have been added on along the way are very strong, such as Principle, System, Strategy, Procedure, Rule or Policy and imply strict adherence. The only exception to this is Approach, which I prefer myself as it seems less rule-bound. Grammont is mentioned a few times, particularly by Hamers and Blanc (2000) although it was once attributed to Ronjat by Bain and Yu. The most striking difference is the inclusion of the word 'parent' as opposed to 'person'. Which began around 1980. This minor but significant change could affect the success of the approach since it implies that the parent is the only linguistic role model in the child's world. Grammont chose to label it *une personne; une langue* with the wider implication that it could be any person – an extended family member or employee such as a nanny who only uses one language too. The final stage is to abbreviate the sometimes wordy 'one person; one language' and make it OPOL, as seen on bilingual family websites and in *The Bilingual Family Newsletter*. Although we don't always know if the 'P' stands for *Parent* or *Person*.

Research Done on Child Bilingualism

In most case studies of children growing up bilingually with simultaneous acquisition of two languages we see the term OPOL being used. So what exactly does the OPOL approach mean for these researchers? How have recent researchers redefined the term in accordance with their own insights and research? We look at some of the most prolific authors on child bilingualism and their comments on the OPOL approach.

Josiane Hamers and Michel Blanc (2000: 51) in *Bilinguality and Bilingualism* describe it as 'Grammont's Principle. . . . According to which each adult should use exclusively his or her mother tongue with the child.' They also clarify that the Principle is only an 'assumption' given credence by child biographers such as Ronjat and Leopold, and 'lacking in psycholinguistic proof'. They add that it has been 'adopted as a proven rule rather than as a hypothesis'. Hamers and Blanc cite two studies, which found no differences between families using the OPOL approach and those who did not (Bain & Yu, 1980; Doyle *et al.*, 1977). They propose that the child's social networks and available linguistic role models are more important for developing bilingualism in a child.

Suzanne Romaine (1995: 193) discusses the 'one-person-one-language method' in her book *Bilingualism*. She labels this kind of family Type 1, saying: 'The parents have different native languages with each having some degree of competence in the other's language. The language of one of the parents is the dominant language of the community. The parents each speak their own language to the child from birth.' Romaine also mentions that the most common outcome of the OPOL method is children who can understand both languages but only speak the language of the community where they live. This is particularly true if the language is a minority and only spoken by one parent for example. She notes that the success stories such as Ronjat and Leopold describe children whose parents are often educated linguists adding 'The majority of detailed longitudinal studies . . . deal with elitist or additive bilingualism.' Romaine concludes that quality of language input, especially from the fathers, is more important that quantity.

Leonore Arnberg (1987: 87) in her book *Raising Children Bilingually*, aimed predominantly at parents, agreed with Romaine over the issue of supporting the minority-language through the 'one-parent/one language strategy'. Leonore cautioned that '. . . it is of my opinion that the best results will be achieved if both parents use the minority-language when addressing one another. In this way hearing spoken language the child's exposure to the minority-language is increased. In the case of a minority-language, that the other parent simply cannot or will not learn, then the minority speaking parent must be "absolutely consistent" in their language use to the child or the child will lose motivation and use the majority-language with both parents.' Arnberg also points out the difficulty of maintaining consistency for the minority speaker, for example, when talking to people in the community or not embarrassing their child by sounding very different in public. She mentions a study by Ramjoue (1980), which showed that even young children do accept and understand the reason why a parent has to switch languages when they can see a reason for it.

Colin Baker (2000: 44–5) in his book for parents bringing up children bilingually, *A Parents and Teachers Guide to Bilingualism*, defines the 'one-parent-one-language strategy' as a way of giving clear linguistic boundaries to the child. He notes: 'Experts on bilingualism have traditionally placed stress on the importance of keeping the context of children's languages compartmentalised.' Baker remarks on how the separation of languages makes it easier for a child to know when they should speak which language to which parent. However the choice of language between parents and the language chosen by siblings can make one language more dominant. Like Romaine and Arnberg, he therefore recommends the parents use the minority-language together thus giving the under-used language more exposure.

A parent and linguist Traute Taeschner (1983) wrote a detailed case study on her two German/Italian daughters living in Rome in *The Sun is Feminine: A Study on Language Acquisition in Childhood*. Employing the same style as Ronjat and Leopold she gives numerous examples and diary evidence of Lisa and Giulia and their emerging bilingualism from birth up to five and four years respectively, with further observations up to nine and eight years old. Taeschner is a Brazilian of German origin, who was brought up in a German-Portuguese community and is bilingual herself. She uses only German at home and her husband Italian. Regarding her use of a parental strategy she says (1983: 234): '. . . with the one-person/one-language procedure the child does more than just ensure a consistent source of information. He organizes the world of his knowledge and shares it with the adult . . . which leads to a better understanding between the child and his interlocutors.' Traute also notes that the OPOL stage is temporary, becoming redundant when the child's grammatical errors fade away. After that, the child is more willing to speak either language with either parent, or switch as necessary. Like Louis Ronjat and Hildegard Leopold, Lisa and Giulia appear to have become positive and well-balanced bilinguals by the end of the study.

George Saunders (1982) wrote about his three children in *Bilingual Children: From Birth to Teens*, which is one of the most well known case studies. Saunders is Australian and wished to bring up his children bilingually speaking German, although it is not his native language. Trained in languages and linguistics like Leopold, he took on the task of passing on a minority-language alone and recorded the data from birth to around the age of ten. Although he accepts that it would have been easier if it were the mother who spoke German, since the children have about six times more exposure time to her language use than his, especially at the pre-school age. Nevertheless he persevered and taught German to Frank, Thomas and Katerina almost single-handedly with great success. George Saunders (1982: 49) concludes that consistent use of 'one-person-one-language system' is a 'considerable advantage' because '. . . this ensures that the children have regular exposure to and have to make use of each language. This is particularly important for the minority-language, which has little outside support.'

Susanne Döpke (1992a) in *One-Parent-One-Language: An Interactional Approach* gave several detailed case studies on families in Australia, like Saunders' family, where one parent spoke German and the other English. There were three German native-speaking mothers, two mothers were second-generation German-speakers and one father who spoke German as a foreign language. She followed the progress of six children, who were aged from two years and four months to two years and eight months. Susanne Döpke believes that there are two main factors for successful bilingualism – parents' 'consistent adherence' to the appropriate language and the insistence that the child respects the one parent-one language principle. The two children in her 1992 study, Fiona and Keith, who achieved the highest proficiency scores, did have this consistency and separation within their families. However, it is important to note that both Fiona and Keith had parents who made extra efforts to make contact with German-speaking people, find German books and music and even, in the case of Fiona, organised trips to Austria to meet native-speakers. Döpke, therefore, concludes that a parent who provides enjoyable 'interaction' with a child is more likely to succeed in passing on his or her language. However, Susanne Döpke (1998: 49) recently remarked that the OPOL approach is a 'framework for language choice, not a strategy'. This framework 'provides a macro-structure, which needs to be realised through micro-structure moves'.

There are several journals that also publish articles on child bilingualism and shorter studies on bilingual families that will be mentioned in this book. Some of the most relevant ones are the *Journal of Multilingual and Multicultural Development*, *The International Journal of Bilingualism*, *Journal of Child Language* and *Bilingualism: Language and Cognition*. *The Bilingual Family Newsletter* also has many case-studies and brief descriptions of current research in the field. See the section at the end of the book for a fuller list of journals and the areas they cover. Many of the journals can be accessed online now, or read in a library reading room.

What the Parents Think About OPOL . . .

In my survey of nearly 100 bilingual and trilingual families, I asked the parents what they knew about the OPOL approach. It was an open question so they could write as much as they liked. At least half of the fathers replied 'Nothing!' and several mentioned that their partner had explained the concept to them, which was enough for them. On the other hand, many parents had done some extensive reading and research into the topic. Many families mentioned books, which had given them some guidance, such as Colin Baker's *Parents and Teachers Guide to Bilingualism*. Here is a selection of the parents' comments:

What Exactly is the OPOL Approach?

'It means what it says.'

'It's where each parent speaks their own language to their children.'

'The thing I understand is that you have to insist on talking your own language.'

'Consistency is the key to success, and a lot of varied input in both languages.'

'Each person should stick to their own language exclusively. Although in our family with three languages sometimes it's not really possible.'

'It's the most efficient way to pass on the languages.'

'It's the approach my parents used when I was growing up and I have since done some reading up about it. The two crucial things to me seem to be that: (1) Both parents at least understand the other's language, and (2) They try to stick to their chosen language.'

'One parent uses one language and the other parent uses another. It seems like this approach works best when the minority-language-speaking parent has as much support as possible.'

'This is the most promoted advice for helping kids with learning two languages ... there are families that swear by it and others that are more flexible with continued positive results.

The Best Way to Raise Children Bilingually?

'I did some reading before starting (*c.*1963) and was convinced by that that OPOL was the "safest" way so as not confuse the children. After more than 30 years of practice – still following OPOL today – I can report it has been successful for me and is also the sole reason for my own continued fluency.'

'I heard that it was a good method to raise a child bilingually, but I've never really investigated it.'

'I know it seems to be the preferred method of a lot of bilingual educators/families, and tends to be successful at producing well-balanced bilingual kids.'

'At least in our circumstances (it is) probably the best strategy. Also generally seems to be considered as a good approach.'

'I have heard that many people have been successful with OPOL because each parent consistently uses the language that he or she speaks best. We decided to use OPOL before we knew anything about bilingualism.'

'I have read it's the best strategy to follow, but as my own parents did it I knew it worked.'

'I understand the benefit of each language being identified with a parent.'

'Is the best way to help her learn and separate both languages. . . .'

'It is a very effective way (but not the only way) of bringing up children bilingually.'

'It is usually an effective method. I think that sometimes it is a problem if the father speaks the minority-language – since often fathers are home with the kids less than mothers.'

'We have read that it's the most common approach used by bilingual families. We decided to use it before the birth of our daughter. We use a minority-language for communication between ourselves.'

'A strict method, but successful in our case.'

We Found Out About It From Word of Mouth or Books on Bilingualism . . .

'I read a few articles or books (about OPOL) saying it's positive. I haven't seen anything negative or if I have, ignored it!'

'We heard (about OPOL) from a friend of ours, who has two children – now 11 years old, and asked how they did it.'

'I have read one of Colin Bakers' books about bilingual families and read many comments and opinions in *The Bilingual Family Newsletter*. All this was after we started and just did what came naturally!'

'I heard just a little bit about it on the Internet. The only thing I really know it's the only system we can use and that it means each parent speaks their own language to the children.'

'Prior to (our son's) birth I had read that it was recommended by many experts to be the most effective way to raise a bilingual child. I also had reinforcement from other bilingual families we got to know.'

'Some literature from the Internet, indicating the general approach and benefits of such a method. It's really the only method our family can use, since I do not speak a second language.'

'I knew nothing but I have discussed it with my wife. Also have personal experience of a family (French-German) where a mixed approach did not work – one language was dropped.'

'I heard about it long before the birth of my children, and I have always considered it was the most natural way to bilingualism.'

Adapting OPOL to Suit the Circumstances

'I used it flexibly at first, but found a more pragmatic approach more relevant – though it is still the backbone of our family strategy.'

'It seem to be appropriate in the first years of a child's life, but can successfully be adapted to the family's circumstances later on.'

'It seems to be the thing to do, though I feel it's only really important to start like this. Actually the fun begins when you can mix (the languages) without getting lost and everybody knows which language they are using at any time!'

'It s very effective. I do not think that its that important to stick to it 100 per cent though. I don't want it to be a dogma.'

'We have found it too regimented and restrictive especially in the presence of visitors in the house.'

'I personally don't think this is a viable approach for a family with a minority-language living in a "strong" language environment (i.e. Finnish-speaker in England). It needs some extra Finnish from the other parent.'

'I used to feel uncomfortable speaking my language to my young baby son for the first few months. I have been more successful in speaking the same language to him since he was six months of age, but I still mix the two languages particularly in social situations. I speak the majority-language with my husband.'

Part Two: Mixing and Code-Switching Within the OPOL Approach

When Grammont proposed the one-person-one-language method one of the benefits would be that the child would be *less likely* to mix languages. Mixing of languages has often been seen as a sign of weakness and inability to speak both languages 'properly'. It is particularly offensive to monolinguals who cannot understand the other language or feel excluded by such language use. From a monolingual point of view, the bilingual must have two equal and separate languages. Equally mixing and code-switching can be seem as a laziness and lack of correction from parents leading to 'messy' and incomprehensible speech. It took until the 1980s before mixing and code-switching in children was investigated in detail by researchers such as Meisal (1994), and shown not to be a sign of retarded speech.

Nowadays mixing is a well-documented area of child bilingualism with mixing reported in nearly all case studies in various degrees. We see ourselves as parents that from an early age, children combine words from each language to form hybrid words or short sentences. Suzanne Romaine (1995) confirms that this is 'part of the normal process of growing up bilingually' and nearly all children growing up bilingually go through a stage of mixing. Bilingual families are now able to justify their child's mixing as 'a stage' and feel confident enough to accept. it. They are also able to laugh at some of the more amusing combinations of mixing that bilingual children come up with and see which words the child chooses from each language.

But what exactly is mixing in bilingual children? In the bilingualism literature we see the terms language-mixing, code-mixing and code-switching. Children's early dual language use (usually under two or three years of age) is generally referred to as mixing or language-mixing. These are usually two or three word mixed language sentences. Most language mixing involves lexical items; familiar words from the child's world such as toys, food or close family names. This would be expected, as there are a high percentage of nouns in a young child's vocabulary and a young child has not yet learnt many verbs or adjectives. Some examples of early mixing are given here:

*Das **petit** tiger* (That little tiger) – French/German, 2; 1	(Meisel, 1994: 431)
*Mer **paper*** (More paper) – English/Norwegian, 2; 0	(Lanza, 1992: 643)
*Balloon **vermel*** (Red ballon) – Catalan/English, 2; 3	(Juan-Garau, 2001: 70)

Mixing is often unintentional as the child probably does not know the appropriate word in the other language as in *vermel* or may find a word in one language easier to pronounce than the other like *tiger*. There are overlaps between languages too, such as similar sounding words like *mer*/more, which the child could confuse initially. At this young age, children are usually so keen to communicate and tell the world what they are thinking that they don't stop to think whether it makes sense. Under three-year-olds are cognitively not able to consider whether the person they are talking to understands everything or whether they are using the 'right' language.

As the children grow older their mixing becomes more like adult code-switching. This requires proficiency in both languages and it is a skill that takes time to develop. Jurgen Meisel (1994: 414) an expert on child mixed language use, defines code-switching as:

> ... a specific skill of the bilinguals' pragmatic competence, that is, the ability to select the language according to the interlocutor, the situational context, the topic of the conversation and so forth and to change languages within an interactional sequence in accordance with sociolinguistic rules and without violating specific grammatical constraints.

Some examples of later mixing/code-switching in older children are:

*No, she wants to go for **kai-kai*** (. . . a walk)	– English/Baba Malay, 4; 8 (Foley, 1998: 135)
*Go like this **et apres** foot's clean* (. . . and after . . .)	– French/English, 3; 8 (Jisa, 2000: 1374)
*Sann og ny **diaper*** (Like that and new diaper)	– English/Norwegian, 2; 3 (Lanza, 1992: 650)
*Et puis Pattis a **sein arm gebrochen*** (and then Patti has broken his arm)	– German/French, 3; 7 (Meisel, 1994: 435)
Doch, wir Fleisch . . . fasulye yedik etlan (Yes, we [ate] meat . . . we ate beans with meat)	– Turkish/German, 7; 2 (Pfaff, 1998: 106)

The older code-switching child chooses a language to suit the purpose; it can be because he or she is with another bilingual person or the child wants to talk about something related to one language. Sometimes a certain word has a special relevance for them, like the English/Norwegian child, whose mother is American; she uses the English word 'diaper' specifically, as this is a word associated with the mother. Fred Genesee (1989: 166) commented that: 'Mixing may decline with development, not because separation of the languages is taking place but rather because the children are acquiring more complete linguistic repertoires and, therefore, do not need to borrow or overextend between languages.'

One interesting features of code-switching in children is their ability to use it to effect. As Colin Baker (2000: 48) remarks: 'Children are amazingly adroit at knowing when to switch languages. Partly for this reason, bilinguals seem to have some degree of social sensitivity that monolinguals do not have to have in a social situation.'

He describes it as a 'third subtle language' and notes how code-switching can be used in several different ways: making a point, stressing an argument, reporting a conversation authentically, highlighting a friendship and sometimes to exclude other people from a private conversation. We can see therefore that code-switching is not just a linguistic phenomenon but a social feature which bilinguals, both children and adults, use to create a bond between themselves and other speakers. One important fact to remember is that bilinguals rarely code-switch when monolinguals are present for the simple reason that they would not understand or appreciate it.

Mixing, Code-Switching and Parental Acceptance

A criticism of the early case studies and research done on bilingual children by Ronjat and Leopold is that they rarely reported what the other parent, other siblings or the nanny were saying at the time. Diary extracts usually report on the child conversing with one parent, such as Leopold, in his work on his daughter Hildegard. We have very little information on the dynamics of the whole family or how brothers and sisters talk to each other. Since in the bilingual family one parent needs to speak both languages there is a likelihood that one parent will mix or code-switch languages too. Does this role-model of a parent or a sibling switching languages regularly affect the children's code-switching too?

One of the first researchers to look at such a link between parental mixing and code-switching was Naomi Goodz (1989). She videotaped four French/English children aged from around one to four years with the all the family and came to some interesting conclusions. She reported that in some families mixing can be used as a strategy in itself – to allow easy family communication and in some cases as a way to get attention, discipline or to emphasise a point. Parents with more tolerant or flexible parenting attitudes would accept and even encourage mixing. This, for example would mean that a tolerant parent would allow a child to use language X with a Y-speaking parent either as a mixed sentence or as part of their conversation. Whereas other less tolerant parents would correct the child or take a monolingual stance, using only language Y.

Naomi Goodz (1989) also found that in families where the father is the only minority-language speaker in the family, he often does not support or accept mixing and code-switching in children aged three or more. Assuming that by now the child has a basic grasp of his language the father is more challenging when conversing with the child. He tries to have a more monolingual context with the child and reacts negatively to switching from the child, although he may be bilingual himself. We see that following the one-person-one-language rule is not enough; the minority-speaking father must actively engage with the child and insist on getting the responses he wants from the child.

A short case study done by Satoko Mishima (1999) looked at a minority-speaking mother instead. The subject was a Japanese/English bilingual child, Ken, with a bilingual mother and monolingual English father. She predicted less mixing with the father and more with the mother, which proved to be correct. Mishima (1999: 338) adds that the parent's acceptance or response to mixing was also an important factor saying '... language mixing phenomena are strongly related to how the parents deal with the child's mixing'. In this family the father's (and close family members) lack of knowledge of Japanese supported the monolingual stance and Ken even began using more English with his mother, who readily accepted it.

This is supported by research that Rose-Marie Adjani did on parental language use, which found that the parents' stance on discipline in the home could actually have an effect on the child's use of languages. Her article in *The Bilingual Family Newsletter* (1998, Vol. 15, No. 1) discussed how stricter parenting could lead to more 'language policing' at home and more emphasis placed on using the right language appropriately. Therefore parents with more rigid attitudes would be more against code-switching as a sign of laziness or lack of competence in their language.

Elizabeth Lanza (1992) did a case study on Siri, an English/Norwegian two-year-old and found that the little girl was very sensitive to languages when aged two and could change her language appropriately to suit the situation. Siri rarely mixed languages with her bilingual American mother, who preferred a monolingual inter-action between them. But she mixed with her Norwegian father, who encouraged Siri to speak both English and Norwegian with him. The father was probably trying to help the minority-language mother by speaking English as well. However, the mother often slipped into Norwegian when responding to Siri's requests, and she was often unaware she was code-switching herself. Lanza called this either a *Bilingual–Monolingual Interaction Strategy* with varying levels in-between as we can see below.

Lanza (1997b) gave five ways that a parent can react to a child mixing. These are:

Monolingual				Bilingual
Situation				Situation
Minimal Grasp	*Expressed Guess*	*Adult Repetition*	*Move-on Strategy*	*Code-Switching*

The monolingual situation actively discourages mixing and creates the necessity of participants in the conversation only using one language at a time. In the mono-lingual situation we see *Minimal Grasp* when the parent reacts to the child using the other language by saying 'What? I don't understand you!', forcing the child to say it again in the right language. A parent making an *Expressed Guess* signals that they may understand what the child has said, but question it, for example my son, Marc, might say to me 'On y va chez Francois?'. To which I could say 'Go, where?' implying that he needs to give more information in my language to get a reply.

Adult Repetition is simply the parent repeating the child's utterance in their lan-guage, in the hope that they will get it right next time. This is often seen while read-ing together as a child names a picture in language Y and the parent gently repeats it in language X. The *Move-on Strategy* is where a child says something in language Y and the parent listens, and understands but replies in language X. This could be my son Marc saying to me 'Ou est Papa?', to which I could reply 'He's at work.' Finally a bilingual parent preferring a bilingual situation could *Code-Switch* back to the child, allowing whichever language is more suitable or comes up first to give the lead for language choice. This would clearly value the use of two languages within dialogue,

These ways of reacting may change with age and the parent's adjustments of what kind of language they want to hear back from the child. *Adult Repetition* seems to be suited to younger children who are absorbing language, while the monolingual strategies of *Minimal Grasp* and *Expressed Guess* are well suited to a parent wanting their child to speak more or his or her language. The other end of the continuum is most likely when bilingualism is established as in older children and accepted by all parties.

Parental Language Use With Their Children

As we have seen with Siri, she quickly become aware of which parent spoke which language. Blessed with an innate sense of language awareness from birth young children often observe and analyse language. Parents are around most of the time and offer lots of interesting interaction, not only when talking to the child but together or with other people. Although as parents we think we are following the OPOL approach rigidly by only speaking in our language to the child, he or she is (silently in the first year) watching us chat to family, friends, shopworkers, neighbours and our partner. This information gleaned will have an effect on the child's eventual language use.

In my study I questioned parents about which languages they use with their children. Interestingly more mothers mix languages with their children as the data in Figure 1.1 shows. It gives five scenarios based on where the family live:

(a) Child talking to a father living out of his country.
(b) Child talking to a father living in his country.
(c) Child talking to a mother living out of her country.
(d) Child talking to a mother living in her country.
(e) Child talking to a mother living out of her country, who mixes languages.

As we can see the fathers appear to not mix or accept the mother/country languages much when talking to their children. Those who do have young children who may not have yet learnt to separate the languages. This could be because they are have more monolingual attitudes and expect monolingual standards as they are usually living in their own country. Mothers, on the other hand, more likely to be bilingual-orientated since most of them live outside their home country. A typical family in my study would be a father in his country (b) and a mother living outside of her country (c). They probably use the country language more with visitors, children coming to play and to fit in socially with native-speakers. The 17 mothers who regularly mix would be expected to have children who mixed back, but actually some children choose to follow a more OPOL approach themselves and use only her language in response. We must also remember though that many parents are not aware of their mixing and would not report it, which is why studies such as Elizabeth Lanza's are important as they show the reality of the bilingual family compared to how they see themselves.

Finally another interesting case study is by Harriet Jisa (2000), who studied the mixing patterns of two young French/English sisters. Odessa (three years and six months) and Tiffany (two years and three months) who have an American mother and French father. They live in France and attend a monolingual pre-school there and their dominance is clearly in French. For this study Jisa reports on a two-month stay the girls had, along with their American mother, in California. Harriet collected data on their initial 'linguistic shock' to be in a monolingual English-speaking society and how the girls mixed languages. Odessa, the older child, used quite sophisticated

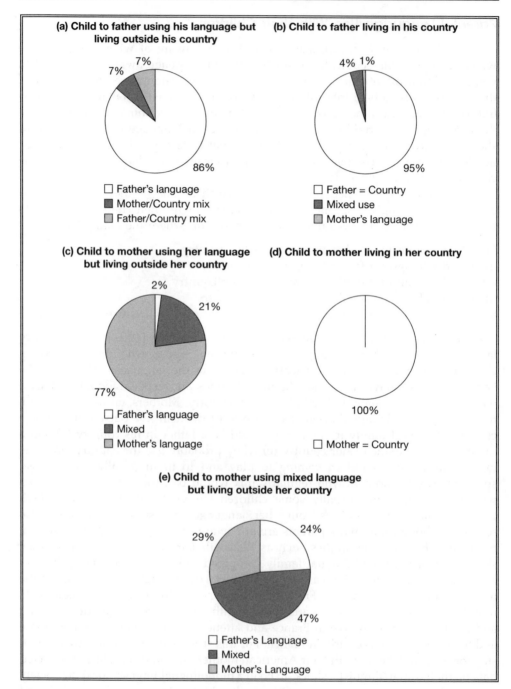

Figure 1.1 Parent to child language use patterns

mixing; inserting one or more French words into long English sentences for her age. Some examples are: *a daddy avec a child on his shoulders* (a daddy with a child on his shoulders), *on va push, ok?* (we are going to push, ok?) and *tu do what avec la table?* (You do what with the table?).

Odessa, quickly began to use the right language for the appropriate person using what is sometimes referred to as *situational code-switching* with her monolingual American family and friends in California. Her younger sister, Tiffany, continued to use mostly French or French mixes to everyone, regardless of their language. As she is only two years old her sentence structure is much shorter and aimed at getting what she wants in general. However, the 'roots of code-switching' for social purposes can be clearly seen here, where Tiffany realises that mixing is not appropriate or tolerated by monolinguals. Some examples of Tiffany's speech are: *coffee a mommy* (Mummy's coffee), *see le kitty* (see the kitten), *I wan pas chair* (I don't want my chair), *c'est cold* (it's cold) and *met Odessa high chair la* (put Odessa's high chair there).

Regarding the mother's role Harriet reports that the mother '. . . spoke English to the children but made no effort to force them to speak English'. Within the close family a lot of French is used between the girls and their bilingual mother and she obviously understands what they are saying in either language. In this way she encouraged code-switching in the home, whereas it was seen as a negative trait with other family members. At the end of the two months the two girls did use significantly more English than before and were able to switch languages if necessary with monolinguals.

We can see therefore that the attitude and acceptance of the parents is important. The gap between families who are tolerant and bilingually-orientated and those who are stricter and prefer monolingual standards can be wide. Having a parent who chooses a certain way of reacting to mixing will probably affect the child's output. Interestingly most parents claim that they rarely mix with their children and it is only when detailed taped observations are made that it becomes clear they are more in a bilingual situation than a monolingual one.

What Do the Parents Think About Mixing . . .?

The 93 families in the study were asked what kind of strategy they followed. Choosing from 'pure' OPOL, mixed language use or mainly using one parent's language. There was no great difference between mothers or fathers except that mothers mixed slightly more than fathers did. However, what is evident is an increase in mixing with age, as Figure 1.2 shows, going from 20% in the youngest age-bracket to over 40% with the oldest children. The stricter less-tolerant OPOL approach seems appropriate for younger children as some researchers have found (Taeschner, 1983). The gradual decline in the use of OPOL and an increase in mixing languages in the home comes with age. This could be a choice of the child, who is now bilingual and able to switch easily from language to language. Equally, the

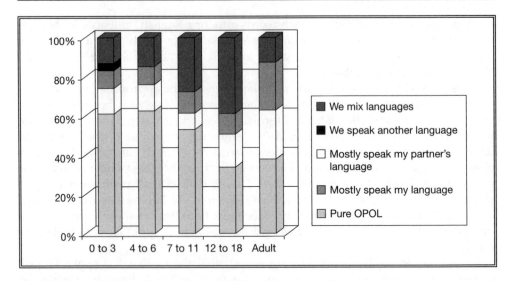

Figure 1.2 Relationship of age and mixing patterns

parents may feel that since they have successfully established the two languages they can relax language enforcement or 'policing' in the home.

Secondly, I asked parents what they thought about their child or children mixing in an open question, where they could write as much as they wished. They were more or less split into three groups:

(1) Parents, who were quite happy, accepting and even amused by the strange combinations or new words their children created. They found the mixing quite natural and some even said they mixed themselves so they could understand the child.

(2) Those who had children who had 'passed through' the stage of mixing. These parents generally had an older child aged five years or older. This made them much more relaxed with the second one and convinced that it would sort itself out.

(3) Those who didn't like it and preferably wanted their children not to mix. These parents were often minority-speakers trying hard to keep their language strong against a dominant community or school language, which they felt 'interfered' with their language. They may also have strong views on speaking a 'pure' language as against a monolingual standard.

Here is a selection of the parents' replies, with the ages of the child included, because mixing is generally seen as more of a 'problem' at around age three to five. This is when parents are more aware of it and are often unsure if it is a passing stage or a pattern for life.

(1) It's Fine by Us ...

'She's only two years old so this doesn't worry me' (2 years).

'It does not worry me at the moment, in fact for the time being it reassures me that German is "taken in" as Caspar will only use certain words in German, for example, "We are going to the *spielplatz*"' (2. 5 years).

'Inevitable' (3 years).

'Amazed and patient' (3 years).

'No problem at this stage at least. She's still needing to develop her vocabulary and speaking skills. I might be more concerned to structure things later if she doesn't begin to distinguish. She already translates my instructions in Spanish into English for her father' (3 years).

'Hazuki mixes Japanese and English when she does not know words in the language she's speaking. When she uses English words in Japanese sentences I realise what is missing in our Japanese conversations' (3 years).

'I find it amusing' (3.5 years).

'Not worried, happens very seldom-usually only when child is not familiar with Finnish word and corrects sentence straight away when given Finnish word. Take it as a normal part of language development' (3.5 years).

'Quite tolerant as we do it ourselves!' (4 years).

'No problem – It's actually sort of funny sometimes and causes laughter. I also mix with other bilingual adults, and think "code-switching" is very natural. I am sure my son(s) will grow out of it someday, and I don't see it as a sign of weakness in a language – I see it as being resourceful and creative' (5 years and 1 year old).

'No problem at all, why should it be? We are quite relaxed about the bilingualism. Our son may choose ANY language or combination. COMMUNICATION is what matters, not language. And in the long run he'll sort out the languages perfectly – no doubt' (5 years).

'I think it's quite funny when they do. Our first-born girl has been very slow with her speech development whereas the younger boy appears to be somehow linguistically gifted. Pia has always been more worried about mixing the two languages, but Tom can come out with sentences like *Tässä podissa on Thunderbird four, se on submarine*' (6 years and 4 years).

'It's usually done as a matter of expedience. When it's done with the feeling of not knowing or temporarily forgetting the word I supply the word usually within the continuity of the conversation' (6 years and 3 years).

'Happy if they do it for social reasons, unhappy if because it's easier. It's a fine balance, often not easy, but we're getting there!' (7 years and 5 years).

'She only does that when she can't find the right word and that's rare. In that case we supply the missing word or sometimes continue to use a German word in English because it's a German concept that's hard to translate, such as 'Where's your *Krankenkassecarte*?' (14 years).

'She only ever does that with people who understand both languages so that's fine' (12 years).

(2) Our Child Used to Mix, But Now It's Less and Less

'Until about two months ago our son mixed English and Spanish sometimes. It bothered me. I kept reinforcing the Spanish only by repeating what he would mix in Spanish only and asking him to repeat it back to me. He does not mix any more. He only speaks to me in Spanish now. I am very happy with his progress' (3.4 years).

'Recently our first child has begun to clearly separate the languages, she rarely mixes now. We were concerned until this milestone was reached' (3 years).

'I used to be unhappy with it. I wanted both languages to be 'pure'. Today Ophelia is so fluent that she hardly ever mixes her languages and I am much more relaxed about it' (5 years).

'I don't feel very satisfied. I try and correct their 'mistakes'. I used to be a bit nervous. By now, it rarely occurs, so I feel much more relaxed about it' (5 years and 3 years).

'This does not happen much anymore. It worried me earlier, up until just about age three' (3.5 years).

'I have got used to it. With the oldest one, I used to worry at first, but both the older two are bilingual at this stage, and do not mix within sentences. They seem to change easily from language to language' (6 years, 3 years and 9 months).

'Eleonor (our middle child) is the only one who mixes. I repeat the phrase correctly for her and she then corrects herself. I think she's now mixing lots!' (6 years, 4 years and 2 years).

'They now rarely mix the languages. If, for example, they use a French word while speaking English, I simply repeat the phrase with the English word in it' (9 years and 7 years).

'Initially I worried about my children mixing their languages although the results were sometimes very funny. Now that the children speak both languages so well it's not an issue any more and I don't worry if they occasionally use a German word in an English sentence. I very seldom corrected the children's language use when they were younger, and now with my youngest child, and only fill in the word in the correct language now if the children want to know it or if they are being lazy' (10 years, 9 years and 4 years).

(3) We Would Prefer If Our Children Didn't Do It . . .

'Emotionally I dislike it, but rationally I accept it as part of a bilingual child's development at this age' (2 years).

'I don't like it and tend to correct him despite the fact that I am fully aware that it's totally normal' (3.7 years).

'We do not want our child to do this. We ask our child to speak only one language' (4 years).

'Up to now I don't mind so much, but I have been trying in recent months to correct him' (4 years).

'I feel a little rejected and disappointed if they don't use Spanish' (4.5 years and 2 years).

'I don't like it at all. My 6-year-old spends all day at school where English is spoken. Thus, the amount of time she spends with me and uses my language is reduced tremendously. That's why I am very strict about them not mixing the two languages and try to make her tell me stories about school related topics in the non-school language' (6 years and 3 years).

'Sometimes frustrated because I put so much so much effort into teaching them Brazilian Portuguese but mostly I'm thankful that they have a complete and equal understanding of both languages' (4 years and 21 months).

'I worry about the implication for proper grammar and vocabulary development in the weaker language' (5 years and 3 years).

'I'd rather they don't. This occasionally happens if they don't know a word in one language or another – then I just try to tell them the word, and then have then repeat the sentence' (6 years and 3 years).

'I don't like it. It reminds me of second generation Japanese-Americans who can't speak pure English' (6 years and 3 years).

'It's best to speak both languages correctly. If they want to speak English, speak English. When they want to speak Japanese, speak that' (6 years, 3 years and 9 months).

'Not too happy though I know it's inevitable. I have always picked her up on it though. When she was smaller I used to say that her grandparents wouldn't understand her if she put French words into English sentences. Now she accepts that it is laziness and tries not to do it. She wants to speak correct English' (12 years).

Summary

We see that Grammont certainly raised the status of bilingual families. His advice helped many bilingual families, such as Ronjat's and Leopold, to publicise the positive advantages of bilingualism in a political and social climate that did not appreciate it. Grammont's legacy has changed over the years and although it is the base of many case studies researchers look at it from different viewpoints. It remains in general an accepted and useful approach. The parents in my study appear to have a good grasp of what OPOL is and have done research themselves or thought about it carefully.

Mixing is seen as a normal stage nowadays and not something to hide or discourage. However there are differing levels of mixing, as we see in under-threes and older children. The younger ones are often not able to separate languages yet, while older ones employ code-switching as a social tool effectively with other bilinguals. We see that families adapt to increased mixing as their children become more articulate and able to discuss how they want to communicate within the family. Parenting styles do appear to have an effect, as they do on many areas of child development, although it is impossible to say which one is best.

Chapter 2

The First Three Years and Establishing the One-Parent-One-Language Approach

In this chapter we look at the first three years, which are extremely important for the bilingual child. This is the time when they *acquire* languages and link each language to a person. This time-frame is fascinating because we can see rapid development in the child from babbling to making short sentences. Language input is still relatively structured and controlled by parents so the effects of language use on a child are evident on a daily basis. Often parents find this a challenging and exciting phase as they see their new baby begin to talk. Parents have a high level of interest at this stage in bilingualism and are watching their offspring carefully in anticipation of verbal skills.

We first question in Part One whether very young children are in fact better language learners? Are they particularly sensitive to languages at a certain age? We then look at getting started and the use of motherese and fatherese in relation to bonding with a new baby. Making a decision about which language and adjusting input along the way is discussed too. In Part Two we see how young children refer to each language and begin to separate them. Some thorny issues are covered, such as what do you do when you child refuses to answer you in your language? Should we translate words and how can we make sure new words are learnt in both languages? Finally as children near age three we look at the effect that starting pre-school and nursery can have on language use. At the end of the chapter there are five case-studies of families with young children, showing how they got started and any problems they encountered along the way.

Part One: Very Young Children and Language Learning

There is a universal belief that young children are better than older children and adults at learning languages. Children exposed to two languages from an early age generally acquire a good native-speaker like level with apparently little effort. Their correct grammar, good accent and pronunciation are the envy of older learners. We now know that children are sensitive to languages from birth and there is probably an optimal age for learning languages from birth to around puberty (Hamers & Blanc, 2001). Some researchers link this optimal age to work done by

Noam Chomsky on how language develops within the child's mind. Chomsky proposes that children have an innate ability to generate languages from birth until puberty and they are 'pre-wired' to do so. He calls this the *Language Acquisition Device* (Chomsky, 1964). The LAD is not a real device as such, simply a theoretical way of describing the brain's organisation of language within a child. The brain facilitates acquisition by allowing the child to generate and form grammatically correct sentences without structured teaching. Young children in particular have very little correction and formal grammar lessons yet at around age five they are able to use grammatically correct sentences quite easily. However we cannot prove the existence of these two hypothesises and some recent research has reduced the age limit to toddlerhood only (Werker, 1997). Bilingual children certainly do appear to pick up a language quickly if say, their parents move to another country or use a different language with them, but is it as easy as it looks?

In his review of the 'age factor' in learning languages, David Singleton (2001) concluded that the evidence available does *not* consistently support the hypothesis that either younger or older language learners are globally more efficient and successful. In the long run, the younger ones generally achieve higher levels of proficiency, but this could be simply a question of more time spent familiarising themselves with the language. It is worth bearing in mind that as adults we demand much less of a two-year-old bilingual than say, a seven-year-old, who we would expect to be able to hold a conversation with us. Therefore the younger child has more chance to listen to other speakers and learn the social structure and appropriate language use before conversing fully.

We do know that young children do have a higher neurological capacity as they are at a stage of learning many new concepts, which they have to 'decode'. Learning is still a game where they discover, experiment and test out ideas as Smith, Cowie and Blades report on in *Understanding Children's Development*. Studies involving scanning brain waves show that bilingual's brains have more 'plasticity' or flexibility and are more open to new concepts. Children also benefit in terms of 'superior input', simply as they are 'talked to' more by adults or older children and are not expected to answer back fluently or have such a high level of ability. Mistakes, such as grammatical errors, are accepted as part of the learning process of a child. Many adults chatting to a three-year-old in English would not be shocked to hear the child say 'I goed home' instead of 'I went home' as we understand they are immature and the correct form will come later. Children are not really expected to produce sophisticated language until they start formal education. Most young children are keen to interact with other children and adults and by doing so, gain important role-models.

The one area that children do excel in is 'sensory acuity'. They nearly always have a good 'native' accent and can perceive and recognise sounds very well. Nevertheless the time frame is short; as Rod Ellis (1995) warns, the critical age for acquiring a native accent is only up to age six and must be accompanied by wide exposure to languages in a naturalistic setting. It seems that young children are

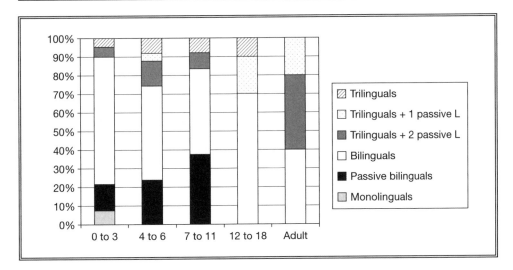

Figure 2.1 Age and language proficiency in children

not necessarily 'better' language learners but use different strategies by utilising their in-built cognitive and biological advantages, which they can access from birth to around starting school age. So an early start could benefit bilingual children and establish patterns for the future. Nevertheless as Figure 2.1 shows the older children are just as competent proportionally as the youngest age group, and only monolinguals are seen in the lower age-spectrum. Bilingualism remains steady at around 60–70% in all age-groups, although the number of passive bilinguals rises up to age seven to eleven, a subject we will discuss more in Chapter 3.

Bonding and Talking to a New Baby in Two Languages – Motherese and Fatherese

When we have a new baby, particularly with the first one, it can seem quite strange to 'talk' to it. This particularly affects parents who have used a second language frequently with their partner, at work or in the community and suddenly revert to using their first language again. Nevertheless, those early days are vitally important in establishing a language relationship. The baby is 'tuned' in to the mother's voice and loves to watch her face. In basic terms to ensure his survival he needs to attach himself to one close person.

Studies on very young babies have shown that two to four-day-old babies have already acquired 'sensitivity' for recognising their mother's languages, even when strangers speak it. A study done by Moon, Panneton-Cooper and Fifer (1993) on Spanish/English and Irish/English two-month-old and six-month-old babies showed that they can discriminate between 'their' two languages but not between another two foreign languages. Another study on babies by Dehaene-Lambertz and Houston (1997) tested two-month-old monolingual American and French infants for 'orientation' or reaction towards selected sentences from the classic child's story *The Three Little Pigs*. These sentences were either read normally, filtered or mixed-up. The babies were able to recognise in less than one second their 'native' languages. Therefore, it appears that babies are highly sensitive to intonation and prefer continuous natural speech to segments. Young babies absorb language deeply, even in the early months, and input from the mother or father or the country language will become productive a year or two later. The importance of parents using their own languages is evident even though results do not come through immediately.

The unique way in which a mother talks and bonds to her children is often described as motherese. Typical motherese is use of non-linguistic features such as eye contact or games with a linguistic element. Babies love to see adults clapping their hands, sticking out their tongues and generally being a bit silly! They like rhyming sounds like 'Coo-coo' and the game of 'Peep-po!' or making animal sounds to amuse the child. It can also be those typically baby comments we hear from mothers and doting onlookers such as 'Ooh! You're such a cutie!', and 'Hello, sweetie-pie' and other such culturally linked expressions and terms of endearment. It is often done in a soothing high-pitched voice that is not normal and often sounds quite musical. David Crystal (1987: 53) comments that: 'Far from babies copying their parents noises in the first year, it seems that more often the parents imitate the children, producing the range of baby-talk that acts as a marker of intimacy between parent and child.'

Often this comes naturally to parents; others may find it all quite strange. However, in the bilingual family, there is a risk that the father sits back and waits for his child to talk, whereas he needs to indulge in a bit of fatherese too. The father's language needs to be established by him spending time with the baby, ideally on his own if the parental language of communication is different so it doesn't interrupt him. He can use songs and music to support him too as all babies enjoy music and rhythm. He can also indulge in some non-linguistic play using gestures, funny faces and sounds. Fathers can also try to interpret what the child is saying to have some of that close language contact that the mother initially has. When the baby begins to crawl, walk and actively touch things the time is right for telling the baby the names of objects, toys, food and people around him. By now the baby is smiling and enjoying the attention so there is usually a good rapport between parent and child. This is something mothers seem to do instinctively and fathers need to be encouraged too, because it is an excellent opportunity to bond with their child.

This wonderful ability does decline with age, but usually by the end of year the baby begins to make few sounds that can be clearly heard by parents as distinct words. Within the bilingual family often each parents 'hears' his or her own language in the child's first babbling or words. In the beginning I was sure Marc was saying things in English, while Jacques heard French! Whatever, it doesn't matter, as long as you react to the child positively more and more words will come in both languages. As this is a pre-verbal stage, parents or families hoping for a bilingual child may give up early as they cannot 'hear' their own language. But lack of time or effort for such activities with a baby could possibly precipitate future passive use, as an affective bond has not been made between language and person.

When the child does begin to use one or two familiar words, such as 'milk' or 'cup', then the mother will often help the child extend the few words into a sentence. Hearing *'milk ... cup'* the mother might respond with *'Oh! You want some more milk in your cup?'*. The mother is highly tuned in to the sparse and often random words that the toddler utters and second-guesses what the child wants. Mothers and fathers try to translate and enlarge the child's sentences into what they expect, predicting what they will say and reacting to their needs. In this way a conversational rapport is formed, even if the parent does most of the work. This process is very intimate between parent and child and often visitors or strangers will have no idea what the child is talking about.

Consistent Language Use at Home

Children need to form a strong parent-language link and have the security of knowing who speaks what. Therefore consistent language use is important in the first three years. Most parents make a decision either before the birth or soon after. In fact about 80% of the parents in my study stuck to the same language strategy from birth onwards. Consistent language use means a child can hear a good quantity of each language and he or she can bond with a parent through language. For many families it is a 'natural' choice to follow some kind of OPOL approach, where each parent speaks his or her own language. Parents do need to think ahead to how much input they can actually give – which means quality time talking, singing and communicating with the baby or young child. Ideally they should consider the amount of minority-language and majority-language input used within the family and whether they wish to increase one language by living in that country or speaking it together.

In an extensive study looking at the success of the OPOL approach, Bruce Bain and Agnes Yu (1980: 305) tested eighty-eight young children and their parents from Alsace, Alberta, Canada and Hong Kong. They compared monolingual and bilingual families and gave some 'tutoring' to selected families on how to effectively apply the OPOL approach. They also asked the minority-language-speaking parent to spend at least one hour a day (more at weekends) and 'engage the child in play-talk activities'. Bain and Yu noted how '. . . the practice of each parent dialoguing with their child in a distinct language apparently sensitises the child to the system as a whole'. They conclude that the OPOL parents did achieve bilingualism in the first three years if only they put in enough effort.

Recent studies on bilingual babies and toddlers, aged eight months to two-and-a-half years, acquiring languages simultaneously showed that the amount of language exposure was correlated to the amount of active vocabulary the child produced. Pearson, Fernandez, Lewedeg and Oller (1997), found that with 20% language exposure some active words develop but to have a balanced bilingual development 40–60% exposure is needed in each language. As many parents are busy working and simply don't have so much time with their children, there is a risk that language exposure be reduced. This can be counteracted by employing a nanny or au pair in the home, who speaks one of the languages, like Jules Ronjat who hired a German nanny for his son, Louis, or Charlotte Hoffmann who employed Spanish and German au-pairs in her trilingual family. This should ideally be in the minority-language as this one is going to get less input. If the father is not around as much as the mother then having someone whom speaks his language can be a benefit too. Parents can also choose language-linked childcare, like a nursery or extra activities like dance classes to give extra exposure to one language or perhaps they could even move to the minority-language country for community support.

Getting Advice and Increasing Exposure to One Language

I asked parents about how they helped their children to be bilingual in practical ways. Many parents said they needed some advice when getting started and nearly all of the families read books or searched the internet. Some other practical ways they used to meet other parents in the same position and share advice were email lists, join or even set up minority-language playgroups and talking to other families in the same situation. The top ten ways to help a child become bilingual and increase input in one language were:

---

(1) Reading books for bilingual families.
(2) Surfing the internet and websites for information on bilingualism.
(3) Subscribing to bilingual family email lists.
(4) Subscribing to *The Bilingual Family Newsletter* or another newsletter for bilingual families.
(5) Meeting other bilingual or minority-language families at local support groups where a parent can use his or her language socially (such as a mother-and-child playgroup).
(6) Asking family and friends for advice.
(7) Asking other bilingual families for advice.
(8) Asking bilingual colleagues at work for advice.
(9) Enrolling child for classes, such as sport or dance, where minority-language is used.
(10) Having a subscription to a comic/book club for minority-language material.

More information on relevant books, internet sites and newsletters can be found at the end of the book.

In general, most parents appear to choose a certain language pattern and stick to it, but as a mobile population due to employment, bilingual families often change countries. This may mean an adjustment of the balance of languages as one parent loses or gains the support of living in country where his or her language is spoken. In our family we have adjusted language input through the help of other people and the location. The biggest problem for us was to have enough input in French. When Marc was born in Hungary we had a French au pair for six months, because Jacques was working away most weeks on projects and he would have struggled to reach 20% of input. I joined several English-speaking playgroups whilst living abroad and found that it is a great way to increase English input. The weekly singsong and craft activities encourage participation and interaction with other children in a natural way. Nevertheless the best way to increase an under-used language is to be immersed in it. So when we had a chance to spend a year in France on sabbatical we all benefited from having French spoken all around us. After struggling hard to reach 20% French, we then had to make an effort to keep up our English input.

Parents lacking language support can change this situation by considering extra 'organised' input. One option is to employ a nanny, au pair or babysitter using only one language who will establish a direct personal relationship with the child, thus encouraging him or her to use that language on a daily basis. This is a good example of the one-person-one-language concept in practice. However, this is an expensive option and problems may arise with au-pairs or babysitters using the majority-language not the minority one, if they are in the country to learn it. Unfortunately, if they feel the child is more comfortable using the majority one and will revert to that too, so parents will need to be strict with language use.

Many parents with young children regularly go back to their home country, for up to a month, enjoying the daily native-speaker contact and family networks there. They may also cultivate friendships with other native-speakers families living near them through a group of mothers and babies or toddlers. It may not force children to actively use a language but it forms an important reminder for the children and parents and a focus for extending activities at home. Other parents opt for a crèche, nursery or pre-school which uses a particular language.

Elizabeth, mother of a two-year-old German/English boy, has organised a German-speaking playgroup near to where she lives in England as a way of supporting the minority-language and meeting other mothers. Janet, an English mother, who brought up her three English/German children in Germany, helped set up a national group for bilingual families, with playgroups, a newsletter and a way to get in touch with other new families. She started the group when her oldest girl was two years old and has gained a great deal of support from the group over the last ten years. Another mother in London, Izumi, is also part of a Japanese-speaking mother-and-toddler group. Izumi has also opted for a Japanese-speaking nursery for her oldest daughter, who is three-and-a-half, so she can participate in Japanese culture and use the language daily with other children.

• See also *Case Study 1: Richard and Elizabeth, Case Study 3: Janet* and *Case Study 5: Izumi* at the end of this chapter for more details on these families.

Part Two: Stages of Development and the Emerging Bilingual Child

As with all developmental steps in a child's life stages can overlap and change depending on circumstances. This is only a rough guide to your child's linguistic development. Parents should not be concerned if a child is delayed or does not go through a certain stage. The stages are based on information from case-studies and observation of young bilingual children.

Stages of Development (From Age 0 to 7 Years)

• As a newborn baby the child is aware of two languages and may well have heard them in the womb too. He or she is sensitive to his direct carers' language use in the first few months as a survival technique – he must respond to his carers for them to feed and look after him.

• From three to six months onwards a linguistic rapport is set up between mother and child, with the baby preferring her voice and being soothed by it. He or she will smile, gurgle and babble in response to being talked to or sung to. The father's voice will also be recognised and reacted to positively.

• As the child reaches it's first year the languages sensitivity is reduced and a wider outlook on life appears as the baby sits, crawls and walks around exploring the world. Objects and concepts can be labelled and talked about at this stage. First words appear, usually close carers and objects within reach such as *Mama, Papa, spoon, cup, teddy* etc.

• Around age two, the child becomes aware that communication can take place in two languages. He or she realises that some people speak different languages or some speak only one language. The toddler realises that objects may have two different labels. The child may mix languages in an attempt to communicate and lacking enough words he or she may substitute or borrow words across his two languages.

• The child then becomes aware of language differentiation and that each language is different (i.e. Finnish is different to English) around age two to three. He or she will try to respond in the appropriate language to the right person. The child still mixes sometimes as a way of communicating, or when with bilingual speakers who understand both languages.

- At around age four the child then gains more social awareness; talking the right language to a speaker. He or she begins to follow the social norms of the culture in different formal settings (at nursery or school, in shops or with strangers etc.) or informal settings (playing with other children, with family and friends, neighbours etc). Mixed language use fades out with monolingual speakers as he or she realises it is simply not appropriate or accepted.

- As school starts the child begins to grasp the use of the language in the wider society outside of his or her family and friends. He or she will make an effort to choose the appropriate social form with prior knowledge. The school child understands clearly the role of formal/informal language. He or she may refer to the language by name, such as 'I speak French' and explain to people why he or she is speaking a certain language.

- Finally at about age six or seven the child reaches a stage where he is capable of switching languages according to speaker, topic, setting, language hierarchy and the social norms. This takes some time to reach and requires fluency in both languages and familiarity with social etiquette gained over previous years and empathy with another speaker in which language is understood and can or cannot be used. He or she begins to read and write and explore the world through text and writing.

Language Differentiation – 'Mummy says milk, *Papa dit lait*'

The stage when a child actually realises it has two languages is, according to researchers, an important part of their development. It is often referred to as language differentiation. In general, case studies report a growing awareness of the two 'systems' from age two to three, depending on the child and it's use of language. Ronjat mentioned that Louis became aware of his dual language heritage at around age two and Leopard had a similar age for Hildegard. Fantini's son, Mario, was noted to have reached the stage at age two years and eight months and by aged three he was able to make a 'clear and consistent separation of Spanish and English'. Up to the late 1980s it was believed that because children mixed languages they only had one 'fused' storage area in their brains. They had to grow into separate language use with age.

Jurgen Meisel (1989), Fred Genesee (1989) and Annick De Houwer (1990) have studied the subject in great depth and believe that children differentiate between the two linguistic systems from a very early age. Recent studies done by Johanne Paradis (2001) and Elena Nicoladis (1998) confirm this, showing that children do have a knowledge of two different languages from birth (possibly even in the womb too) and mixing is simply a stage of development. When we examine closely the child's mixing it is often grammatically correct and follows distinct rules. As I discussed in Chapter 1, the child often uses mixing as a way to communicate with both parents simultaneously. He or she often borrows or transfers words from each language that either he or she doesn't know yet or prefers in a certain language.

As the young bilingual child gains more and more vocabulary he or she will need to work out which words are appropriate for each parent. As this vocabulary learning is closely linked to the environment we often see child-orientated lists, with food and clothing words linked to the mother, who often is involved in the feeding and dressing of the child. Initially bilinguals have a smaller vocabulary than monolinguals but this is hardly surprising, as the bilingual child has to learn most words twice. One benefit is that such children have an early understanding that a word can mean two different things, i.e. water can just as easily be *l'eau* or *aqua* or *wasser*. Thus the bilingual child has a cognitive advantage in seeing words as 'arbitrary' and not only linked to one object, as a monolingual child might presume.

How do children label each language? Children under about the age of three or four are too young to be aware of the subtleties and the nationalistic value of saying 'English', 'Russian' or 'Japanese', they naturally link a language to a person. Charlotte Hoffmann tells that her two German/Italian/English trilingual children to differentiate between each language used the terms: *'so wie Mami'*/*'como dice Papa'* (Like Mama/How Papa says). The younger child even applied the same terms to his English friend Ian next door too saying: *'so wie Ian/como dice Ian'*.

Fantini's (1985: 50) Spanish/English son, Mario, said of his Spanish: *'Como estoy hablando ahora'* (Like I'm speaking now) and *'Como hablan los nenes'* (The language the children speak). Mario used this phrasing until he was aged three-and-a-half, when he then referred to it as *espanol*. At age four-and-a-half Fantini reports on a more reflective child asking *Papa, como se dice . . . en ingles?* (Papa, how do you say . . . in English). Usually by age three or four the child has learnt the more formal way of identifying each language, as both Marc and Nina began to ask me for translations, saying, 'Mummy, how do you say that in French?'.

This brings up an area of concern within the OPOL approach – should a parent be giving out translation in the 'other' language? In an ideal world we would have double phraseology within the family such as: 'Mummy says milk' or *'Papa dit la lait'*. However, if we only say a word or phrase in one language then we run the risk of the child never finding out how to say it in the other language if the other parent is not present. Some more curious children may ask a specific question such as: 'But how does Papa say "milk", Mummy?'. To which the parent can then decide, depending on their level of second language fluency or strategy whether to answer: 'Papa says *'lait'* or *'Papa dit la lait'* or 'Ask your father!'.

Consequently early language learning is often very patchy, with children making great strides in one language, simply because one parent spent more time labelling things for them. So bilingual parents, aware of this asymmetry need to make sure someone is filling in the gaps and aim for a wide range of input material. They also need to be aware that children sometimes may not accept the 'other' word and resolutely stick to one name for an object or person.

Traute Taeschner (1983: 37) describes two small experiments when a word remained attached to each language for Lisa, then aged two-and-a-half. Traute made big efforts to teach her daughter the words 'wardrobe' and 'mirror'. First the Italian father taught Lisa the word '*l'armadio*'. Two days later Traute showed her photos of wardrobes, saying '*Das ist ein Schrank*' (That's a wardrobe) and then saying '*Was ist das?*' (What is it?). Lisa replied correctly several times. Then two days later the father was in the bedroom and pointed to the wardrobe. Lisa replied in Italian '*Madio*' (a short form of 'Armadio'). The mother went into the girl's bedroom and pointed to the wardrobe. Lisa replied '*Madio, madio . . .*', but when given the word '*Schrank*' used that one too.

Sure that they had both succeeded, the parents test her one more time – and they find that Lisa links '*Schrank*' to the wardrobe in the children's room, and says '*Armadio*' for the parent's wardrobe! The same thing happened with a mirror – for a month Lisa uses Italian for the bedroom mirror and German for the bathroom mirror. As we can see she is making a clear link to place and word and although she has double-input it makes no difference; she has made the distinction herself.

All in all this stage is quite confusing and messy for everyone and most parents are grateful when the child has become aware of the two different languages. They will also be happier when the child can ask directly for translations and they do not have to worry so much about 'pure' language use, that they cannot give vocabulary items in the other parents' language without risking language confusion.

Language Refusal and Reluctance to Talk in Young Children

One topic often discussed in *The Bilingual Family Newsletter* is the problem of children refusing to speak one of the languages. I have seen this in practice too, with friends talking their language to a child and it replying in another, which is usually the country language. There are several different levels, ranging from children absolutely refusing to speak the language to children to simply avoiding using the language. Here are some typical child language avoidance techniques:

Child Language Avoidance Techniques

- In conversation the child refuses to speak a particular language, usually by answering back in another language.

- The child uses 'avoidance strategies' such as ignoring people or leaving the room when a certain language is being used.

- The child prefers to use non-verbal communication such as gestures or mimes to get what it wants.

- The child may severely reduce language use to single-word responses such as 'yes' or 'no', restricting conversation with a parent.

- The child may simply repeat what is said to them, without making any effort to respond or re-phrase the sentence.

- The child can interrupt conversations in a particular language by talking about another topic or subject in the other language. For example, they may choose a subject directly linked to one language such as a video or a friend.

As we can see some of the language avoidance strategies can be linked to lack of knowledge of vocabulary and can be remedied by more input. Other strategies are used to annoy or upset a parent, who wants to talk to them. Pre-school children are by nature quite argumentative and rebellious around the age of two. The child is in between babyhood and childhood. He or she feels independent but in reality the child is still heavily dependent on the mother for emotional and physical support. Children of this age often have tantrums, scream, cry or hit other children or out of sheer frustration that they can't have what they want! Language is intrinsically linked to behaviour and as the child realises the power of words he or she tries to control a situation. Nevertheless long-term avoidance and under-use of a language will lead to *passive* knowledge of a language and the language will cease to be used in the family over time.

Some level of language avoidance is to be expected in all families and we have experienced several of the above-mentioned techniques over the last six years. Marc, at around the age of two to three, chose to go for the non-verbal option, where he simply smiled, grunted, growled or used gestures to get a drink or food. After moving to England when she was two our daughter, Nina, sped ahead in English but lagged behind in French. Although she heard French regularly from her father and brother and several French visitors, she used only single-word responses, typically *oui* or *non*, which enabled her to give the impression she was conversing. In actual fact her active speech was very low, although she certainly understood French because she was able to give the right 'oui' or 'non'! We solved the problem by asking more complicated questions where she was obliged to give an answer: '*Tu veux lait au chocolate ou lait au fraise?*' ('Do you want chocolate milk or strawberry milk?'). She couldn't just say yes or no! Later we tried to enlarge the sentence: '*Tu veux ta lait chaud ou froid? Dans une verre ou dans un tasse?*' ('Do you want your milk hot or cold? In a glass or in a cup?'). She began speaking more and more words and gained confidence as she saw she could get more by responding.

Una Cunningham-Andersson (1999: 47) says this is a typical situation when the father is the minority-language speaker in a majority-language country. She also mentions the problems of language shift within the family, which goes from minority-language to majority-language around the age of two-and-a-half. This usually happens when the minority-speaking parent uses both languages when addressing the child. This may sound like a contradiction of the OPOL rules but it happens often without parents realising it. Una describes a typical scenario where monolingual majority-language speaking local children come round to play; something families will start to encourage from toddlerhood onwards as it benefits the child and the parents too. Una says the minority-speaking parent has three choices:

(a) saying everything twice, once in each language;
(b) speak only the minority-language and risk letting the majority-language children feel left out or letting the children who know both languages translate for them; and
(c) speaking only the majority-language to all the children.

As she says the last option is most often taken as the diplomatic way out but the result is that the child replies in the majority-language and will continue in this way if it is not stopped.

We can also see language avoidance or refusal techniques in periods of change, for example, when a child starts school, goes to visit family in another country or has visitors to stay. The child may reduce its usual language output until settled and at times may seem unresponsive or rude to onlookers. In that case some explaining is needed and time for the child to adapt. Most importantly the circumstances should not change and everyone should continue talking as they would normally to the child. George Saunders' son, Thomas, when he was three years old didn't like his father speaking German to him when he collected him from kindergarten. Equally his daughter, Katerina, when she was three and on a six-month trip to Germany only spoke German to her father and some of the children at the kindergarten she attended. She refused to speak German to the teacher or anyone else. A trilingual family in my study who lived in France while the youngest child was a toddler found him reluctant to change from French to using the mother's language of Norwegian. As Helen reports:

> During Kevin's phase of passive Norwegian and refusal to speak this language at age two, I explained to him that it was important to me to be able to speak my language at home. His reply was '*Mais, Maman, ma langue à moi est le français*' (But Mummy, French is my language). Even when his competence in Norwegian had improved, he still remained a monocultural person. Recently I asked him whether he was French, Norwegian or English. His answer was clear – he felt French.

Even young children can also be embarrassed at having their parents use a minority-language in front of them in public and prefer to be monolingual in front of friends. One Scottish mother told me how her three-year-old English/Italian child, who attends a French *ecole-maternelle* in France, asks her to speak only French at the school gates. This is also difficult because when the parent begins speaking the majority-language to please the child, he or she is agreeing that the language is not worthy of being used outside of the home. This can lead to the child using less and less of the language and eventually having just a passive knowledge of the language.

The False Monolingual Strategy

One answer to language refusal or passivity is the False Monolingual technique of 'pretending' not to understand the majority-language, in the aim of forcing the child to use more of the minority-language. This is mentioned several times in studies on bilingual children and Leopold, Saunders, Taeschner and Juan-Garau and Perez-Vidal all used it temporarily as a technique for balancing languages. Its' main purpose is to give sufficient exposure to the minority-language whilst keeping the language 'pure' and free of mixed utterances. We generally see the False Monolingual strategy comes into play when the child begins to mix languages. This alerts a parent to the fact that his or her language is either under-used or is being reduced to one-word insertions into a sentence in the other language. Bilingual parents can fake monolingualism to reduce over-use of the majority-language and mixing and then return to a more realistic code-switching mode later when a more equal bilingualism is established in the child. So how do you do it?

Maria Juan-Garau and Carmen Perez-Vidal (2001) report on their project in Barcelona with Maria's Catalan/English son, Andreu (aged from one year and three months to four years and two months). In the case study Maria used a bilingual interactive strategy and did not disapprove of the child mixing languages. But as she collected data for her case study she realised that Andreu was rapidly losing his English as he had exposure only from his father. The father frequently accepted the child talking to him in Catalan, not English, because he understood Catalan.

However, when Andreu was three the father decided to 'impose' a monolingual strategy so as to improve his English skills. The restriction worked and Andreu's English levels soared. First they spent three weeks in England being 'immersed' in the language, and then back in Barcelona the father became strict. He asked more for clarification and demanded a translation when Andreu used Catalan. He bought two toy puppets 'Sooty and Sweep', who only spoke English. An example of this is when Andreu is three years and two months old and playing with the puppets (2001: 77):

Andreu:	*va buscar, vol menjar peixos*	(he's looking, he wants to eat fish)
Father:	what's that?	
Andreu:	*vol menjar peixos*	(he wants to eat fish)
Father:	well, he doesn't understand that Sooty	
Andreu:	*vol menjar peixos*	(he wants to eat fish)
Father:	hey?	
Father:	then, ah, well no, I'll talk to Sooty (he translates Andreu's words into English and whispers them to Sooty)	
Father:	he wants to eat fishes!	
Andreu:	to . . . to eat pishes!	
Father:	Fishies!	
Andreu:	*ui, ui, ui*	(oh, oh, oh)

Maria Juan-Garau (2001: 84) says that her husbands effort were important, saying: 'No doubt the father's preserving and consistent choice of language has had a major role to play in Andreu's development . . . had the father surrendered to code-switching English would soon have lost ground and eventually disappeared form the child's linguistic repertoire.'

German-speaking linguist mother, Traute Taeschner (1983: 200), used what she called the *Wie* strategy with her two bilingual German/Italian daughters, who were then age three and two, as she explains:

> Their mother began pretending not to understand most of what they said in Italian. When they spoke to her in German she answered immediately and fulfilled their desires. But when they spoke to her in Italian, she answered *'Wie bitte?'* (What, please?) or *'Was hast du gesagt?'* (What did you say?) or simply *'Was? Wie?'*.

In the beginning the two girls thought their mother was going deaf! They would repeat the same words, only louder or even shouting! Traute would cover her ears and ask *'Wie?'* again. Eventually the girls began to replace the Italian with German. This technique did work eventually, after getting tired of saying everything twice the girls just spoke directly to her in German. Traute advises: 'The child should not be subjected to this *"Wie?"* tactic before he has reached a certain level of linguistic organisation.'

For example, it should not start until the child actually knows the equivalent words or conversations will not be possible. She gives an example of the how the technique can also help the child learn new vocabulary. Here Guilia (age two years and one month) is talking about some scissors:

Guilia:	*Das da per tagliare*	(This here is for cutting)
Mother:	*Was ist das?*	(What is that?)
Guilia:	*Per tagliare*	(For cutting)
Mother:	*Wie heisst das?*	(What's it called?)
Guilia:	*Per tagliare unghie*	(For cutting fingernails)
	[pretends to cut her fingernails]	
Mother:	*Das ist eine Schere*	(These are scissors)
Guilia:	*Eine Schere, ja Mami, eine Schere*	(Scissors, yes mummy,
	'bianca', eine Schere 'lote'	white scissors)

Traute goes on to say that the technique only really works if the child is relaxed, happy and when interaction is 'not compromised' by the tactic. If the children were upset, anxious or angry then she let it drop. Also it works best when the child is interested in the conversation and wants to please the parent. In brief it is also not an effective way to correct mistakes rather simply a way to encourage more use of the minority-language at home.

Susanne Döpke (1992b) looked at a German/English child's struggle to comply with the OPOL approach. His mother was his only source of German (three after-noons a week with her) and the parents spoke English together. Around aged two, the German-speaking mother wanted him to speak more German to her. She did this by clarifying the two languages as 'Mummy's words' and 'Daddy's words'. As Döpke (1992b: 470) says the mother, '... made the "one-parent-one-language" rule operative in the family explicit to the child'. When the child used English with his mother she would gently remind him to use 'Mummy's words'. This conse-quently had an effect, as Döpke measured the amount of German and English vocabulary the child produced. Around age two he used more German in his speech but two months later the level dropped again. Susanne thinks this might be a reaction to the mother's 'demand' that he use German when English was his dominant language. Luckily this struggle was resolved and the child at age two years and two months used much more German when alone with his mother.

Colin Baker (2000: 75) cautions over-use of the False Monolingual technique saying: 'It's often impossible and usually unwise to compel a child to speak a language.' For parents who say they don't understand when a child speaks the other language he cautions: 'Unless this is handled tactfully and skilfully, the result is that children learn that language is an imposition, a part of authoritarian power.' However, if parents can simply influence language use 'latently' rather than impose a language strictly they may have more long-term success.

As we can see the general age when parents consider this false-monolingual strategy is around two to three years, when children can be rebellious and aware of the effect of language. It can work on a short-term basis. The refusal to use one parent's language can be a reaction to all the other things happening in the child's world and given time the minority-language will probably reassert itself if there is sufficient motivation for the child. On the other hand, children can be quite lazy and may need a little prod in the right direction. We often use this technique with young children to improve their manners, for example when we pretend not to hear a request without the magic word *please!*

As the toddler grows into a child we see many cognitive and emotional changes in the child. He or she begins to feel more independent and ready for more challenges in life. Monolingual and bilingual children alike begin to understand their role in the family and the wider world too. Curiosity levels are high and questions about how things work or are made fill the child's mind. The child is more curious about his or her language use too and after age two-and-a-half some kind of decision has been made, at least in his mind, over which language to use with which person. There may be a preferred language or one that is connected with fun activities or friends. Children nearing three years old have already amassed a great deal of information about the two languages in their brains and have the majority of it stored in their memories. However, what they need to learn now is *when* to use each language, with whom to and how to fit in socially with their world.

We saw in Part One that children under the age of three generally prefer the mother's language. A pattern often appears of a child using a mother's language predominately and reaching a good level by age three. At which point they (or the parents too) aim for more of the father's language. Father's can really enjoy this stage, answering all their questions, talking to them about the world and inter-acting with them in a different way to the more caring and nurturing role of the mother. Three-year-olds love to talk and having a father who is willing to chat and play games will boost their language input no end.

These children are ready for more stimulation in their world and in most coun-tries some kind of organised group for children is available, be it a nursery, pre-school, a kindergarten, or a regular meeting of children for activities and singing together organised by parents. This is usually part-time and involves lots of free-play, reading stories, artwork and physical games and outdoor play. Children benefit from the routine and the freedom to explore new things.

The choice of language for the child is important, particularly in the case of a minority-speaking parent, whose child will attend a majority-language nursery or pre-school. In this case they will have to take care that the language does not become passive or the child refuses to use it. Social pressure from other parents to use the majority-language or increased use in communicating with teachers and assistants can quickly precipitate a downward slide into majority-language speaking only children. Una Cunningham-Andersson, the English-speaking mother of four English/Swedish children living in Sweden, reports that her four children were all English-dominant until they began pre-school at the age of three. Since starting school, Swedish has become their dominant language. This is reflected in the case histories of Charlotte Hoffmann whose two trilingual children became dominant in English (the country language) when they began school. Such parent's need to accept that the school language is important and the child may find it hard to talk about his or her day in a different language or may possibly feel frustrated at being different or having a lower vocabulary than the others have initially.

Traute Taeschner (1983: 211), in her report of her two bilingual German-Italian daughters, mentions the importance of motivation for emerging bilinguals around age three years. They are able to imagine the past and the future and by doing so can think about the fun times they had with say a grandparent or a friend who used one language. That can increase their desire to keep on speaking the minority-language even when surrounded by the majority-language. As Traute says 'Lisa and Guilia no longer showed the highs and lows of the earlier period when their bilingual production was directly proportional to the quantity and richness provided by the environment.' She goes on to say that the persons connected with the child can inspire the child to use their language '. . . which the child remembers as a concrete setting instead of momentary contact'.

Summary

Before moving on to hear about children starting their formal education in school in Chapter 3 we can conclude that it is a benefit to begin bilingualism as soon as possible, if only to give a child more exposure and a chance to absorb languages without pressure to be verbal. The highly sensitive baby responds well to language input, especially from the mother. She should profit from the first three years while she has the baby's full attention, as later on the father and school languages can take over. However, the father's language should not be neglected or allowed to become passive and he needs to continually use his language even if the child does not respond.

We have seen how very young children can refuse to speak a language, and how they sort the languages in their brains. These steps are important in letting the child take control of a language and see what effect it will have on the world around him or her. This age group is prone to mood-swings and temper tantrums, which will hopefully fade out over time and parents need to stay motivated and not give up at this stage.

Seeing our children grow up and become independent is inspiring, but we must respect their language immaturity, mixing and swings from one language to another. Gaps in knowledge will be there, even with the most dedicated parenting and all that can be done is to explain to the child how to ask for the word in another language. The balance of languages begins to change for the growing child as school and new friendships beckon.

Case Study 1: Richard and Elisabeth – A Bilingual Upbringing for Max's Mother and Strong Family Support

Richard, 37, is American and married to Elisabeth, 31, who is American/German. They currently live in Faringdon, near Oxford, England with their son, Max; who is two-and-a-half. Richard is a software engineer and Elisabeth does freelance translation work. The couple met 12 years ago in France, where they were both studying French. Their language of communication is English together, although Richard has a good level of German and understands everything Elisabeth says. He says 'I would like to speak German to Elisabeth and Max, but we have decided that I should stick to English, at least in the beginning.' Elisabeth was brought up bilingual, as her mother is American and her father German; the family lived in Germany and spent one year on sabbatical in America. Her parents are both bilingual too and great role-models.

I asked about Max's language development and Richard said 'Max began speaking English and German almost at the same time. We try to tie a word closely to a person, and we are amazed at how clearly he sees the difference between English and German.' Elisabeth mentioned that Max often uses her as an interlocutor, for example, when they are at local playgroups and activities. Elisabeth also meets up with some German mothers in Swindon, giving Max exposure to other German-speaking children too. Although bilingual and bicultural herself Elisabeth is currently emphasising her German side to establish Max's bilingualism. This benefits her as she notes, 'My German has actually improved since I had Max. Before, I used German very little in everyday life (after leaving Germany at the age of 19) and my father and my German aunt accused me of losing it on several occasions! It seems that even though my main conversation partner is a two-year-old, just the fact that I speak German every day seems to keep the cogs oiled and I don't forget as many words.'

The family goes back to Germany at least twice a year Elisabeth's family often visits them in Oxford. Elisabeth's American mother is particularly supportive of their strategy, having been in a similar situation. Most of Elisabeth's family speaks both languages fluently and when together they often code-switch and mix German and English together as their way of communicating. They even jokingly refer to it as *Germish*. The choice of language is linked to experiences too, as Elisabeth explains 'Since Max was born in England when I talk about having a baby I'll slip into English because it's more natural.' However, at home with Max she makes an effort to set a good example and not speak Germish, although Max enjoys playing with words and meanings. As Elisabeth remembers, 'When he was about 15 months old and just learning parts of the body, I asked him whether he wanted some *Eis* (ice-cream) and he thought about it and very solemnly pointed to his eyes!'.

They go to visit Richard's family in California every 18 months, where Elisabeth is seen more as an American who speaks German and she fits in perfectly there too. As multilinguals the couple are keen to open Max's horizons to other languages and periodically speak or read French or Russian to him. Their next challenge will be to decide whether to stay in England or return to their native countries and keep the German language strong when Max begins English-speaking school. Max is lucky to have such parental role-models, especially in his extended family and like his mother he already seems to feel at home with both languages and cultures.

- See also *Case Study 12: Mary* in Chapter 4 on Elisabeth's family.

Case Study 2: Vilma – Keeping Spanish and French Strong Whilst on Sabbatical in Canada

Vilma, 42, is Costa Rican and married to Jean-Pierre, 44, French. They are both scientists and are currently on a year sabbatical in Toronto, Canada. They met in Heidelberg, Germany while studying for a post-doctoral qualification in cellular biology. They have also lived in France and intend to return there when their sabbatical is over. Vilma has had direct experience of bilingualism as she went to an American bilingual school in Costa Rica and then went on to study Biology at University in England. She says: 'My parents are very supportive and encouraging, because for them knowing several languages has always been a priority.' Most of her family is bilingual and it is part of normal family life.

The couple have one child, Alexandre, who is nearly two, and has just begun talking. He goes to an English-speaking day-care centre three days a week. Vilma has had some problems convincing some people that he would be bilingual! At his 15-month check-up in France their paediatrician advised her to 'drop a language', as he thought three languages would be too many for Alexandre. Vilma asked other bilingual families to help, particularly through an Internet website for bilingual families, who convinced her she should follow her instincts. Vilma thinks his dominant language is Spanish as she reports. 'He knows about 100 words in Spanish and is starting to use two or three word sentences. His vocabulary in French is more limited, maybe about 30 words and English is the same. He speaks English exclusively at the day-care and never with us although he likes to watch Thomas the Tank Engine videos in English at home but his comments are always in Spanish!'

The main issue now is to find suitable education for Alexandre when they move back to France. The couple say: 'We plan for him to go to a French ecole maternelle [Pre-school] but he will stay with Vilma on Wednesdays to reinforce Spanish. When he is ready for Primary school we would prefer a bilingual English/French school, if there is one nearby.'

While in Toronto Vilma is speaking French to Jean-Pierre to reinforce French for Alexandre, but in France she will revert back to Spanish only at home. However, Vilma sometimes finds being the only 'minority' language Spanish speaking parent hard, and hopes that the French community and culture doesn't overwhelm her language. They plan to go back to Costa Rica at least once a year for a month to reinforce this and visit family over there. Vilma sometimes finds it hard to keep speaking Spanish when everyone around her is speaking French, as she herself is fluent in French. Nevertheless this young bilingual family is very positive, saying that being a bilingual family makes them: '. . . more open to other cultures and exploring new ways of doing things' and with the background knowledge Vilma has of being a bilingual child she will certainly be an excellent role model.

Case Study 3: Janet – Helped Found the ImF Support Group for Bilingual Families in Germany

Janet, 42, is British and lives in Morfelden, Germany with Helmut, 56. They met in Moerfelden in 1984, Janet had moved there after studying French and German in England. Since they met in a German environment and Janet's German was more fluent than Helmut's English they always spoke German to each other. They married in 1987 in Frankfurt. Their first child, Jennifer, was born in 1990, Alyssa two years later and Dominic in 1997.

From the beginning it was clear that the children would be brought up bilingually – Janet says: 'We didn't really plan how our children would learn to speak. It was never a question of whether they would learn English or not – I just couldn't imagine visiting my parents without my children speaking English.' The OPOL method seemed most natural for them, and gave the children plenty of opportunity to hear and speak English as Janet stayed at home with the children. At first Janet says: 'I felt a bit strange speaking English in a completely German environment but this soon changed and it became completely normal.' Looking for other mothers in the same situation in 1992 Janet helped form a weekly English-speaking playgroup, which supported the children's English language. Through structured play and activities to encourage talking in English they could see for themselves that it was quite natural to hear and speak English regularly with adults and children outside the family. Janet's original idea still exists – there is a national group of multilingual parents called ImF (Interest Group for Bilingual Families in Germany) who publish a regular newsletter, helping families all over Germany get together and share advice.

As a small child Jennifer had no problem understanding and using both languages and soon knew which language to use with which people. As Janet remembers her first words were from both languages, often with language mixing within a sentence such as 'My broken plate *ist kaputt, Daddy muss es rasieren*' but only for a short time. Alyssa was born when Jennifer was nearly two, so both girls were at home together before Jennifer started German kindergarten. By this time Jennifer's English was more advanced than her German but she never used English at kindergarten and her German was as good as her peer group. Everyone warned the family that once she started at kindergarten her English would deteriorate rapidly but this was not the case at all!

Alyssa's and Dominic's language development was similar to Jennifer's although Alyssa's English was far better than her German for quite a while. Dominic had more German input at an early stage since the German grand-parents lived with Janet and Helmut by the time he was born, but this did not harm his English. Although Helmut and Janet still speak German to each other the children usually speak English together, unless German friends are present. Jennifer began reading at an early age and still prefers English books if she can get her hands on them. She is very proud of the English part of her and is inter-ested in English history and other aspects of English life. Alyssa also likes England but doesn't make such a distinction between the two cultures. Dominic, now five, likes English and insists on anyone who can speak English doing so when he is around! Janet's positive contribution to the community has greatly benefited her family and she continues to advise and inspire other English-speaking parents living in Germany.

To contact the ImF group email: ImF-e.V@gmx.de

Case Study 4: Martine and Nicolas Changed From Using Dutch Together to Support French Learning

Martine, 30, lives with her French husband Nicolas, 34, in Veldhoven, the Netherlands. He is an engineer/designer and she works as an occupational ther-apist. They met in Holland ten years ago. Martine is Dutch and they have one child, Rémi, who is two-and-a-half years old. They are expecting their second child in a few months. Both parents understand and speak each other's languages, and as a couple spoke mostly Dutch together before Rémi was born because they felt it was the best thing to speak the language of the home country, and also for Nicolas to learn Dutch.

When Rémi arrived the couple decided to speak French to one another to balance the languages. Martine continues to use Dutch to Rémi when she is speaking directly to him. I asked them why they changed languages and Martine said 'It is important because French is the minority-language and we want to give Rémi at least some extra input in French this way.' Living in a Dutch speaking community and having a Dutch nanny, Rémi benefits from hearing more French from his parents. Martine describes the their life at home as being quite French culturally saying that 'It's more important to support my husband in passing on his culture, since he is the one living in a foreign country.' As a family they visit family and friends in France frequently, at least six times a year, usually for short three-day trips or a long holiday. They also have some French visitors staying with them from time to time, and know a few French–Dutch families locally.

For Nicolas it felt very natural and comfortable to speak French at home, especially to his son. Also he wanted Rémi to learn his language to be able to communicate with family, friends and for a possible future in France. As he says 'It's a gift having the opportunity to pass on two languages and cultures so we should make an effort for that, it's so much easier when learning young! Besides it can be handy to hide secrets here between father and son, speaking French while others around don't understand.' At home Martine enjoys hearing Nicolas singing childhood songs and talking to Rémi in French, which she thinks is much more natural. As an added bonus Martine is also learning some extra French and since she understands, doesn't feel 'apart'.

I asked the couple about Rémi's progress and they reported, 'Rémi started talking around his first birthday and has never stopped since! His first language is Dutch but French started around the same time, although he knows less French words. But in the holidays when Nicolas is around more his list of French words explodes then! Some words are always in French because he learned them first (or only) from his dad. Now, at two-and-a-half years old, he speaks well. Dutch is still his first language, but if dad asks him what he means, he translates it without a blink!'.

This family has made a great start and by changing the parental language and aiming for a more French ambience at home they are actively supporting Nicolas's language and culture. Supplemented by trips and a supportive extended family the French is well established and the next issue is what kind of school to choose and how to keep the French going for Rémi and his new brother or sister.

Case Study 5: Izumi – Japanese/English Family Keeping Japanese Culture Alive in London

Izumi, 38, is Japanese and married to Andrew, 39, who is British. They live in West London, England and have two children, Nadia, three-and-a-half and Tatiana, nearly two. They are expecting a third child in the next few months. Andrew is a university professor, where he uses Japanese in his work while Izumi employs her excellent English skills as an interpreter. Together the couple speak English, although Andrew speaks Japanese too and the children mainly speak Japanese together. Within her family Izumi has a sister in Tokyo who is also married to an Englishman and is bringing up her children bilingually. This has helped Izumi, as her sister's experience has shown bilingualism can work and the Japanese grandparents are very positive. The English grandparents were a little concerned until Nadia began to speak but since then they are supportive too.

Nadia currently attends a Japanese-speaking nursery where she is able to gain a strong sense of Japanese traditions, festivals and culture in context. The family plan to continue the girls' education in the Japanese school in London, which offers them a linguistic and cultural balance. It is very important for both Izumi and Andrew that they learn to read and write fluently in Japanese and gain good literacy skills. Izumi comments: 'We have come across quite a few Japanese people who have been brought up abroad. Most of them feel very inadequate in a Japanese context because their Japanese literacy skills are either non-existent or very limited.'

I asked Izumi how she passes on her Japanese culture at home and she told me 'It's too expensive and exhausting to go to Japan regularly with very small children, so we don't have the option of long visits. We don't like children watching television, so watching Japanese videotapes are not an option at the moment. Instead, we read a lot and sing Japanese songs too.' She went on to explain to me about the children's names, 'One's name is the basis of one's identity. We absolutely insist that our children should be called by their Japanese (middle) names in the Japanese-speaking environment. For example, Japanese speakers call Nadia *Nozomi* and Tatiana *Hikari*. Most of the Anglo-Japanese children we know use their English names only.' The children also have a double surname with both parents' surnames as a way to keep their dual identity.

Izumi makes a positive contribution by attending and editing a newsletter for a local Japanese baby and toddler group. She also runs a Bilingual Family Register, which puts new foreigners in contact with each other in her local area and gives advice on bilingualism. She remarks, 'I don't know whether being involved in these activities has helped or changed in any way how I think about raising my children bilingually, but my motivation is that, if I can offer something, I would like to help others in the same situation.' This young and growing family values bicultural identity and bilingualism highly and is keen to create an equal balance as shown in the choice of two names. Appreciative of each other's cultures and languages Izumi and Andrew have made a great start in blending their two different worlds together.

Chapter 3

Starting School and Becoming Bicultural – One-Culture-One-Person?

In this chapter the focus is on school-age children and becoming bicultural. The first section looks at the choice of school and the change in children's language patterns when they start formal schooling. From comments in the study and *The Bilingual Family Newsletter* I found four areas of concern that arise when a child starts school:

(1) The other parental language is likely to be discouraged in a *monolingual school*, particularly so if it is the father's language and it can remain relatively invisible in the eyes of the teacher/other parents.
(2) Parents need to understand and *communicate* with teachers and other parents in the language of the school, particularly with regard to reports, tests and information sent home.
(3) After the age of six or seven most schoolchildren will start with *homework* and reading in the evening. Parents need to be aware of this and work out a strategy for dealing with this.
(4) The school may at some point begin teaching the child's other parental language as a *foreign language* or expect the child to learn a third language at school.

I also wondered if it made a difference whether the child is male or female. Are girls more receptive to language skills and adapting to formal schooling? I investigate the gender difference and the peer group effect at school too.

The second part discusses the role of a parent's culture for a bilingual child. How do families see themselves culturally – monocultural, bicultural or multicultural? After establishing our languages how do we then transmit our culture to our children? We see how parents feel about passing on their culture and the efforts they make to do so. What happens when a child feels at home in only one country? How can we balance the cultural input? Can a child have a bilingual identity too? Finally there are comments by parents on how their children have reacted to growing up bilingually and five case studies of families with diverse cultures who have created their own unique blends of cultural balance in the home.

Part One: The Parent's Choice of School

When a child starts full-time formal education at around age five or six there is usually an effect on their language use. By this point he or she has a good command of language and is able to ask appropriate questions to find out about things. School certainly encourages this new curiosity and can provide many answers and new things to think about. A large part of the day is taken up with school and peer-relationships and friendships. School opens wide horizons for children with the learning of alphabets, numeracy and literacy. But there is a subtle difference between the language that is used at home, outside of school or at nursery and kindergarten and that which is used in a formal classroom setting. In this respect children have a new set of rules to learn and follow and different standards of language use.

Within the multilingual family we have four options for schooling – a monolingual school using the majority or minority-language, a bilingual school using both or a school using another language. A monolingual school would usually be a local school, linked to the community. The choice of father or mother's language would depend on where the family lives and whether they want a school using the majority or minority-language. A majority one would allow the child to fit in very well with its peer group, reserving the minority-language for home/family. A minority-language school would support this language and ensure active use, but may alienate the child from local friends living nearby. However, a minority-language school could be chosen because parents know they may well return to that country in the future and want the child to be familiar with that education system. This might be the case for a child living abroad and attending, for example, a British or American School, or a government-sponsored Lycee Francais or a Japanese school.

A bilingual school would seem an ideal option for those able to find the right language combination as theirs. Unfortunately truly balanced bilingual education is rather sparse across Europe and America and usually restricted to special schools such as the European Schools, which are funded by the European Union and for the children of government employees. There are some good Spanish-English bilingual schools in America, where Spanish is prevalent as a second-language. Successful French-English 'immersion' schools have also been set up in French-speaking parts of Canada where either half or all the tuition is taught in French. Although agreed on in principle by governments and with ever-increasing numbers of children speaking more than one language, the concept has never been fully integrated into educational planning. In the European Union alone 10% of the school-age population have a different language or culture to the country in which they live in (Romaine, 1995). Sadly a good bilingual school is only an option for richer families prepared to pay for education. Some countries, such as Switzerland, Belgium, Luxembourg and the Nordic countries of Norway, Sweden and Finland are positive towards bilingualism and make an effort to include such policies within the state system. Monolingual countries like France and England leave it to the private system for funding.

Colin Baker (2000: 93) discusses the different options for bilingual education in his book *The Care and Education of Young Bilinguals*. He says that the only way to retain bilingualism and biliteracy is through a classroom situation where both languages are used. This encourages maintenance of the minority-language, linguistic pluralism and enrichment. A majority-speaking speaking school, even one that offers extra classes in the other language is not sufficient and leads only to limited bilingualism. The end result of a minority-speaking child in a majority-language school is assimilation to one language and culture and eventual monolingualism.

I asked the parents in my study with school-age children what kind of school they chose for their children. Surprisingly, 92% of the children are attending a monolingual school using the majority-language. So why do so many parents choose a monolingual school? Most big cities such as London, Paris or Geneva have the choice of education in the minority-language in schools such as British or American International schools abroad or government sponsored schools like the Lycee Francais or German or Japanese schools. We can see the advantages of a minority-language/bilingual education in three of the case-studies. Cornelia's German/French daughter attends a German school part-time in France. Izumi, a Japanese mother in England with two young daughters, is keen to have her children attend Japanese school in London. A French mother, Diane, also based in London, chose a French-language school to 'counteract the effect of English in the family' for the two oldest children in her family. But these are privately funded options and are possibly not available to all families for reasons of cost and proximity to such a school.

• See *Case Study 5: Izumi* (Chapter 2), *Case Study 6: Cornelia* (this chapter), and *Case Study 25: Diane* (Chapter 7).

Since nearly all the parents chose a majority-language monolingual school this risks pulling language use in one direction only and making it the child's dominant language. As Figure 3.1 shows this is generally the case. Those who are still using their mother or father's language are often attending a school using a minority-language or still quite young.

After talking to some of the families it appears that the parents are happy about their decision and want their child to fit in and identify strongly with at least with one culture. Some see it as a temporary stage and intend to return to another country at some stage. Several said that they could not afford a private bilingual school. Other parents didn't want their child to attend an 'elitist' private school and preferred a more 'normal' local school. Their children may also have made local friends who attend the same school and if the family intends to stay long-term then that is a more settled option too. They may also remember their own monolingual schooling and want to replicate that too. The majority of parents had a monolingual education, although many studied second languages at university. Only three fathers and three mothers have had a bilingual education themselves. Five of those were parents brought up in Catalonia in Spain, Wales, the border of

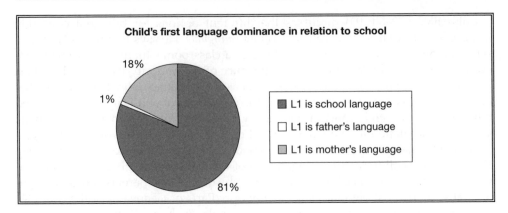

Figure 3.1 Influence of school or parents on first language

France/Italy and the border of Finland/Sweden. These are areas of territorial bilingualism, where pressure has been put on government to fund such education. So bearing in mind that most children are in monolingual schools we look in more detail at the consequences of such a choice.

Monolingual School Environment

Such schools set high standards of monolingual language competence, which if not reached will result in some kind of remedial or specialist help. Therefore the child is obliged to perform to monolingual standards, something he or she might have not done before. The gap between the home language and the school language may be wide, depending on the similarity of alphabets and writing systems in the family. At home, the close circle of family may accept the child's grammatical mistakes, code switching and lack of knowledge about social etiquette. Whereas the school requires uniformity and conformity from the children. Teachers are often too quick to point out small speech problems or unintentional mixing that may well fade away with maturity.

This can cause family pressure and a feeling within the family that their child is not 'normal' or 'right'. Other parents and teachers can reinforce these fears from having rather traditional ideas that monolingualism is best, based on lack of knowledge about other cultures or languages.

All teaching takes place in one language, with the teacher usually a native-speaker of the country. All books, workbooks and tests are in one language as are all the instructions and praise for children. On top of the stress of starting 'big school' the child may be bewildered by information never heard before within the family.

Subjects such as maths, geography, history, art and physical education will be new to most children and the phraseology surrounding these subjects will have a strong effect on their language use. As monolinguals we often take for granted these things but for a bilingual child he or she, if not given the equivalents, will stick with the school language only. Take, for example, some basic maths concepts, in English we count up in units of: *Sixty . . . sixty-five. . . . Eighty, eighty-three . . .* In French, after seventy, the order changes and we say: *soixante-dix, soixante-quinze . . . quatre-vingt, quatre-vingt-trois . . .* (sixty-ten = seventy, sixty-fifteen = seventy-five, four twenties = eighty, four twenties + three = eighty-three). In German, the numbers are slightly different too: *Sechzig, funf-und-sechsig . . . achtzeg, drei-und-achtzeg . . .* (sixty, five and sixty, eighty, three and eighty . . .).

Parents need to think about whether to try to translate simultaneously equivalents for alphabets, mathematical concepts and literacy terms. Grammatical structures can vary widely from language to language. Over-simplified or mis-use of tenses or verbs can give the impression a child is unable to speak the language well, when they may simply not have been exposed to such sophisticated language use. Parents may choose to delay equivalents until the school-language concepts have sunk in. Either way one parent is going to have to be a teacher at home too and find a way to explain such new ideas appropriately to a child.

The other side of the predominately monolingual school is the teachers and other parents' reaction to a bilingual child. This varies dramatically from enthusiasm and interest in the child's other language to complete ignorance. The teacher and parents may anticipate problems that may not exist, such as potential speech problems, language delay and stuttering. Teachers generally grade and test children in only one language and a bright bilingual child may be graded lower in comparison to a monolingual. Other parents may see the child as different and not wish their children to socialise with the child after school. Children also can be cruel too, especially when they don't understand the situation and make nasty comments, leading a child to hide one language and possibly stop using it temporarily to fit in. On the bright side, children catch up fast and learn to adapt to their situation. A helpful understanding teacher can make the child feel special and interesting. In our family we have had generally positive reactions from the English teachers, who have welcomed a real 'French connection' and asked for French songs and music to play for the class.

Parental Involvement

Schools generate a lot of paperwork, frequently sending home newsletters, reminders, requests for help, school reports. This is done in the language of the school and parents need to be aware of this and be able to react to them. Not sending back a reading record or a request for permission for school trip can cause problems for the child. Therefore, if a parent's language skills are not so good then this might give them reason to seek improvement.

Parents' evenings and chats with teachers can become very hard work if a parent cannot talk about their child with the teacher. This is when the majority-speaking parent needs to step in and accompany them or if necessary, translate for the other parent. Although mothers' are traditionally the ones who deal with all the school stuff, the father needs to be just as involved too and perhaps put in more of an appearance to show family agreement on the child's bilingualism. Important areas such as testing, reporting and sorting out problems need a joint understanding and parents may need to discuss these areas carefully together. Often parents who are living outside of their culture have no idea of how a certain school operates, for example, a minority-speaking mother whose child is attending a majority-language school may feel unsure of the goals and objective of the school. The starting age, age-related targets and ways of teaching subjects such as reading may be completely different and this is an area that the parents must discuss together.

Homework

Homework is introduced at different ages in schools around the world. It can start off with a simple reading book for home or a spelling test and quickly spiral to long detailed projects demanding research, presentation and lots of work in the evening. Most schools have a homework policy and can advise parents of what they are likely to get. The issue in the OPOL family is how to split the tasks. In a monolingual family both parents may take it in turns to read, say or help with the subject they are familiar with or prefer. One English/German parent, whose two children are being educated in French and Arabic in Morocco, found the OPOL approach just too much and said: 'Once my children started to have homework regularly I abandoned the one-parent-one-language rule for good. It's no help to them if I insist on using English vocabulary to explain concepts they are unsure of in French and Arabic.' Other mothers said they simply could not do phonetic work or spellings in the school majority-language through their minority-language.

In that case the parents may temporarily switch languages or translate when necessary. However, often one monolingual parent is restricted to knowing only one language or does not want to use the other language at such an academic level due to lack of familiarity with the terms used. A good conversational language level may hide grammatical and spelling errors, which can be glossed over in speech but are clearly evident in writing. The child may then lose out on vital parental help that is needed to support school studies. The parent speaking the non-school language shouldn't get away with doing nothing though! He or she can get a good idea of what the child is doing at school through their homework and at least try to talk about school with the child. The child will be helped cognitively by rethinking through concepts learnt at school in another language and this it can benefit overall learning skills. This may be an uphill struggle though especially with a tired child at the end of the day. Some parents mention setting aside time. Weekends are a good time to use more minority-language informally with a parent or family member. Some parents opt for an organised extra class, such as a Saturday minority-language school for older children.

When children begin to learn to read and bring home books for practice or pleasure there is the problem of which language do you read in? We want literate bilinguals of course and a dual-language bookshelf representing the family. Nevertheless, many parents find this a tricky issue. Translation is possible in the younger age-range books but becomes messy when you are reading complicated or longer length books. One parent commented that the child would correct them as they read since they knew the story better than the parent did! Another English/Spanish speaking parent, Nicola, who is bringing up her daughter in Spanish, commented that sometimes she is unfamiliar with the equivalent words herself – such as *splish, spolsh!* in a children's book. Even the best bilingual parents can get stuck on certain vocabulary or unfamiliar storylines. So the parents need to decide who does the homework reading and if the person speaking the school language is simply not around enough then extra help may be needed perhaps by employing someone else to read with the children.

Foreign Language Classes in a Parental Language or a Third Language

This area can be frustrating for parents, as they are often unable to do much about it. Most schools offer a second language to children, although the starting age varies widely from country to country. Some may start in primary school around age seven; other education authorities wait until children begin secondary school. On top of this many children do private lessons in popular languages. For parents whose child is about to learn the *other* parental language at school the main problem is boredom and lack of motivation. The child has already learnt the language and will not want to be taken through the tedious routines of *Hello, my name is . . .*, and basic vocabulary learning when he can hold a full conversation with an adult.

A 15-year-old German/English schoolgirl, Franziska, wrote about her personal experience in Germany in *The Bilingual Family Newsletter* (1999, Vol. 16, No. 1). She began learning English when she was ten and found the class frustrating as she tried to stay at the beginner class level and not upset the teacher by saying too much. She was even excluded from class games, as her side would invariably win! As she says: 'You have to be so careful not to sound arrogant when your teacher knows less than you do.' Pragmatically she realised the usefulness of learning the grammatical rules in English and saw her English knowledge as a bonus.

Language classes often include dry, over-simplified unnatural texts designed for grammatical content and testing. One mother, Edith Steffan, whose children who had to learn a foreign language at school wrote to *The Bilingual Family Newsletter* (1999, Vol. 16, No. 2) saying:

Bilingual children, however, having a genuine sense of what their language is about, will naturally rebel against these alien synthetic constructs in their textbooks, which bear no relation to the truly living mother and father tongue in their minds.

Other parents have commented on the child's higher knowledge of the language than the teacher and the ensuing 'corrections' given to say, idiomatic expressions not known by the teacher. Teachers can be very sensitive about their standing in the classroom and may resent criticism and changing their teaching style for one child in the class. Some schools allow the child to skip the classes, go and sit in the library or take the appropriate exams early in a higher-age group class. Other more open-minded teachers may use the child as a teaching resource, asking him or her for translations and helping other children.

Larger schools may have another language option available, which the child has not yet learnt and would be at the same level as his or her peers. But for many parents struggling to keep two languages alive at home having their child start a third language class is the last thing they want. Some parents react strongly against it and try to take their children out of classes while other accept it on the basis that it should be relatively easy for a bilingual child to pick up another language. Depending again on the teacher the child may be allowed to miss classes. But in most cases the rules state that that the children have to attend school like the other children. A German/ Danish family living in England are trying to educate their four children at home in equivalent reading and writing skills to equip them for an eventual move back to either Germany or Denmark. When the mother asked for time off to do this it was refused.

• See *Case Study: Judith* (Chapter 5).

On the other hand some parents welcomed the Foreign Language classes which coincided with the minority-language spoken by one parent. Families with an English-speaking parent living away from England have quite a high probability that their children will have *English as Foreign Language* on the curriculum. Particularly for children who only speak the language and have not mastered reading and writing, the parents may hope the class will remedy that. Consequently they see this as an added bonus and a way to support the home language. However, some caution is needed, as the classes can be completely different to the child's previous experience of the language and too formal to be interesting. The child may be reluctant to join in and may do badly in tests etc which can cause tension with the parent. All in all it seems best not to rely on the school for topping up the child's language skills but better to work at home, keeping as closely to the current learning pattern as possible.

Gender Differences

School age children are known to congregate in either gangs of boys or groups of girls in the classroom and in the playground. Although teachers make efforts to mix them there is often a wide cultural divide between the two sexes and friends are generally from the same-sex group. The gender of a child is not set from birth; a child only becomes aware of his or her gender around age three. Sarah Brewer (2001) notes that by age five most children are in a period of gender stability and begin to act in a gender related way, i.e. being macho or feminine. By age eight most children have developed similar gender stereotypes to those held by adults. Although the social environment of the child can affect their identity, the stereotypical idea of boys being more aggressive, loud and noisy and girls being quiet, calm and enjoying role-playing exists still. One myth that exists is that girls begin to talk earlier and to talk more. This is fuelled by the belief that adults, especially mothers, talk more *to* their children especially at a young age to which girls respond well and copy. Conversely fathers generally use more direct challenging speech with lots of information and commands more suited to boys. Suzanne Romaine (2000: 123) remarks that:

> Girls use language to create and maintain cohesiveness, and their activities are generally co-operative and non-competitive. . . . Girls use forms such as 'let's, we're gonna, we could', to get others to do things. This alongside the girl's use of narration, storytelling, role-play and singing, more often than boys, points to a higher awareness of language in girls.

Joan Swain in her book *Girls, Boys & Language* (1992: 51) discusses in great depth the differences between the two sexes, in particular the primary school age children. In terms of language use it appears that a very different kind of language use will be evident in boys and girls at this intensely gender-aware stage in life. We can all probably remember typical teacher gender discrimination from our school days, such as allowing boys to be more disruptive and encouraging reading and writing in girls and scientific experimenting for boys. These patterns are often perpetrated by teachers unconsciously, and often supported by the same logic in the home and society too.

I summarise Joan's findings below, although it should be noted that her book is about monolingual English children in the UK and patterns may be very different in other countries. For example, in the UK, reading and writing are often perceived as feminine subjects and sport and science masculine. The majority of primary school teachers are female and boys often lack role-models at school.

Gender Differences in Children

- While there are quiet pupils of both sexes, the more outspoken ones tend to be boys.
- Boys tend to 'stand out' more than girls; disaffected boys make trouble while disaffected girls sit quietly at the back of the class.

- Boys are generally more assertive than girls; one study found that boys were eight times more likely to call out in class than girls were.
- Girls and boys tend to sit separately.
- When they have the choice, girls and boys often discuss or write about gender-typed topics.
- Boys are often openly disparaging about girls.
- Teachers often make distinctions between girls and boys – for disciplinary or administrative reasons or to motivate pupils to do things.
- Teachers believe that girls talk more (without evidence).
- Teachers accept certain behaviour from boys (such as swearing) but not from girls.

The few case studies, which cover both girls and boys, do tend to report a difference in language use. We see differing patterns in George Saunders (1988) study of his two boys and one girl, where the girl was particularly sensitive to speaking German for social reasons, not wishing to exclude anyone. Charlotte Hoffmann (1985) had a girl and a boy and they were linguistically very different, with the girl being trilingual and able to communicate very well, and the younger boy taking much longer to talk and getting frustrated along the way.

Tracy Tokuhama-Espinosa (2001) noted the wide difference between her trilingual eldest daughter, Natalie and the two younger brothers. Natalie had a much higher vocabulary count than her brother, Gabriel, and enjoyed using language much more than he did, adapting easily to different language speakers and environments. Tracey describes her as a 'natural translator' and 'chatty and sociable'. Tracey thinks that, on average boys begin speaking much later than girls and are less verbal in general. However, boys catch up at around aged eight so any damage is not permanent.

In terms of bilingual parenting this change in attitude and strong gender bias means that one parent may feel rather left out temporarily. Parents who once had good relationships with their children may find them uncommunicative and using certain school-language forms such as swearing to fit in. Our son, Marc, age four, after starting English school quickly adopted the common playground dropping of *th*, saying *fink* instead of *think*. He became very masculine, joining in with a macho gang of boys who saw themselves as super-heroes and fighters. Marc identified very much with his father and male role-models, which brought him closer to his father and his language as they talked more together.

It is therefore worth remembering that minority-language extra material at home should be gender-appropriate. While trying to teach or support a minority-language at home the job will be much easier with books, music and media that are suited to the child's gender. Barbie sticker books won't go down well with boys nor will space-men or dinosaur comics for the girls. Literacy, mathematical and grammatical practice can be done with girl or boy-based material, as long as it catches their attention and interests them.

In my study I had 82 girls and 65 boys. I measured their language skills against their gender as Figure 3.2 shows:

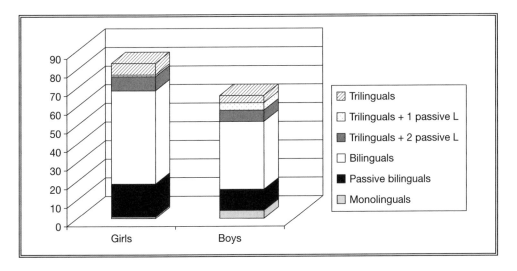

Figure 3.2 Language proficiency – boys and girls

Figure 3.2 shows some differences between the two sexes, but is not as great as I had imagined. Looking at the ages of the children too there is a higher percentage of very young monolingual boys. This is acknowledged by child experts who agree that boys generally speak later than girls do, although they soon catch up. Interestingly girls and boys are extremely similar around age four to six. They show almost equal degrees of passivity, bilingualism and trilingualism. From seven to 12 girls become much more passive in both bilingualism and trilingualism, but the boys stay steady until age 12. The conclusion to be drawn here is that the boys are certainly not behind the girls. They may develop languages differently and be affected by different external factors such as friends, school and parental involvement at different times. However, the boys are as linguistically able as the girls and are making as much effort to communicate.

The Effect of the Peer Group

Alvin Fantini (19855: 89) comments on the change in attitude when his Spanish/English son, Mario, started school at the age of five years: 'Mario showed more and more effects from contact with peers. His behaviour, which had been influenced up to this age primarily by his parents, was now affected by the attitudes of others.' Fantini goes on to report on how Mario began to have distinct preferences for certain clothes, food and hobbies like other children he knew.

With younger children parents are able to handpick their children's friends (and language) but as they get older it becomes more and more difficult. New friendships form at school and bilingual children may sense that they are 'different' or not the same as the other children. This change is seen in monolinguals too, who around age five or six, begin to follow fashion or trends in line with their peer-group instead of their parents wishes. Many of them are international trends we have all heard of cleverly marketed at children around the world and often linked to film or television. Think of world-wide recent trends such as *Pokemons, Spiderman, Action Man, Barbie, Playstations* and *Winnie-the-Pooh*. Children need to build an identity and these brands and styles give them a way to fit in, particularly at school.

Sometimes as children get older they may become less willing to use the minority-language in public or in front of friends. Several parents mentioned this, as one parent put it: 'He doesn't want me to speak my language at the school gates or in front of his school friends.' Although Fantini, Ronjat, Leopold and Saunders managed to maintain the use of the minority-language at home, other studies report a dramatic drop in minority-language use at this stage. This is sometimes temporary and the child will adjust back to using two languages eventually, when he or she feels part of the group.

Frequently children find it hard to re-adjust to another language when they come home after school. Laura Sager did a project on 18 bilingual families in Germany regarding the impact school had on the children and the fact that their new experiences take place in the majority-language of German (*The Bilingual Family Newsletter*, 1999, Vol. 16, No. 3). She remarks that 'When starting school most children began answering in German when addressed in the minority-language.' The children feel they can't explain their experiences in the other language as it wouldn't mean the same thing. However this puts the parents under extreme pressure to keep the minority-language alive at home.

Finally, the Caldas family gives a snapshot into the world of older bilingual children and their perception of languages. Stephen Caldas and his wife Suzanne Caron-Caldras (2000) taped their family having dinner together over a three-year period. The three children, John, age 12 and twin sisters, Valerie and Stephanie, aged ten, were recorded while all together around the table. The family lived in Louisiana, America but spent long summer holidays in Quebec, where they all immersed themselves in French. Suzanne is a French-speaking Canadian who teaches French, and Stephen is American. Both parents are bilingual.

Suzanne Caron-Caldras initially spoke French to her children and English with Stephen, but when John was 18 months Stephen changed to speak only French at home and with Suzanne. In the study, we see that the twins attend a (50%) French partial-immersion school in Louisiana so they are already ahead of John in speaking

French. The recordings show a huge seasonal increase in the summer of French being spoken around the dinner table. This is reduced to almost nothing for John in the winter but the girls stay steady. Apparently, the more French the children spoke the more the father spoke too, showing the children affecting him not vice versa. The girl twins often 'berate' John for not speaking enough French at home too. Overall the twins (counted as one person) use 68% French while John uses only 23%. The difference between the children seems to be the location for John. As he nears adolescence he is less keen to speak French because he says 'it's not cool to speak French in school'. But it could also be because he is a teenage boy and sees speaking a foreign language as a girl thing too.

Part Two: The Cultural Heritage of the Parents

After about age five, the child will already have a good grasp of at least one of the parental language and hopefully the other too. As one parent in my study commented: '. . . by the time that my daughters were six and seven they had worked out who spoke which language and they adapted their speech accordingly'.

The hard work is over now regarding language acquisition, as children begin to use each language appropriately and switch when necessary. Now the child needs to have an understanding of the culture that is intimately linked to the language. It is important for the child to identify with the particular language and country. Cultural acquisition is something rather under-rated, yet it is an important motivational factor in keeping older children going with their two languages. Indeed, one of the best ways to keep the minority-language alive is to spend time in the country and with family and friends, however, some cultural knowledge is needed to 'fit in' there. It can be simple things such as knowing how to greet people accordingly, eat in a certain way and say please and thank you. Children are very sensitive to being different and want to fit it so having some background knowledge of what people expect will help them greatly. A basic idea about the geography and history of a country and knowing what kind of food they eat there can benefit too.

Children generally see a parent's culture and background through his or her parents. Thus the parent living in the majority-language-speaking country usually has to do very little, while the minority-language parent has to work overtime. As Una Cunningham-Anderson (1999: 15) says:

> In the case of a mixed marriage where one partner is from the country of residence, the children's picture of their parent's childhood can be very unbalanced. The children might meet their grandparents, uncles, aunts and cousins on, say, the father's side very often, perhaps even daily. . . . The father will be able to share his childhood with his children in a very concrete way. If the mother gets no opportunity to share her upbringing with her children, they may have the impression that she has no background.

It is therefore important for the minority-culture parent living away from their family to make regular trips back to the country if possible, invite visitors to stay and supplement that with telephone calls, letters and in general talking about their childhood and life in that country. Parents can also encourage the child to make comparisons about the countries, discussing what is similar and what is different. This is easier as the child gets older and can have a proper conversation but it can be introduced early as part of say, bedtime stories or around festivals or special days when the other country is more in the child's mind.

One factor that seems important is how the family see themselves – are they monocultural, bicultural or even multicultural? Does the parent living in the majority-language country accept or take an interest in his or hers partner's culture? So I asked the parents in my study how they saw themselves – as a family with just one culture, one culture which is deeper, two equal cultures or three or more? Figure 3.3 shows what I call the cultural description of the families:

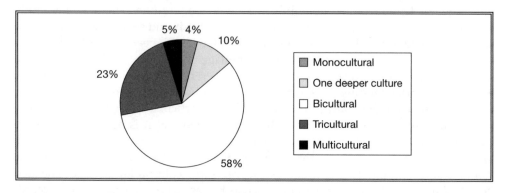

Figure 3.3 Cultural description of the families

This gave me an idea of how bicultural they were and their perception of this within the family. There are very few monocultural (4%) parents and most consider themselves bicultural (58%). This is interesting because in fact a third of the fathers rated themselves as monolingual (i.e. speaking only their native language). So it appears that although these fathers are not able to speak their partner's language, many consider themselves part of that culture. The mothers are mainly bilingual or trilingual (with only two monolingual mothers). Similarly they are culturally plural, with nearly a third being tricultural or multicultural.

I found these results extremely positive for the families, especially that the older children would see clearly that both parents had a positive attitude towards biculturism and the minority-parents culture. This is important because all too easily a parent can stop fully supporting his or her culture and not bother to cele-brate special festivals or days or talk about their country to the children. In the long-term this is implying to the children that the one culture is 'worthless' or not important and they will follow suit. Positive partners made encouraging comments such as:

Comments from Culturally Positive Partners About Their Partner's Culture

Father: I am consciously more concerned with the transmission of my wife's (Catalan) culture in an English environment (Catalan/English family in UK).

Father: We live in Japan, so [the children] must know my culture. Of course, the English culture of my wife's country (New Zealand) is also important' (New Zealand/Japanese family in Japan).

Father: I feel the strongest influence on their culture is the education environment. But we certainly feel it essential to retain a 'Frenchness' about the family (French/English family in UK).

Mother: I don't have to put much effort into it since we live in my country/culture at the moment. I feel that it's more important to support my husband in passing on his culture (being in a foreign country) (Dutch/French family in the Netherlands).

Mother: We live in 'my country', so there aren't any difficulties in passing my culture. But I feel it is important that the children learn about their Dad's culture, too (Finnish/English family in Finland).

Mother: [Our child] gets it automatically, because we are living in 'my' culture. I also find it important to pass on the culture of my partner too (Dutch/Swedish family in the Netherlands).

Importance of Culture for the Parents

I firstly asked the parents who are living away from their culture whether it was important for them to pass on their culture? Sixty per cent of these parents were mothers living in their husband's or partner's country, compared too only 10% of fathers. In general this question created a lot of discussion and comments. The majority of parents were highly concerned about the necessity to pass on their culture. Some were not so bothered about the whole thing, because the two family cultures were quite similar, like German and English, or they had purposely left their culture for their partner's country and were more focussed on being part of their new culture than keeping the old one going. There were some perceptive comments about the worth of an individual culture or that of a bigger entity such as 'European' or 'American' culture too. Some of the comments I received were:

Culture is Very Important To Me . . .

Mother: Since we are not living in France, it is even more important. I would like my daughter to have the best of both countries/cultures. I would like her to feel French as well as English (very difficult to achieve) (French/English family in UK).

Mother: Especially in Britain where there's not much emphasis on foreign/European culture. I find it's vital for me to do my best to bring my children up as 'European citizens'. Also of course I am hoping that my children will be able to integrate when visiting family in Germany (German/English family in UK).

Father: I feel it's a gift we (parents) have to pass to our children, make them understand that there's a diversity of culture/meanings/opinions in the world (Dutch/French family in the Netherlands).

Mother: You are formed by your culture. In our case the cultures are not all that different. There are (subtle) differences though and I find it important that the children are exposed to all (Dutch/Welsh trilingual family living in UK).

Father: I think a big part on passing on language is exactly so that culture can be passed on. If we move away from Hungary, this will be difficult – because Hungarian [culture] is hard to be exposed to (French-Canadian/Hungarian trilingual family in Hungary).

Mother: With more languages and cultural understanding I think our child will have more opportunities in the future. Also when I'm older I will probably appreciate someone who shares the same language and culture in the same family (Japanese/English family in UK).

Mother: It's part of me. If the children would not know my culture they wouldn't know me (Finnish/English family in UK).

Mother: Denying the culture of one parent's is denying the child's identity as a whole (French/Dutch family in the Netherlands).

Father: It's important for me that the children learn the three cultures of the family (Dutch/Italian family living on Italian/French border).

Mother: I think it's important for [our daughter] to know people's basic behaviour pattern from a culture to avoid unnecessary misunderstandings or confusion (Japanese/English family in Japan).

Mother: Absolutely. That's why we started our own playgroup and organise regular community events that help make Brazilian customs closer to and more integrated with Australian customs (Brazilian/Australian family in Australia).

Father: It's an integral part of who I am and by extension who my daughter is (Russian/English family in UK).

Mother: It's paramount that my children become bilingual and bicultural (Italian/English trilingual family in Singapore).

Mother: We are living such a long way from Australia, I want the children to have an identity of both of their families. We also move around a lot and not being able to put down our own 'roots', it's important that they have a strong cultural identity (Australian/French family in France).

It's Not a Big Issue . . .

Mother: To a degree I enjoy celebrating special holidays, such as Nikolaus, Advent and Fastnacht the German way and others such as Thanksgiving and the 4th July the American way (German/American family in UK).

Mother: I do not continuously feel very strong about my culture but what I like about it I suppose I enjoy passing on, like family habits of ways of celebrating birthdays, Easter, Christmas, St. Martin. I try to repeat with my kids what I loved when I was a child and what I miss (French/German family in France).

Father: This is a multicultural world that should have one culture and moral (French/English family in UK).

Mother: Basically we have one culture – not much difference between Swedish and English ones (Swedish/English family in UK).

Mother: I don't feel passionate about it. I feel so at home in England that I 'forget' my French roots (French/English family in UK).

Father: My culture has good and bad sides. The good sides and the knowledge of how to interact with others must be passed on. The bad sides not necessarily (British/Danish family in Belgium).

Father: I have acquired a mixture of Russian, Jewish, Greek, general European and general North American cultures and I believe the children will have no difficulty to select their own cocktails (Greek/Israeli and Russian family in Israel).

Mother: No special effort is made – it happens spontaneously and naturally. Our child is aware that a different cultural reality exists in the home as compared to the surrounding community. He is not only bi/trilingual but also bi/tricultural. We don't try to impose one culture at the expense of another – he has the whole package! (German/English trilingual family living in French-speaking part of Belgium).

A Wider View of Culture As a Whole . . .

Father: It's important to a certain degree. However, I do not want my daughter to feel that she is 'American' in a narrow, exclusionary, sense of the word, since she is also Japanese. I'd rather pass along an 'English-speaking' sense of identity, and hope that her sense of cultural identity is something broader than feeling simply 'American' or 'Japanese' (Japanese/English family in Japan).

Mother: Certainly there are aspects of American culture that I wish to transmit to Felix, but there are also many that I am hopeful he will not assimilate. I would like him to have the best of both British and American literature, humour, music, etc. I suppose it's a 'transatlantic' or perhaps one could say 'Anglo-Saxon' tradition that I am trying to pass on to him, not necessarily directly related to either country (English/German family in Germany).

Parents: Since we have travelled extensively, and lived overseas, I would say we have a mixed culture family. That means our lives are guided mostly by our American culture, but with good mixes of several other cultures. We have a great openness to other cultures, cultural ideas and ways of living (American parents bringing up child in Swedish).

Father: I think the cultural differences between neighboring European countries are rather small these days (German parents bringing up child in English).

Father: It's more important to help your children grow up as good human beings rather than teaching them special things from our cultures that might not be relevant to anything (Dutch/English family in UK).

Father: It mustn't be a goal in itself. It has to fit in [our son's] interests, it shouldn't be something he has to consume just because I or we want it (Swedish/Dutch family in the Netherlands).

Mother: I don't really feel that it is reasonable to refer to 'English', 'French, 'German' or 'Moroccan' culture – cultures are wider, i.e. Western/Christian/secular on one hand, Arab/Middle Eastern/Muslim on the other. Because our children are Muslim, Arab/Muslim culture is dominant in our family. On the other hand, almost all the books, videos, audio cassettes in our home are European and so are most of our values and ways of dealing with people (German/Welsh/English trilingual mother and Arabic father bringing up children with French in Morocco).

Secondly, I asked parents to describe in what ways they passed on their culture. The options included books, films, videos, music, singing etc. The table below shows the practical ways parents employed to enrich cultural knowledge of their country for their child:

Top Ten Ways of Supporting Cultural Heritage

(1) Trips to visit family and friends in the minority-language country.
(2) Reading minority-language books together.
(3) Watching minority-language videos or films together.
(4) Singing songs or listening to music together.
(5) Talking about the family history and stories and looking at photo albums together.
(6) Celebrating festivals linked to culture.
(7) Arranging for child to attend minority-language school when on holiday or go to a summer school.
(8) Meeting up with other minority-language speakers locally.
(9) Satellite television/CD ROM's and Internet use in the minority-language.
(10) Cooking and passing on traditional recipes.

Some other ways that were also mentioned were regular phone calls, reading a newspaper or comic together, attending Saturday school and going to a church. Looking at the 60% of mothers, who are living out of their country, all but two mothers made regular trips back to their country. They all read to their children too. Watching videos/films scored extremely highly too for both parents. While mothers prefer to celebrate festivals, cooking and arranging to meet up with other minority-speaking children. The 10% of fathers living outside of their country like videos, television and surfing the internet together. Some fathers took their children to museums and exhibitions or to the theatre.

We can conclude that the parents do seem to be trying very hard to pass on their heritage, both by thinking about the issue and actively passing on culture through the ways mentioned above. This was also confirmed in the case-studies too. Several couples are in partnerships, which are very different culturally, and yet they manage to blend it together for a unique family cultural base. Louise, for example, is from New Zealand and wants to retain her cultural background while living in Japan. Her Japanese husband is very positive too, and Louise is able to travel back regularly and even enrol her oldest child in school there for a real taste of New Zealand life. Caroline is Dutch and has moved to Qatar, where her husband is from. Living in a Muslim country she keeps her heritage strong with visits back to Holland and introducing the children to Dutch food. Within Europe, Christine and Jane are very integrated in their respective Spanish and Finnish communities, but take care to keep their British roots strong and regularly visit family and friends back in their native country. Many families appreciate this cultural difference and say they enjoy having the best bits of each culture.

• See also *Case Study 7: Christine, Case Study 8: Jane, Case Study 9: Caroline* and *Case Study 10: Louise* at the end of this chapter.

Bicultural Identity and Anomie

Societies, particularly monolingual ones, require a high level of cultural awareness alongside linguistic knowledge of a language. The ability to be both bilingual
and bicultural is often the true test of fluency. A major concern for parents is
whether their bilingual child will develop a double identity alongside intellectual
capacities in two languages. Pressure to conform culturally is subtle and can come
from a country or from a parent. Children with parents using two languages are
under the same pressure to be bicultural from each parent as the children growing
up in a second language country.

Living with two or three cultures can even cause a conflict of emotions or *anomie*,
which is a breakdown or absence of social norms and values that an individual
associates with a certain situation. Anomie can be described as having feelings of
disorientation, social anxiety and isolation, and is commonly seen in bicultural
adolescents or young adults. It does not usually appear until the bilingual has
reached an almost 'native speaker' level. The older child or adolescent often
has to conform to the norms of a parental minority-language and at the same time
behave as a native speaker would in the community or majority-language culture.
Lambert, Giles and Picard (1975: 127) give an example of this:

> . . . it is difficult to be both Jewish and Russian, or Algerian and French and
> this is so because the person involved realises that two separate networks of
> valued people expect him to show unambiguous signs of allegiance to one
> group or the other. It is extremely painful to be caught in the influence systems
> of two or more ethnic groups and to be 'tested' by members of one's group
> or the other who demand evidence of one's true colors.

Child (1943) did one of the first studies on biculturalism on teenage Italian-
Americans. As second-generation children of Italian immigrants, they were all able
to speak both languages fluently. Both Italian and American cultures have strong
identities and pull adolescents towards a certain lifestyle, expecting commitment
and following of certain traditions or cultural norms. Child recorded 'symptoms
of bewilderment and frustration' and 'conflict of loyalties and aspirations'. The
young adults consequently withdrew from the Italian community or American
society. Some refused to attach themselves strongly to either identity, seeing themselves as hybrids or *Italio-Americans*. Wallace Lambert, Giles and Picard (1975) also
studied French-American children from mixed marriages, for signs of conflict and
indifference to one culture. Expecting similar results to Child they found a fourth
group, who coped well with both cultures. This group had healthy attitudes, showed
no signs of personality disturbance, social alienation or anxiety. They compared
these bilinguals to homogenous monocultural children and found no differences.
The bilinguals had developed what they called: '. . . a dual allegiance that permits
them to identify with both their parents'. Whether all children are able to develop
such attitudes is not known as this research has mostly been done with prestigious
language bilinguals.

As with languages the level of cultural understanding between the parents, and empathy for the other culture is important. Sometimes the gap between parental cultures is not recognized until children are born and a parent begins to assert his or her culture as the language is acquired. This is more frequently seen as differences in parenting, acceptance of behaviour and inter-family relationships. A child needs a wide range of cultural input to be able to fit in each community as Una Cunningham-Andersson (1999: 85) says: 'It is far more difficult to arrange for children to acquire knowledge of a culture in the same uncontrived way.' While parents alone can give children a second language, they will not be able to give them a second culture without the help of others and the support of society.

In some situations a child may become closely attached to one culture, therefore isolating the other parent. Ideally both parents want to see their children not only speaking their language but appreciating cultural jokes, family histories, fairy-tales, songs or participating as they would in celebrations of special occasions such as birthdays, Christmas, Easter, Thanksgiving, Mardi Gras (Carnival) or Ramadan. The bilingual or multilingual family must accommodate all these cultural issues and compromise to suit all family members, in order to build their own individual family culture. Often as parents we don't realise how important these things are to us until we have children. Like languages we cannot just assume the child will just 'absorb' our culture; it needs to be identified and time dedicated to bringing up bicultural children. The good part is that it can be fun and satisfying and it helps the children adapt when visiting family and friends overseas.

This stage of anomie can be temporary but often causes a reappraisal of the languages. The bilingual may consciously or unconsciously or may drop one language if he or she feels he can never live up to the standards expected. He or she may wish they had 'normal' parents and want to associate only with one culture. An article about *The Trials and Tribulations of a Bilingual Teenager* by a 20-year-old Finnish-English bilingual Tommi, highlighted some of the difficulties of simultaneously belonging in two cultures (*The Bilingual Family Newsletter*, 1997, Vol. 14, No. 2). Describing himself as 'bi-national' Tommi was brought up with a strong attachment to both cultures. As a teenager in England he missed Finland and says '. . . this made my patriotic pride of everything Finland reach almost fanatic proportions'. His English classmates did not appreciate this enthusiasm and teased him. On the other hand between ages 16 and 19 he felt growing irritation with all things English and was annoyed to have to live in such a 'horrible country'. This dilemma was resolved by travelling alone for a few months, seeing that all countries have their good and bad sides. Tommi concludes by saying: 'I will always be a foreigner wherever I am, but I will also be at home in two countries, a valued member of the community with two different outlooks.'

An even wider cultural gap was experienced by two English/Japanese teenage children described by their mother, Mary Goebal Noguchi (*The Bilingual Family Newsletter*, 2000, Vol. 17, No. 4). Mary tells how 14-year-old Amy and 11-year-old Dan coped with their double-identity in Japan, where foreigners are seen as very different from the norm. After some initial teasing and being called *gaijin* (foreigner or literally 'alien'), the children benefited from parents who openly valued both languages. Their teachers also admired them and their frequent trips to the United States to visit family proved to be something their friends envied. As Mary says: 'I tried to make sure that the children had a wealth of positive experiences to associate with English and American culture.'

This reaction from other children tends to be restricted to those whose minority-language is English and is familiar to them as a school or after-school extra subject. As Louise, a New Zealander living in Japan with three children comments: 'The children at school think its "cool" to speak English.' Her children, like Mary's are able to use this to their advantage.

• See *Case Study 10: Louise.*

How Our Children Reacted to Growing Up With Two (or More) Cultures

The following comments show what the families' thought when I asked, 'How do your children react to living with two or more cultures?'. I wanted to know how the children had coped with being part of a bicultural family. This open question again provided food for thought. On the whole parents fell into two camps – those children were under school age and those to whom the cultural issue had simply not affected them yet. They usually answered 'Too young to know the difference' or 'Not known'. The other families with older children all seemed delighted in their child's progress! I have not actually found any negative comments although I was expecting many more 'problems'. Many fathers have responded positively to this question too, showing a strong interest in their children's ability to fit into both worlds.

Children's Reactions to Growing Up with Two Cultures

Father: Our daughter likes it. Is pleased to have what she calls 'A Dutch half and an English half' (Dutch/English family in UK).

Mother: Proud when they are in Germany. Occasionally embarrassed at home in England. All in all they take it for granted – it's how they've grown up (German/English family in UK).

Mother: Tania (aged six) finds it perfectly normal and adapts to the English culture. Kevin (age four) claims he's only French even if he speaks Norwegian and participates in Norwegian activities (Norwegian/English mother and French father trilingual family living in UK).

Father: It makes me feel good says our 6-year-old with a big smile! (French/English family in UK).

Father: She seems quite comfortable and is proud of having 'two flags' when her parents only have one each! (Catalan/English family in UK).

Mother: It seems to be natural to them. They easily switch between Jamaican big-happy-family-city-life and the Hungarian quiet sort of village life (Hungarian/English (Jamaican background) family in UK).

Father: They don't think there's something special about it! (Greek/Dutch trilingual family in the Netherlands).

Mother: Interestingly a recent change in my daughters attitude to her nationality – at primary school she used to say she was French only – as a result of being teased as 'la British' – even by a teacher. Now she says she's British and has a very definite attitude to anti-Brit remarks (English/French family in France).

Father: My daughter is perfectly at ease with this. She talks proudly of being Russian and English. She separates the two well (Russian/English family in UK).

Father: Two cultures are fun, enriching for all! (Japanese/English family in UK).

Mother: Our children like to compare differences or similarities. They are proud (sometimes boastful) that they know two languages (Japanese/English in Japan).

Father: They rather seem to enjoy the variety, all opportunities of trips, relatives' visits. They like 'crêpes' and 'wafel', the strictly vegetarian cooking culture of 'Mama' and going fishing and eating pike with 'Papa'! I don't think they are so aware of the peculiarity of their situation. I'm convinced they will still enjoy it as much when they grow older. Even when both parents come from the same town and speak the same language, they often come from two different 'cultures' (German/French family in France).

Mother: At this stage, they seem to take it for granted. We know lots of other bicultural families, through various groups, so they know they are not that unusual. I think the oldest child (age six) is proud of his bilingualism/biculturalism (New Zealand/Japanese family in Japan).

Summary

This chapter on the school-age children has proved illuminating in that discovery that most parents choose a monolingual schooling for their children. We can see the reasoning behind this – proximity of schools, wish for their children to fit in with the local community, high fees charged for a private minority-language education and the parents own experience of a monolingual education themselves. However, as we saw, the monolingual school does create some problem areas; communicating with the school in a second language, homework, testing and how to deal with a child learning a parental language at school or a third one.

Although there are differences between boys and girls they seem to even out over time, although the boys may start talking later. What is more important is to be in tune with peer-group pressure and use gender-specific teaching materials at home so as to get the child's attention. Temporary dropping of one language may occur as children try to fit in with their classmates and not be too different. The dynamics of the class and the teacher's attitude can help too.

We saw how bicultural or multicultural the families are and supportive of each other's culture. There is nearly always one parent living away from home, or two in the case of some trilingual families where both parents live in a third language country, and a positive partner can help greatly. The parents commented on how they pass on their culture and how they feel their children are coping with such a lifestyle. Bilingual children are adaptable and accepting of both cultures, given sufficient input and opportunities to be immersed in both cultures. In Chapter 4 we see how family members like grandparents, cousins and siblings can benefit the child both linguistically and culturally. Giving the child a rounded view of parental languages and background is essential if language use is to continue and grow.

Case Study 6: Cornelia – Increasing German Input by Their Choice of School

Cornelia, 36, is German and works as an export manager for a textiles company in Le Pecq, near Paris in France. Her French husband, Denis, 38 is a telecommunications engineer. They have one daughter, Ophélia, who is six years old. Their family language is French and they have a German au pair. Both Cornelia and Denis are able to speak each other's language and English too.

Cornelia wrote an article for *The Bilingual Family Newsletter* about her struggle to bring up Ophélia bilingually and be a working mother over the last six years. From Ophélia's birth the couple used the OPOL approach and because Cornelia worked they employed an Algerian French-speaking Nanny for the first three years. This meant that Cornelia only had a short exposure time with her daughter, although she supplemented this with three annual trips back to visit family in Germany. Ophélia certainly understood German, but was rather unwilling to actually use it, with French being so dominant in her life. As Cornelia battled on with using German some of her French friends would wonder how Ophélia managed to understand that 'strange language!', and her French in-laws had some difficulties with her speaking German in front of them, especially as she is a fluent French speaker.

The couple decided it was time to take some action so when Ophélia was three they enrolled her two days a week in an International School near Paris, alongside French 'école maternelle' the rest of the week. Ophélia blossomed at the school, which has a very high reputation, and felt at home with her mixed-marriage friends. As Cornelia says: 'She became aware that she was just like so many other bilingual children.' They also hired a German au pair for more input at home, especially for childhood songs and cultural background. Her German improved dramatically and Cornelia felt confident enough to send her to Germany alone for a holiday, with Cornelia's sister.

This worked so well that 'Today Ophélia feels so at home in Germany that she even goes there by plane on her own during her winter or spring holidays!'. In Germany, people think she is the daughter of Cornelia's sister. After trips to Germany she continues to speak German at home, even urging her Papa to speak it too! Ophélia now wants to get start learning English as she says: 'Please Mummy teach me English now, my German is good enough!'. Cornelia now can relax and enjoy Ophélia's bilingualism, and speaking German together brings them even closer. The whole family are supportive and grateful for their close contact with their grandchild. As Cornelia concludes: 'It takes time, patience, practice and goodwill to raise a child bilingually, but it is possible, even for a full-time working mother like me.'

• See also Cornelia's article – 'Hope for working mothers' in *The Bilingual Family Newsletter* (2001, Vol. 18, No. 4).

Case Study 7: Christine – Scottish-Spanish Blend of Cultures in the Galician Region of Spain

Christine, 42, is Scottish and works as a translator. Her husband, Jesus, 40, a university lecturer, is Spanish and they live in Spain in the region of Galicia, in the north-west of Spain, where the dialect of Gallego is spoken. They have two children, David, eight and Elena, six. They met in Aberdeen, Scotland where Christine was working in a laboratory and Jesus worked there for a year.

Gallego as a language is quite similar to Portuguese and has gone through periods of prohibition and now resuscitation. In the times of Franco, the teaching and use of regional languages were prohibited, then in Spanish society there was a stigma about speaking Gallego because it was associated with being uneducated. However, in the last 20 years or so, there has been a big effort made to encourage people to speak Gallego and to publish children's books, etc. in the language. Jesus learnt Gallego at home, and considers it his first language, although his schooling was in Spanish. Christine understands Gallego, but does not speak it, however in her local community, people are very tolerant of this and often conversations are a mixture of Spanish and Gallego.

At home the parents use a mix of Spanish and English depending on the circumstances, although Jesus only speaks Spanish to the children. Christine tells me that she speaks Spanish to them 'for the benefit of other people', such as when shopping locally, with Spanish friends or with her husband's family. This is has evolved though as she remembers that when David was very young she was much stricter about speaking only English to him in public.

I asked Christine about the children's bilingual schooling and she explained 'They now attend a small rural school and, like most of the schools here, they are taught in a mixture of Gallego and Spanish. They have Gallego as a subject, but how much the other classes are taught in it depends on individual teachers and schools. Up until last year David and Elena went to a much larger school in a small town and more classes were in Spanish than at the school where they are now. Now the majority of the children in their classes speak Gallego as a first language and the teachers tend to speak mostly Gallego to them.'

Her extended family are very supportive of the children's bilingualism, although in the beginning there were some difficulties. As Christine says: 'When David started to speak my mother-in-law realised that I was speaking to him only in English and was a bit annoyed – she said that I should be teaching him Spanish!'. However, seeing the results she is now very proud of the children's bilingualism. Sometimes family members may feel a bit 'awkward or left out', but as Christine remarks it is probably more due to a difference in cultures rather than languages. Christine goes back to Scotland once a year to visit her mother and two brothers, and the children feel very much at home there too. There are some similarities between Scottish and Galician cultures, such as the folk music and she says funnily enough David is learning to play the Galician bagpipes now, which shows him blending the two cultures effortlessly, and pleasing both parents at the same time!

Case Study 8: Jane – English Woman Settled With Her Finnish Family and Local Community

Jane, 45, is English and lives in Muhos, northern Finland with Hannu, 45. She is a teacher of english as a foreign language at a vocational college, and Hannu has his own business. They have three boys, Samuli, ten, Pauli, eight and Terho who is five. The couple met in 1981 at an International Centre in Finland, where they were both studying. Jane has now lived in Finland for 15 years, and can get by in Finnish in everyday situations. Using the OPOL approach has benefited Jane as she has learnt most of her Finnish from her husband and children when hearing them speaking together. She feels very much at home in the local community.

The family also run a small-holding, and in the summer have volunteer workers staying with them who speak English and also friends from all over the world who use English as a lingua franca. As the school holidays are ten weeks in Finland this has naturally created a 'season' of English, so to speak! Jane recounts a charming story about Samuli and these summer workers: 'When Samuli was about three and we first got volunteers, he appeared to have internalised the concept that English was for *female* visitors and Finnish was for *male* visitors. So with our first male helper, he tried to speak to him in Finnish for about a week. I asked him to speak to Brian in English like he did to me. But Samuli said he couldn't! Luckily, after a week he started using English more freely.' At that time, Samuli's main role models for English speech were his mother and grandmother – so it obviously felt wrong for him to use English with a man!

Jane's mother was very relieved that right from the start she was able to have good contact with her grandsons; as through the OPOL approach the children naturally learned to use and understand English alongside the Finnish. However, Jane remembers one trip to England . . . 'I took Samuli and Pauli to England, then aged four and two, thinking it would be good for their English. They tried speaking Finnish with everyone they met – obviously missing their Finnish language terribly- and probably their father too!'. Now Jane's mother can really see the advantages of bilingualism, and is very positive about the situation. Jane goes back to York, in England, to stay with her mother about once a year, usually taking one child with her and her mother visits the family at least once a year.

Hannu's side of the family have had more experience with bilingualism as his sister lives in Sweden, where their child is growing up bilingual (Swedish and Persian). His family also sees learning English as an advantage as most children in Finland learn English at school and appreciate the value of having a second or third language. Jane tells me that 'English is very "high profile" here, and we have always been supported, even admired or envied by some people in our community.' As Jane says: 'With our language combination in a Finnish context the children can see themselves as Finns and also part of the rest of the world.' Feeling part of a close-knit community and also part of the English-speaking wider world should produce secure bilinguals who can profit from their language skills and feel at home in many situations.

Case Study 9: Caroline – Mix of Dutch and Arabic Cultures in Qatar

Caroline, 38, is Dutch and lives in Doha, Qatar with her husband, Ali, 41, who is a marketing manager. The couple met in the Netherlands and later lived together in England for three years, Ali reading maritime studies, while Caroline took business and finance studies. They now have two children, twin boys Tariq and Omar, who are five-and-a-half. Ali and Caroline both speak fluent English, which they use at home together. Caroline says her Arabic is 'limited' and she has always spoken in Dutch to the children. However, Ali used a mixture of English and Arabic to begin with Tariq and Omar, until they were four years old. After that he made an effort to use only Arabic. As Caroline says: 'I am happy Ali speaks his language to the children. I want my children to be fluent in his language; I can understand most of what they are saying. Hopefully it helps me learn Arabic too!'.

For the first four years of the children's lives the family lived in Japan, where Ali was based with his company. Both children were born there. They didn't have many Arabic-speaking friends, so Ali was the main source of Arabic language input for quite a while. However, as Caroline recounts he was working long hours and had many business trips abroad and even when he was around he often used English. When they returned to Qatar nine months ago, Caroline said the boys' Arabic was 'very limited'. Realising their need to integrate quickly into their father's culture Caroline asked the family to speak only Arabic, but instead they often spoke English. Caroline tells me: 'My children usually speak Arabic mixed with English, particularly to their father. They will say the English word if they don't know the Arabic word.' She is not too worried though and thinks that in time the mixing will decrease.

The children are now attending an English-speaking international Montessori school in Doha, with Arabic options. As Caroline says, 'They know now all the Arabic letters with the corresponding sounds and they can read and write them. They started to read simple three-letter words but no sentences yet. Their reading and writing skills in English are more advanced while in Dutch they've none.'

In Qatar, Caroline cooks Dutch food and brings back Dutch treats from her trips back home. She follows traditional customs like Easter, Christmas, etc., even though she is living in a Muslim country. Caroline goes back to Holland as often as she can, and when her mother was alive visited more often to care for her. Caroline thinks that it is important to keep strong links with Holland, for the family over there and for the future if they want to study or live there one day. Living with such diverse cultures could be difficult but for the children they simply don't know any other way and accept it as normal. This family is certainly multicultural, saying: 'We take the good parts of each culture and leave the rest behind!'.

Case Study 10: Louise – The New Zealand Connection is 'Cool' for Kids in Japan

Louise, 33, a freelance writer, editor and university teacher, is from New Zealand and lives in Tokyo with her Japanese husband, Yoshi, 43. He works as marketing director for an automotive company. They have three children, their son, Tsuyoshi who is seven, and two daughters, Reina, four and Marin, one. Both parents speak each other's languages fluently. They met in Hiroshima 12 years ago and started off by speaking Japanese together. In 1995 Yoshi was posted to the US for his work for five years and Tsuyoshi and Reina were born there. Both parents decided to speak English with the children, as they knew they would return to Japan in a few years.

When they returned to Japan in 1999, they changed strategies and Yoshi began speaking Japanese with the children. Louise was rather wary about speaking Japanese with her family and tells me, 'I think me and my kids would have lost out on a lot if we had not maintained the English when we came back to Japan. Our use of English links us in a fundamental way and my relationship with the children seems deeper in English – I suppose because it is my native tongue!'. Louise also reports, 'We both mostly speak only our native languages to the kids, but there is some mixing from time to time since Yoshi and I use both languages with each other.'

Tsuyoshi has started Japanese primary school and when I asked Louise how it was going, she replied, 'Lots of Tsuyoshi's mates study English at after-school lessons at conversation schools, so they think it is "cool" that he can speak English. But he is also careful not to show off too much and to fit in with the norm.' Louise discusses this more, saying: 'As you might know, fitting in with the group and not sticking out too much is crucial to getting along in Japan. Although things have by and large changed for the better as Japan has become internationalised, kids like mine often used to get teased for being a bit "different".' Tsuyoshi has also been able to see what school is like in New Zealand, having attended school there for a about a month each for the last two years, as family summer visits are during the New Zealand school winter session!

Louise has made efforts to meet other families in a similar situation to her, such as organising an English-speaking playgroup in her city, and becoming involved with other groups for inter-cultural families. One such group is B-Sig (Bilingual Special Interest Group) which is an offshoot of a larger organization called JALT (Japan Association of Language Teachers). As Louise says, 'The people in JALT are mainly academic professionals teaching English, but many are married to Japanese and have bicultural kids, and so the B-Sig group is a reflection of that. I joined because of the information on resources for helping our family with bilingualism and biliteracy.' This family, although living with two very different cultures and languages, is able to balance English and Japanese well and to understand bilingualism, as both parents have experienced living abroad and being bilingual. The children are able to relate to life down under, too, and will be able to use both languages to their advantage in the future.

For more information on the B-Sig list see the website: http://www.kagawa-jc. ac.jp/~steve_mc/jaltbsig/

Chapter 4

Interaction Between Family Members and the One-Person-One-Language Approach

This chapter focuses on the interaction between parents, siblings, the extended family and visitors to the house. Firstly, I discuss how the OPOL approach works perfectly in a one-to-one parent–child conversation, but becomes much less evident when another parent is around too. How does a child deal with having both parents there? Do the parents expect the child to say everything twice? Should the child choose one language and expect both parents to understand it? These can be areas of conflict or mis-understanding in the bilingual family.

Secondly, does the extended family have a bearing on the success of the OPOL approach? Indirectly they are very much part of many couples lives, and the grand-parent-grandchild relationship can fail or succeed depending on whether they can communicate. The grandparents can be an effective aid to supporting language and cultural learning too. Equally cousins and friends of a similar age can be a great help in giving essential cultural input.

Thirdly, does having more than one child affect the OPOL approach? With one child, he or she will probably follow the parent's example. Two or more children form their own mini-community and communicate in whichever language they wish. We often see very different language behaviour in second or third children even though parents say they have not changed their strategy. Is there a differ-ence or is it just natural family politics?

Finally, we look at how families deal with visitors. Do families continue to strictly speak two languages in front of someone who doesn't understand one of them? Are parents comfortable applying OPOL in public? How do parents feel when their partner is speaking his or her language? Some parents use a lingua franca, others mix or translate, and many feel uncomfortable because they simply cannot under-stand what their partner is talking about when he or she speaks their own language.

Four case-studies on grandparents and families with experience of the extended family are given at the end of the chapter.

Part One: Conversations With Both Parents and the Children

This is one logistical problem that is often overlooked in the OPOL bilingual family. How does a child converse with both parents at the same time? We have little knowledge of this as most case-studies such as Ronjat or Leopold describe only interactions of one child with one parent. Recent academic studies by Elizabeth Lanza, Naomi Goodz, Susanne Döpke and Maria Juan-Garau and Carmen Perez-Vidal have tried to remedy this with observations of both parents and children. We are now able to see more of how the child alternates and adapts his or her language to suit the situation. This issue seems to be less of a problem in the pre-school years; as a baby and toddler the child is strongly linked to his or her mother and tends to address all communication issues through her. She is happy to 'translate' his or her needs. If she is not listening the young child may try requesting in both languages to get her attention! Later as the child moves on emotionally and mentally he or she wants to share his deeper experiences with the whole family and then problems can start.

The child, especially the first-born, may well believe that the other parent simply doesn't understand the other's language. He or she would specifically address one parent at a time and ignore the other. Children could also repeat the request or comment twice although this needs a higher knowledge of vocabulary and syntax. The child may chose the language that the parents use together, hoping everyone will understand it. As the children get older this dilemma seems to fade out as the children become dominant in at least one parent's language and understand that they can use one language for everyone (usually the language of the country). Older children can either use the 'common' language of the parents, or switch languages according to the topic or person.

Susanne Döpke (1992b: 479) has an example of a two year old German/English boy using his basic bilingual knowledge to ask to be picked up while the mother is dressing him:

Child:	*A:m*	(up?)
Mother:	*Gut*	(good)
Child:	Up!	
Mother:	*sehr hubsch*	(very nice)
Child:	*A:M!*	(UP!)
Mother:	*auf'n Arm?*	(You want to be picked up?)

George Saunders (1988: 54–7) includes lots of examples of typical family conversations between himself, his wife, Wendy and their three children. Sometimes bilingual children just say it twice to be on the safe side. Their son Frank is two years and seven months old. He says, in the presence of both parents: 'I wanna wash my hands [after a barely perceptible pause]. *Ich will meine Hande waschen.*'

George goes on to comment on his children's reaction to talking to both parents simultaneously: 'Faced with such a predicament the children's solution is to address one of the parents by name, establish eye contact with him or her and then proceed in the language appropriate to that parent, knowing that the other parent will understand anyway.'

George also notes that one child, Thomas, would avoid eye contact with the other parent whose language he was not using, but if he did happen to look at them it would create a switch in languages. George says the situation can be resolved by allowing a fluid communication system where each parent can use their language and the children understand. When talking directly to his wife George might begin in English and then add another part specifically for the children in German. Since George's wife, Wendy, understands German this is not really a problem. She often replies in English in relation to their German conversation too or will add an extra bit of information if needed in English to a German sentence.

As Una Cunnigham-Andersson (1999: 31), a mother of four Swedish/English children, in her book, *Growing Up With Two Languages* adds:

> Our experience is that the children ensure that the appropriate parent is listening before they start to say what they want to, by first saying 'Mamma!' or 'Papa!' and waiting for an answer. If the remark is intended for both parents they will sometimes check the other parent's understanding by asking a follow-on question of that parent.

Her children are past the pre-school stage now and have found a way to deal with group language communication. They also know that both Una and her husband Staffan are bilingual and usually they are sure not to be misunderstood by one parent.

Like Una's family, in my family our children both use a lot of eye contact to establish the language too. They usually start conversations with *'Papa, tu sais . . .'* or 'Mummy, do you know. . .'. We are usually gathered together as a family for dinner and Marc swaps languages and eye contact depending on who he is talking to. Nina prefers a more group discussion and mixes both languages somewhat randomly. Sometimes Marc will get quite angry if I respond to something he has said in French, saying 'I'm talking to Papa!'. With a wider group of people (whatever their language) around the table, Marc persists in using one language for each person, while Nina will fit in with the majority.

Here are some real-life examples from our family: you can see we are following OPOL but the language changes in the child, depending on the subject and on how the general flow of conversation goes. The children happily accept this kind of conversation. This only negative side is for outsiders, who may be totally confused by the rapid language changes going on.

From Postman Pat to Penguins and a change of language . . .

Here is a typical weekend family discussion, we are all sat around the television and deciding what to watch next. It begins in English, moves to French and comes back to English at the end.

> **Marc:** (to mother) Can we watch the Postman Pat video now?
> **Papa:** *Non, parce que l'emission de nature est en train de commencer.* (No, because a nature programme is coming on soon.)
> **Marc:** *Ah! C'est pas vrai!* (Ah! It's not true!)
> **Father:** *Tu veux quoi – Postman Pat ou les penguins?* (What do you want – Postman Pat or the penguins?)
> **Mummy:** Oh the penguins are much better and you can watch Postman Pat tomorrow if you want!

What shall we do this Sunday?

Another typical conversation about what we will do that day. Jacques tries to persuade Marc (5; 6) to go with him by using French, and Nina (3; 3) uses English to align herself with me and my day, although it's clear she has understood the French plans for the day.

> **Mother:** Do you want to go shopping in Harrow today?
> **Father:** No, I'll go into London. I'll take one child, who would you prefer, Marc or Nina?
> **Mother:** It's clothes shopping so Nina is best for me.
> **Father:** *Tu veux venir avec moi, Marc?* (Do you want to come with me, Marc?)
> **Marc:** *On va ou?* (Where are we going?)
> **Father:** *A Chinatown. On va acheter des crevettes et puis on ira au Science Museum. Nina tu veux venir aussi?* (To China town. We'll buy some prawns and then go to the Science Museum. Nina, do you want to come as well?)
> **Nina:** No, I want to go with Mummy! I'm staying with Mummy!! I don't want to buy crevettes and I don't like the Science Museum!

Did you understand Mummy?

One amusing feature of family-talk in the family is that the children will often painstakingly translate things, even though Jacques or me understood.

> **Papa:** *Venez ici, les enfants, on va faire de la glace!* (Come here children, we are making ice-cream!)
> **Marc:** *Avec quoi?* (With what?)
> **Papa:** *Les fraises.* (Strawberries.)
> **Nina:** Mummy! Wow! We are making strawberry ice-cream!

The World Cup and divided loyalties ...

Marc (five) wants to tell his father about the World Cup match, which delayed the start of school today but his vocabulary is limited and he soon jumps back into English and phrases he's picked up from school because he doesn't know what to talk about in French.

Marc:	*Oui, nous avons commence ecole a dix heures aujourdhui, Papa!* (We started school at ten o'clock today Papa!)
Papa:	*Et beh! Pourquoi?* (Why?)
Marc:	*La ... la ... World Cup? Comment tu dis ca en Francais?* (The ... the ... World Cup? How do you say that in French?)
Papa:	*La Coupe du Monde!* (The World Cup.)
Marc:	*Oui. C'est ca.* (Yes, That's it) [looking directly at Mother]. Do you know who David Beckham is?
Mummy:	Yes, he plays football for England.
Marc:	He's the best!!!
Papa:	*Non c'est Zidane!* (No, it's Zidane!)

Tasting the plum tart ...

As a last example I show the difference of us being in France, with the French family and the effect it has. The children are using much more French, and Nina picks up on the rhythm and repeats in French and attempts to use more French in general. The conversation between the children and me remains private and although my French mother-in-law, Odile, understands perfectly, she pretends not to and reinforces the French.

Suzanne (to mother-in-law):	*Umm! Ca sent bon? C'est quoi?* (Um, that smells good, what is it?)
Odile:	*De la tarte aux prunes, que Nina ramassee avec moi, c'est vrai, Nina?* (Plum tart, which Nina collected for me, isn't that right, Nina?)
Nina:	*Oui. Les prunes! Beaucoup prunes!* (Yes. Plums. Lots of plums!)
Marc (to mother):	They are plums, Mummy, and they have a special name.
Marc (to grandmother):	*Ils s'appelle comment, grandmere?* (What are they called?)
Odile:	*Des mirabelle.* (Mirabelle.)

Suzanne:	*Est qu je peux gouter, Odile?* (Can I taste it, Odile?)
Odile:	*Oui, vas-y!* (yes, go on!)
Suzanne (to children):	Umm, that's really nice! So sweet and yummy!
Odile:	*Tu l'aimes? C'est trop sucre ou pas?* (Do you like it? Is it too sweet or not?)
Suzanne:	*C'est parfait, suffisement sucre et delicioux!* (It's perfect, enough sugar and it's delicous!)

As we can see the interplay of languages is rarely constant and changes rapidly. Often language change is accompanied by body-language, or someone entering a room. The children rarely misunderstand and if they do ask for clarification. Finally, one important note is to stay consistent with the languages. As I have seen in my own family – if I speak French *directly* to my children it causes discomfort and sometimes confusion about how to reply. This applies to Jacques too, in that he will only use English for clear social reasons. The children will only accept me speaking French to them in certain circumstances:

- With a monolingual stranger, say in a doctor's waiting room, making small talk about the children and me.
- Asking them easy 'yes/no' questions in a public place such as in a restaurant or shop – where it speeds up time for me and everyone else.
- With the French family where I may ask them, in French, if they want more food or if they liked it, as a way to show respect to the in-laws.

Having been conditioned to stick to the OPOL approach it seems that children too like to know where they stand and will change the rules only if they can see a reason for doing so.

Linguistic Ability of the Parents

The language level of each parent is a major factor in the issue of talking to both parents simultaneously, because if both parents are bilingual then the children can choose the language of conversation or switch language, confident that they both speak in the knowledge that they will both understand. If one parent is resolutely monolingual there is only one option. I therefore asked all the parents in my study what they considered their language level to be. Figure 4.1 shows the language levels of the parents, compared to their children. Although we must bear in mind that this is self-reported evidence and it is possible that some parents are over-generous or under-estimate their language proficiency.

Looking at the parental levels of language proficiency the mother's are much more proficient than the fathers, with a high proportion of bilinguals and trilinguals. There are just a few monolingual mothers although we have 50 monolingual

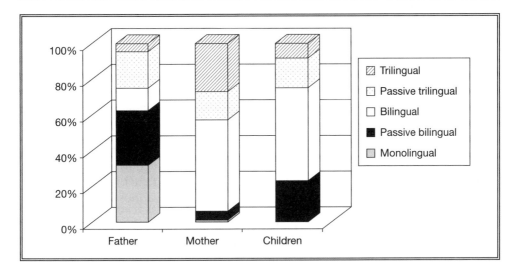

Figure 4.1 Comparison of parent's and children's language levels

fathers. A good number of fathers have a passive knowledge of their partner's language or another language. This is most likely linked to half the families living in the UK, US or English-speaking countries. Over-reliance of English as a convenient parental language may dissuade English-speaking fathers in English-speaking countries from making any effort to learn their partner's language too.

However, in the family where one parent does not have a good understanding of the other language or does not like hearing the minority-language then another strategy needs to be used. In this case the majority-language becomes the lingua franca of conversation. The risk in this situation is that the minority-language is used infrequently and that children see the majority-language as the best way to communicate. In that case some of the advice given in Chapter 2 on language reluctance may help persuade a child to use more of that language. Equally between the parents there may need to be some discussion on how to talk together as a family and possibly asking a majority-speaking parent to accept more of the minority-language around them, as a way to benefit the children.

Part Two: Grandparents and Their Support

Often in a bilingual family parents have married or found a partner from a different nationality to get away from their country, culture and background. In this respect the parents of the couple are often distanced (both emotionally and physically) and have to come to terms with the fact their son or daughter has married a 'foreigner'. This can depend greatly on the distance between the two countries, the personality of the 'foreigner' and the effort they make to adapt. As Dugan Romano (2001: 97) comments in *Intercultural Marriage:*

> Families are not something young men and women shed upon marriage, but usually something they acquire more of. In an intercultural marriage, not only does the couple get a set of foreign in-laws; they also wed a totally absorbing concept of family which will have a great bearing on how they live their married lives.

Our families supported our decision to marry. My English father speaks some basic French and enjoys the gastronomical side of the country while my mother is more monolingual and monocultural in her tastes. Jacques father is originally from Belgium and had a bilingual upbringing as his mother spoke mostly French to him at home. Jacques' parents both spoke good English having travelled a lot and lived abroad with young children. But both sets of grandparents admitted to me that they worried whether they would understand their grandchildren and felt sad that they wouldn't see much of us as we lived abroad.

A large percentage of families stated the main advantage of having a bilingual family is, 'Our children can communicate with their grandparents.' The early days of being a new parent often bring back childhood memories and the grandparents suddenly become important in our lives again. They too are curious to see the mixed-gene baby, with its feet in two cultures and with two languages. However, we do hear about grandparents who simply don't want anything to do with their children or grandchildren or are against the idea of bilingualism. Brought up in a monolingual environment they find the new multicultural generation all too much.

Some conservative grandparents accept the OPOL approach but not in *their* house and will not tolerate the minority-language parents or the child using their minority-language in their home. A Danish mother remembers her Swiss in-laws being against her speaking Danish with them 'because they couldn't understand it'. This doesn't only apply to less well-known languages like Danish, other families reported their parents disliking the use of French, German or English in their homes too. Older generation grandparents may feel out of their depth with the child's second language and culture or feel their grandchild is not really 'theirs' because he or she speaks another language. The new bilingual family, in essence, cannot replicate one cultural norm and is a mix of both, meaning that it may disappoint both sides of the families as it does not duplicate or reflect their culture or values.

Colin Baker (2000: 13) acknowledges the role grandparents can make in passing on a culture saying: 'Not only is the child taught a second language, but the wise and pithy sayings, nursery rhymes, songs, folk stories and traditions of that language can be passed on to the new generation.'

Some grandparents relish the chance to pass on their culture and in the case of a child who has little contact with that culture they are the main source. This can lead too real pleasure for the grandparent-grandchild as they bond together. We sometimes find that the father is less keen to pass on his culture than the mother is and so the paternal grandparents can play an important role in reading, singing, playing games and recounting family stories to the child.

One rather sad case history is from Bent Søndergaard. He is Danish and lives in Denmark with his Finnish wife. His report (1981: 300) on the 'decline and fall' of his son's bilingual acquisition was directly linked to his families' negative attitudes. Søndergaard reports that they gave up bringing up their son, JH, bilingually just before the child was three. He blames the family as the main reason saying: '. . . the parents were under severe pressure from (monolingual Danish) members of the family who maintained that the boy would suffer, perhaps permanently, from this double acquisition of language. It was difficult to resist this, because we could not consult any expert on bilingualism.' This story reminds us of the importance of involving grandparents and family members to gain their support as early as possible.

Grandparents and their Linguistic Role

We hear very little about the grandparents in most case-studies but they are usually there in the background. Leopold and his wife spent six months in her home country of Germany visiting family, which greatly benefited Hildegard. Fantini (1985) reports that they frequently visited the Spanish-speaking family of his wife for one to three months. Their first child, Mario, was very much at home there, quickly picking up the cultural habits and lifestyle of his Bolivian family there. Charlotte Hoffmann took her two trilingual children back to Germany as much as possible to play with similar age children and see family. Traute Taeschner (1983) also mentions several one- or two-month stays with the German-speaking grandparents and the high increase in German vocabulary that it produced in her two bilingual daughters had.

The grandparents do have a role to play in helping language acquisition, especially the parents of the minority-language parent. Such 'pure' input in a real context boosts the minority-language no end. It gives the child what can be described as a *language bath*. It also gives a wide range of male/female, child/adult and group/individual models and justifies *why* the child needs to learn that language. Grandparents often have more time to read books, answer questions and spend time looking at things together. Even the majority-language benefits as the child is away from the dual-language system that characterises family life for them and with monolinguals. Praise from grandparents and their friends for speaking two languages can boost the child although the child should not be forced to 'show off' his or her language skills just to impress family members!

A common problem is that the grandparents expect 'native-like' monolingual grandchildren – twice. Language development can be compared, usually unfavourably, to the monolingual cousins. Other grandparents may criticise the language strategy, especially at the beginning, citing potential speech problems, stuttering or lack of academic skills. They may have had a bad experience with learning languages or heard about children who did not become bilingual. This is made even worse in the mixing stage, when young children combine words from both languages, thus causing confusion and concern that the child can't talk properly.

When our children mixed in France, my French parents-in-law reaction was to speak English to them. It took time to explain that they should stick to French. My parents were either amused or confused by French words thrown into English sentences but would just ignore them and continue talking to them in English. I, like many other families, have found that on arrival in the other country the children usually have rather shaky or limited language skills. They may appear shy and unwilling to talk initially. Taking into account that they are tired or over-excited about seeing their family again it is nothing to worry about. Given time to adjust they will bounce back soon.

Grandparents can feel that they are incompetent at learning languages and may feel threatened by the child's precocious abilities (and also their fluently bilingual daughter or son sometimes). In any case, the grandparents need reassurance that their role is simply to be around and give a natural model of the language. They also need explanations of what strategy you are pursuing and why. The hardest stage seems to be when a child has not yet gained fluency in the second language (usually the minority one from lack of practice). The child simply talks in the majority-language or mixes. It is often hard for the grandparents to remain calm and simply continue talking 'as normal' to the child in the majority-language. They should also follow the OPOL approach as much as possible and try to stick to using one language in the early years.

This is easy for the monolingual grandparents but trickier for those ones who want to try out their language skills on the children. Several parents in the study mentioned that their parents were more positive because they themselves were bilingual or spoke the second language. While it is a great role model to have bilingual grandparents, children cannot really be sent there for a monolingual language bath. Younger children may become confused of the language set-up when seeing their grandparents switching or changing languages and be unsure of how to react. Children may be too honest too; laughing at mistakes or mispronunciation or they may say the grandparents are 'not allowed' to speak the other language.

In my study group I have two families who have grandparents who are actively playing a role in helping their grandchildren become bilingual. One American grandmother, Mary, comes from a bilingual background herself as she was married to a German. Mary lives in Germany and plays a dual role of helping her oldest daughter, who is married to an American and her younger daughter, who is married to a German. For the youngest one, who has a baby, Mary speaks English as a way to help him grow up bilingual. For the other grandchild, age two, and living in England she offers a German environment. Another committed grandfather is Pierre, who is of French origin and lives in England with his English wife. Pierre missed out on the opportunity to bring up his daughter bilingually but is applying a one-grandparent-one-language approach as he successfully helps his seven-year-old grandson acquire and use French well. Nicola is also single-handedly teaching her daughter Spanish so she can feel at home in Chile with her Chilean grandfather and the family there too.

• See also *Case Study 11: Pierre, Case Study 12: Mary* and *Case Study 13: Nicola* at the end of this chapter.

What Parents Said About Their Extended Family

I asked all the parents how they thought the extended family felt about their strategy of bringing up their children bilingually. Most families reported positive attitudes and general understanding that having a bilingual child would benefit everyone. Some families recounted negative attitudes from one side of the family, which could mean a family that is distanced from the children or a family that does not appreciate bilingualism. Several families mentioned the worry that the child would be 'over-loaded' or 'confused' although as the children mature and are able to communicate with them this fear decreases. A great deal of families acknowledged the support they got from a sibling or other close family member, who was also in a bilingual family and could therefore support and validate their choices. A few parents mentioned their own bilingual past or that their parents were also bilingual or spoke the second language as well. Replies from 152 mothers and fathers were received to the question about the level of support provided by their parents, ranging from Not supportive at all, Ignoring partner's language, Accepting and Supportive and encouraging. Figure 4.2 highlights the level of family support:

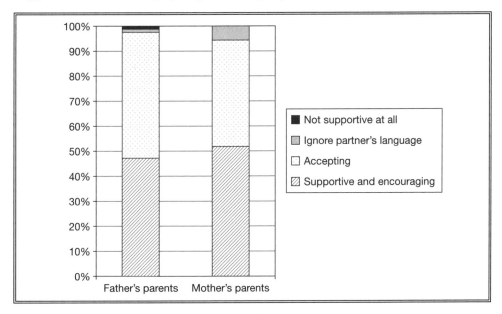

Figure 4.2 Grandparent's attitudes towards parents

The graph clearly illustrates a high level of grandparents who do support their children and grandchildren. More or less 50% of both sides of the family expressed supportive and encouraging views, whilst another 40–50% of grandparents were accepting. Only a very small minority were not happy. There may be a link with grandparents finding it harder with certain languages. As the study shows half of the families are using a language such as Swedish or Hungarian, which could cause some problems in the family since a grandparent in unlikely to have heard such a language before. More global languages such as English, French, German or Spanish may be familiar to grandparents as school subjects or work languages.

We can conclude that the parents are lucky to have such overall support and encouragement from their families. Children can benefit from the extra language input and form strong person-language bonds that will help them maintain their languages, as they grow older.

I also gave the parents a chance to comment on their relationship with their extended families. Here are some of replies I received, divided into four sections: Very Supportive parents, Families where the Father's family expressed some concern; or the Mother's family; and then some general comments about the extended family and it's role.

Very Supportive on Both Sides

Mother: My English family has always been very enthusiastic that my children speak English with them. My sister has selected German as the second foreign language for her children to learn in school. The German relatives accept that we speak English and think it's positive for the children's education (English mother/German father in Germany).

Parents: They are very supportive, even though both our extended families are German. The grandparents do not speak any English but are very proud of April's abilities (German mother and father bringing up daughter to speak English in the Netherlands).

Mother: My mother-in-law is from Welsh speaking family and has given us full support. My parents are very grateful that their grandchildren can speak some Finnish fluently as they don't speak English (Finnish mother/English father in UK).

Father: They are generally pleased we are bringing them up as bilingual, so they can play with their cousins (Danish mother/English father in Belgium).

Mother: Here in Japan, English is very prized, so they think it's a great advantage to learn English as a native language (Japanese mother/English father in Japan).

Mother: My family are very supportive. My children are able to communicate with their extended family in Norway, which is important to me (Norwegian mother/English father in UK).

Father: Appreciate the benefits of the children being multilingual. Enables children to be able to talk to both sides of the family (Dutch mother/English father in Wales).

Father's Family Had Some Concerns . . .

Mother: I am from a bilingual family myself (Dutch/Italian) so for my family it was a natural choice. My husband's family was worried that three languages were 'too much' and that we should speak English to 'help' the children. Now that they see my eldest speaks three languages well, and her English is above average they are very proud (Dutch/Italian mother and English father in UK).

Mother: Although my in-laws find it fantastic that our children should grow up with two languages they struggle with the concept of not understanding what is being said to their grandchildren (German mother/English father in UK).

Parents: The German side is also more or less able to speak and understand French and English, but they would stick to German nevertheless except for speaking to my partner. They are very fond of us and supportive although sometimes challenging the kids as little dictionaries! The French side is not at ease with languages but they are still supportive to our language set up and equally try and learn from the kids the odd words (French father/German mother in France, using English as parental language of communication).

Mother: My husband's family was skeptical about our and our children's ability to deliver on a bilingual strategy. They were (quietly) concerned that the children might get 'confused' (Brazilian mother/Australian father in Australia).

Mother: My German family is 100% supportive. The English family tries hard but can complain about feeling left out when I speak German. We sometimes walk on eggshells! The children are picking this up and often switch to English in social situations now – which I don't mind. It's more important to be socially aware than to be 'right-on' (German mother/English father in UK).

Mother: The British grandparents are more 'impressed' to have a bilingual grandchild – more supportive, or at least more interested in the phenomenon. The immediate French family much less so. For them she's French. They hear us speaking English of course and now basically ignore it. When she was younger there was some hostility; remarks were made about it not being polite to speak a language in front of people who don't understand. But my husband and I were firm about rejecting that attitude and it stopped (English mother/French father in France).

Father: At first, my parents were a bit nervous about this matter though they tried to hide it. By now, they are quite convinced it works out fine for the children. When our children used to speak German to one another all the time, they were sometimes frustrated about not understanding them (German mother/French father in France).

Father: The Austrian grandparents are proud because they consider English to be a language that's essential for the future. The British grandparents, who do not understand German, are impressed with their English, but do not rate German as a necessity. They have said they would be very sorry if the kids could not talk English (Austrian mother/English father in Austria).

Father: My parents are a little nervous when hearing a language that they don't understand (Finnish mother/English father in UK).

Mother: Even though my husbands parents have always been supportive with our strategy they seem to be a bit worried sometimes when I am speaking English to the children. Especially my mother-in-law used to come out with things like. 'Oh, you never know what kind of nasty things she is saying about us.' I think, they have calmed down a lot since they have learned more about Finland. My parents seem to think that it's great that the children can speak English (English mother/Finnish father in Finland).

Mother's Family Had Some Concerns . . .

Mother: My husbands family is very accepting and really want Kyla to be a 'native' Hebrew speaker. My family are accepting, but are more hesitant, because Hebrew is such a 'foreign' language here in the US – especially for non-Jews (American mother/Israeli father in USA).

Mother: In the beginning my mother was not very tolerant of the Finnish and the need for it's use. I think because she doesn't understand, but now she's much more accepting, especially as the children's English has developed well, and she's more aware of the advantages of bilingualism. My husband's family has always accepted our strategy, even if his parents do not understand English. They see learning English in the family as a definite advantage (English mother/Finnish father in Finland).

Mother: It's difficult as Emily does not speak French so my parents can not understand her. My parents are learning English but they are not fluent enough to understand Emily (French mother/English father in UK).

Mother: At first they did not seem to understand the concept of 'bilingualism'. My parents (Japanese speakers) thought (and still do sometimes) it would be rather disadvantageous for Hazuki to have to learn two languages, while other children only need to learn one. This attitude is, however, gradually changing as Hazuki can switch from one language to another with little difficulty. They now seem to be 'impressed' by her linguistic skills (Japanese mother/English father in UK).

Mother: My family (from Australia) were a lot more skeptical than my French-in-laws because they don't know any bilingual families in their circle of friends. Now that my daughter's older and talking fluently in both languages, all their worries about not being able to communicate with their grandchildren are dismissed (Australian mother/French father living in France).

Some Other Concerns and Comments

Mother: Both families are quite supportive but I find that both them and our friends sometimes make tactless remarks about Rebecca's accent or grammar mistakes although we know they are not malicious. It would be nice to hear more praise (Russian mother/English father in UK).

Mother: While being supportive and encouraging people within and outside family occasionally forget that the children are bilingual and should not be compared with other monolinguals. This is particularly true of Mia who's fluent in both languages but would borrow a word if lacking it in another language (Croatian mother/English father in UK).

Mother: The people in my family who can speak English tend to do so with my first son because they see him once a year and he can't express himself in Italian although he understands everything (Italian mother/English father in Singapore).

Mother: The Italian family and friends feel strange if I continue to speak English to baby in their presence or have Marco watch an English language video. They are not unsupportive, just apprehensive and feel a little left out. The younger relatives, six and under are curious to learn a little English so they go with the flow (American mother/Italian father in US).

Mother: My mother sometimes finds it difficult to keep speaking Swedish when the children answer in English (Swedish mother/English father in UK).

Mother: They show interest and they think the children are lucky to be raised bilingually. But it was not always the case and some expressed concern at first. At the first sign of a problem, people tend to blame bilingualism but if the children develop well they accept it (French mother/English father in UK).

Mother: I grew up bilingual myself, so my parents continue the bilingual approach with our son with great success. My parents-in-law are, I believe, slightly bewildered, but they do not openly object (English/German mother and American father in UK).

Parents: Our families back in Germany and Denmark are supportive and very thankful to be able to understand and speak to the children. The German grandmother doesn't mind being spoken to in Danish (which she doesn't understand), knowing that it takes time for the child to figure out, which language to speak to whom (German mother/Danish father living in UK).

Part Three: Studies on Siblings

There are very few longitudinal studies on siblings in bilingual families. The majority of case-studies discuss an only or first-born child as shown in the list of studies done into simultaneous child bilingualism in Appendix 1, where most involved an only child. Studies often end before the second child is born or begins to talk. Although Werner Leopold brought up both his daughters bilingually the six-year age gap between the two girls meant that he had almost finished his work on Hildegard, when Karla was born. Alvino Fantini (1985) mentions Mario's younger sister, Carlina, who is four years younger than Mario but not in much detail. However, we do have a fuller insight on family life with two or more children from Charlotte Hoffmann on her two trilingual children. George Saunders and his three English/German children, Una Cunningham-Andersson, who has four English/Swedish bilinguals and Tracey Tokuhama-Espinsosa, who is bringing up her three children trilingually.

Charlotte Hoffmann (1985) wrote about her two German/Danish/English trilingual children, Christina, aged eight and Pascual, five. Unusually when Christina was three years old Charlotte asked her to speak in German to her new baby brother. This greatly helped Pascaul to hear German from another child and they continued to speak German together until Pascaul started pre-school. When Christina was nearly five she started school and English took over as her dominant language. Her little brother heard Christina play with friends and from around age two he began to speak English actively to join in with his sister. After that he conversed in English to Christina and also used English while playing alone for role-plays. Charlotte describes the children's different personalities as affecting their language use too. Christina is 'more sensitive, thoughtful and reserved' and 'uses the appropriate language to each parent quite consistently irrespective of whether English-speaking children are present or not'. Pascaul is 'more of an extrovert' and '. . . from very early on he has been keen to establish contact with new people and to be accepted by them'.

But Pascaul often got frustrated at his lack of language skills and would use gesture and mime to help others understand him in the beginning. Finally Pascaul used English to talk to his parents. Charlotte thought this was because 'he has just not got the time and patience to stop and think about how he is going to put what he wants to say'.

George Saunders' (1988) book *From Birth to Teens* is one of the best chroniclers of family life with lively descriptions of sibling language use. He observes ten years of family life with his three children, Frank, Thomas and Katerina, who are quite close in age. George single-handedly taught the children German. However, it must be noted that the language of the children when together was English, like their mother, peer-group friends and schools. As he comments: 'That English is the language predominately used, even in private, between Thomas, Frank and Katerina, is a situation which has developed naturally, that is, practically without parental intervention.'

Una Cunningham-Andersson's children are aged 12, 10, 6 and 4 years old. In her family she speaks English to the children, and her husband only Swedish while they live in Sweden. The children all have different levels of language skills as she says (1999: 32):

> Leif (12; 0) and Elisabeth (4; 5) mostly answer in the language in which they are addressed, although their English is heavily laced with Swedish words. They can and will speak more careful English to monolingual English speakers. . . . Anders (10; 3) is very particular about keeping the languages separate, sometimes asking for vocabulary before he starts speaking. Pat (6; 5) speaks only Swedish, although he understands English as well as Swedish.

Una remarks that although all four children were brought up in similar circumstances they have all turned out to be different kinds of bilinguals. Anders has the most aptitude for languages and is able to easily reach monolingual standards for both languages.

Tracey Tokuhama-Espinosa (2001: 86) in her book on multilingual families *Raising Multilingual Children* has three children, Natalie, Gabriel and Mateo, aged seven, five and three in the book. She notes the role of the older siblings as a provider of 'an increased number of verbal exchanges', which can help the younger child. Although she felt she didn't have much time to talk to her second and third children when they were babies the brothers and sisters compensated. They provided role-modelling of social behaviour and use of appropriate language, which is very useful when it comes to code-switching. Tracey tells us how Natalie is more 'maternal' and over-helpful with her brothers. She subsequently becomes the 'official translator' for the boys. Her 'fast-paced, chatty, social' character also overshadowed the quieter second child, Gabriel, who had to shout to have his turn at speaking. The third child, Mateo, seems to have benefited the most, joining a linguistically solid family, with established routines and strategies.

It is often the case that children, who have immigrated to a country, for example Pakistani children coming to live in England, help their siblings in terms of literacy. Charmain Kenner (2002) reports of several such families in London where the young children spent long hours helping each other learn the basics of Chinese, Arabic or Spanish. This was done after a long day at school and willingly. These siblings would also help with homework from their school and role-play being the teacher as a way to help the younger sibling cope with school in a second-language.

Recently Victoria Obied focused on the level of literacy the children had and whether the home language situation was a factor. She observed the sibling behaviour of four very different families in Portugal. Alexandre, aged nine and Marco, 13, are English/Portuguese with two Portuguese half-sisters too. Claudia, nine and her brother Jorge, six are also English/Portuguese siblings. These two families did not have supportive sibling relationships. Alexandre is often 'aggressive in his language use' with his brother and does not feel he can ask his brother for help. Claudia, the older sister, is very competitive with Jorge and often tries to confuse or exclude him in verbal interaction. Victoria describes them as 'out of sync' in regards to family literacy practices.

The other two families were having more success and were 'in sync', Patrick, age 11, and Alison, age six, have an Irish father who loves storytelling. Their shared verbal family interaction was strong, with high value given to the father's culture and language. Martin, 11, Janet, 16, and Justin, 17 are part of a one-parent family (see also Chapter 5 for more on one-parent families). Their Scottish mother was married to a Croatian/American, but now has a Dutch partner. In this family, the younger siblings copy the older ones and there is a strong sense of shared identity and support. Victoria (2002: 9) goes on to conclude that:

> ... sibling relationships may not always foster the development of home literacy. The younger sibling may reject the linguistic and cultural practices of the older sibling and minority-language parent. These conflicts are particularly relevant in the home, as once barriers develop in language use it becomes difficult for the older sibling to transmit literacy practices in the minority-language from the minority culture.

Siblings and Their Use of Language Together

The effect a new brother or sister can have on the bilingual family should not be underestimated. In the bilingual family it would appear relatively easy to control the language use of one child, forming a triad with mother and father. With only one child the language used is more standard, as opposed to the informal often slang-based chat between children. The time the child spends with the parents may be different, with more time for academic skills such as reading, writing or talking with parents, while siblings may play with toys, role-play and share games together.

The arrival of second child changes the power structure and allows an extra dimension – the children can then choose what language they will speak together. On the other hand the second child arrives into a family, which has usually made some kind of decision about what language strategy they will use. Since the average age-gap in Western world is around two to three years between siblings the older child will already be talking, sometimes giving an ideal model for the new arrival. However, as more children join the family the language control gets weaker with the children becoming the main linguistic model for the new baby rather than the parents.

Marc is our first-born and was two years and three months old when his sister, Nina, was born. We had given him a model of language use – English to me and French to my husband. When his sister, Nina, began to speak, their language of communication was English. Since Jacques and I spoke English together as our language of communication this was probably natural. Sometimes they would talk together in French, for role-playing or specifically French games or books. The main difference was that Nina mixed and code-switched on purpose and appeared not to care about speaking one language to one person as long as they understood. Marc disapproved of her strategy, having been brought up rather more strictly to respect the OPOL boundaries and he corrected her, although it made no difference.

The overall trend in my study was for families to have two or more children. Of the total children only 21 were only children, while 60 had one brother or sister and 80 had two or more siblings. This is important because the bulk of research on bilingual families has been done on only/first-born children who may have a very different way of communicating and interacting than children from a larger family.

• See also *Case Study 3: Janet* (Chapter 2), *Case Study 23: Judith* (Chapter 6) and *Case Study 25: Diane* (Chapter 7) for more stories on bringing up two or more children bilingually.

I looked at the languages the children in my study used to find out if they spoke the mother's, fathers or country language between themselves. Figure 4.3 has the results from a total of 110 children (i.e. only children who had a sibling).

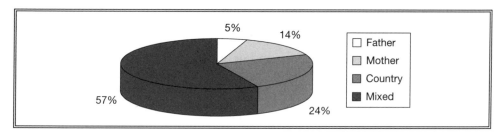

Figure 4.3 Sibling's choice of language

Most children appear to use a mixed strategy – with 57% using some of the mothers and some of the father's language, although we do know the proportions of mother / father language between the children. It could also be either direct imitation of the parents' language patterns, particularly for the younger children who have a minority-speaking mother who will use both languages on a regular basis. The high amount of mixed language use seen in the children reflects an acceptance and acknowledgement of mixing at home, rather than a strict separation of the languages for the children when talking to each other. Only a quarter uses the country language; a percentage that I would have expected to be higher, as the country language often becomes the dominant language of children. The 19% language dominance given to only the mother or father may be a child who is quite young still or a family where one language is much stronger than the other.

Effect on Language Proficiency by Having a Sibling

Does the being the second or third child in the family affect language performance? Anecdotal evidence suggests it does. However, parents may have themselves unconsciously changed their language use and strategy over time and may simply not be as strict as they were with their first child. Child psychologists such as Sarah Brewer tell us that the second or third child is *bound* to behave differently from it's older rival. Communicating in a different way allows the later-borns to be different and challenge the older one's position in the family.

Omark and Erickson (1983) discuss this in their book, *The Bilingual Exceptional Child*. They note that early-borns do better due to standardised direct parental input while the later-borns are subjected to more imperatives and commands, like in a school setting as the parents demand more discipline in the home and more non-standardised child language. However, long intervals of say four or five years between children meant each additional child could have more adult time, as the older one would already be at school. They also comment on the teaching skills of older children, who generally coach the younger ones into following certain linguistic and cultural models of behaviour.

Likewise, Susanne Döpke (1992a) studied six German / Australian children whose families used the OPOL approach, found that *later-born* children often became passive bilinguals rather than active bilinguals. She attributes this to the reduced input of the minority-language that the children receive in comparison to their older or first-born siblings, which would be one-to-one initially. With two or three children using the majority-language the children would have three or more role-models of the majority-language and only one minority speaker.

I therefore compared the language proficiency of the children in my study to their place in the family. Figure 4.4 highlights the potential differences in language proficiency with an only child compared to a first, second and third child. The majority of children are only or first children, with only three third children. The children under age three were not included in the data, as their language proficiency is not yet settled yet.

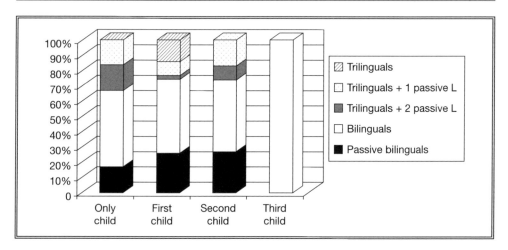

Figure 4.4 Comparison of child's place in the family

The figures show that proportionally the only children are better linguistically, with less passive bilinguals and a good proportion of trilinguals. However there is no major significance and the difference between second and third child is negligible. The low count of only three third children makes it hard to find any conclusions. The third children in the study are generally very young, ranging from new babies to toddlers. We see more trilinguals as first children, but again this is not a major trend and is probably due more to age than anything else.

One advantage of siblings is that they can increase the usage of a minority-language. For parents using a majority-language together the extra input of a child chatting to a brother or sister in the minority-language can give the language a real boost. The minority-speaking parent feels closer to his or her children and language use in the home is more balanced. For parents using a minority-language together the children can join with their conversation, in fact this fact alone may inspire the children to understand the minority-language. However, whether this can be sustained is another matter, the language needing constant input and vocabulary to satisfy the children's need to communicate. Typically when children start school the school language takes over until the minority-language is used for the odd word or expression only.

Cousins and Same-Age Friends

As we can see the siblings make their own language decisions. To help balance this out and allow them some exposure to child language, particularly for the minority-speaker parent, they need to find some similar age speakers. One way is through the immediate family, starting with monolingual cousins or children of close friends, who can count as 'honorary' cousins. If they are similar ages or even a few years apart they can play together and allow the bilingual children a peep into a monolingual culture from a child's point of view.

We have been lucky to have four cousins on the French side of the family, aged seven, five, three and one. The oldest cousin is a boy and close to our son, Marc, who is now six. The second one is a girl, and is close to Nina, now four. Regular visits to the family for holidays have been a chance for our children to see real French children and they are obliged to speak French. We also see an interesting change in child to child interaction, as Marc (first-born at home) becomes number two and Nina (second-born) slides to number four. This allows the older cousins to play a 'teaching role'. Nevertheless, it is obvious there is a linguistic gap and Marc sometimes reverts to miming and gestures to get a message across. The girls, Nina and Manon, enjoy role-playing but Nina tends to repeat everything Manon says which can become annoying for Manon. On the English side there are no cousins yet so we have 'adopted' a few children of close friends, for example the daughter of Marc's godmother and the four-year-old son of my cousin. It has taken time to establish these friendships and it involves quite a lot of effort to meet up regularly and keep the children's friendship alive.

One issue related to cousins is that although parents see a bilingual/bicultural child the more monolingual and possibly culturally limited cousins or friends see such a child as a 'foreigner'. The French cousins refer to our children as *les petit enfants Anglais* (the little English children). Equally they are sometimes referred to as *french children* in England. Children will ask curious questions: 'Why is your dad speaking that funny way?' or 'Why can't I speak French too?' and in the end it is up to the bilingual child himself or herself to explain that they live with two languages and cultures. Lacking cultural input can be hard as discussed in Chapter 3 but children do learn quickly and deal with such curiosity or misunderstandings with grace.

Cousins play a significant role in some of the families in my study. One interesting story involved Cornelia, mother of a German/French girl. Struggling to raise her daughter's level of German she sent her to stay with her sister in Germany in the holidays. This worked very well and the child is very much at home now with her aunt and part of the community. Hedi, mother of two Hungarian/English children with Jamaican roots encourages them to see their Jamaican origin cousins in London. Nicola who is teaching her daughter Spanish as part of her Anglo-Chilean heritage enjoys meeting up with her brother, his Spanish-speaking wife and their two children. Another mother, Lon, with two trilingual Dutch/English/Welsh-speaking children often visits her family and says: 'The Dutch cousins think it really 'cool' that children younger than they are speak such good English!'.

• See also *Case Study 13: Nicola W.* and *Case Study 14: Hedi* at the end of this chapter, and *Case Study 6: Cornelia* (Chapter 3) and *Case Study 22: Lon* (Chapter 6).

If families don't have the chance to interact with cousins then organising holidays around meeting other minority-language-speaking children is a good idea. Many holiday resorts or camping sites organise children's activities or have a play area or swimming pool where children can play with children of the same age. Older children could even be sent alone to the other country for a few weeks in an activity centre, if their language is reasonable and they are happy to go. Although they may only spend a few weeks together long-term friendships can be established and the wide range of activities and informal play mean the children have lots of child to child interaction and see the positive benefit of speaking the language of the other children.

One useful tip here is for the parents to take a back seat and not force friendships on children or interfere too much. However sometimes staff at activity centres are often keen to practise the majority-language, for example, wanting to try out their English on your child. This is acceptable in small doses but really the child needs to fit in and not be 'special' or 'different'. Staff need to know that the child at least has a passive understanding of the language and it may take a few days for the child to adjust and use that language intensively if he or she has not spoken it much before.

Part Four: Communication With the Outside World and Visitors

Here the OPOL family is truly tested on how they use languages. They may have found a way of communicating as parents with their children and as a family but they still need to deal with the outside world and visitors to their home. When visiting other people the strategy may be adapted to suit the circumstances, in a temporary way. Parents may consciously or unconsciously speak less of the minority-language or speak to their children in private, while using the majority-language in public. The situation is different though when they return the visit. As guests in your house they may also find the whole OPOL approach quite bewildering and bizarre and wonder what on earth is going on. Visitors can be various kinds of people:

(1) Long-stay friends and family who are there for a week or more.
(2) Short-term weekend visitors.
(3) Drop-in neighbours and friends and family.

Different strategies may be taken with each kind of visitor. Firstly, with the long-term guests some kind of language accommodation may be needed, especially if the visitor does not understand the minority-language or is uncomfortable and feels excluded when it is used. This could be the case in say a Japanese/English family where the visiting English guests may not understand Japanese at all. A decision could be made to use less Japanese for the duration of the visit. One parent could translate, although this can be tiring for everyone. Parents do need to explain their language strategy and it's relevance to the family. However, being too strict with 'proper' language use may alienate guests, and cause a stressful situation for the children who may be under pressure to use one language when it would be more appropriate to use the guest's language. The visit will have a beneficial cultural effect on the children, which should compensate for any temporary language loss. Visiting aunts, uncles and cousins, godparents and close friends are great company especially if you are living abroad.

The short-term guests will not need so much language accommodation but to make it a pleasurable time the same considerations should be applied as for the long-term guests. Try to explain briefly your language strategy early on and how it works especially for people visiting for the first time. Usually people are very understanding and complimentary but remember it can all seem quite odd to them.

The drop-in visitors and local friends usually speak only the language of the country so parents and children should respect this and not try to confuse them. In the same category as teachers, doctors, shop-workers and local parents the child needs to show social politeness in the majority-language. They will probably not expect to hear another language so depending on the length of visit and their knowledge of the family the conversation can be the country language, with private comments to the children in the minority-language. One French-Canadian parent living in Hungary mentioned how she often used Hungarian when in company with other mothers, as often comments to her child were directed at the whole group.

One uncomfortable situation is when a child doesn't speak the visitor's language very well and appears shy or impolite. Monolingual children can be equally impolite and shy too, but in the bilingual family it is perhaps more obvious. One way to smooth over this is to teach the child some of the non-linguistic cultural norms such as kissing guests (appropriately), offering a drink or biscuits/sweets and smiling at guests. Hopefully such a good impression will distract from the child not talking very much. In the bilingual family children quickly learn which visitors speak 'Mummy's language' and those using 'Daddy's language' and will adapt accordingly, given a bit of time to re-adjust.

What the Parents Said About Group Language Use . . .

I asked parents in my study what they usually did when they had visitors in the house. This was an open question and because group language use can covers many possibilities language use may change depending on who is present. Nevertheless, Figure 4.5 sheds light on the differences between parents in how they interact with other people socially.

The most common response was 'I speak my language to the child', showing that 57% of parents are trying very hard to keep the OPOL approach strong in public. They may do so confidently if people understand the language or quietly and in private if not. Some parents did not want to appear rude or impolite in company by using a language that no one understands. Of those 23% who spoke

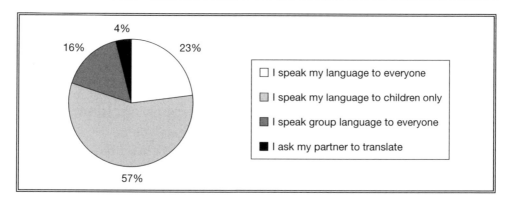

Figure 4.5 Parent's language use in a group

their own language more fathers speak their own language, which is likely to be English. Mothers are usually bilingual anyway and usually speak his language as their second language. Therefore, language use depends on the language levels of the parents, as we saw in Part One, some parents may not be able or wish to participate in a social setting in their second language. Within the minority of parents who ask for a translation no mothers ask their partner to translate, but only a few (monolingual) fathers do so. Finally we can conclude that using the 'language of the group' gives children a model of using language appropriately in social situations, and such switching will be what they are expected to do as adults. It may also be that a group of mixed nationalities will choose a lingua franca and everyone will use that rather than having multiple translations or people feeling linguistically excluded.

The parents commented briefly on such group language use as we can see in the following excerpts:

Comments About Language Use With a Group of People . . .

Mother: I speak the language of the group to the group and my language to the child (Danish mother/German father in Belgium).

Mother: I speak my language to my children, and to the others. If they understand English, but if they don't, I would speak in Finnish as far as I am able (English mother/Finnish father in Finland).

Father: We use English as lingua franca (Norwegian/English mother/French father).

Father: ... it depends on whether or not I feel want others to understand in order to continue the flow of conversation, and also depending if Japanese comes easily to me or not (Japanese mother/American father in Japan).

Mother: A case by case thing. I try to speak in English to the kids as much as possible, but in some cases this would be rude or it's not practical in front of others, so we might switch to Japanese (New Zealand mother/Japanese father in Japan).

Father: I can't switch as readily as my wife can – if we are in a group of German-speaking friends, and I am working hard to be in 'German mode', then I stay there when I talk to the kids. However, at the Grandparent's house or something like that (more extended stay) I speak English. Also I speak English to them in my own home, regardless of company (German mother/American father in US).

Mother: We mix languages and I mix the two languages when addressing the child too (Italian mother/English father in UK).

Mother: My German is presently at an Intermediate level. With bilingual friends or English speakers, I speak English. With those who speak only German, I make an attempt to communicate directly but if I get stuck then I ask my partner or another German speaker to translate. If the whole group is speaking German (even though there may be English speakers within it) I try to follow what's said and join in when possible, in German. Whatever the circumstances, I always speak only English to my son (American/British mother and German father).

Mother: I mostly keep speaking my language to my kids and to the rest I would speak in their language but sometimes I still speak to my partner in our language which remains English (German mother/French father in France – who use English as a parental language of communication).

Mother: I mostly keep speaking my language to my kids and to the rest I would speak in their language but sometimes I still speak to my partner in our language which remains English (German mother/American father in US).

Mother: I try to speak my language to my child but then I forget and then usually use the group language (English mother/Swedish father in UK).

Summary

This chapter tells us of the ever-changing interactional relationships in a bilingual family. From talking to both parents together, forming a bond with his or her grandparents or siblings and dealing with outsiders and visitors the child is constantly updating language use.

We can see that having bilingual parents can make it easier for a child to communicate, but that in such a case we easily slip into a mixed dialogue between parent and child without even realising it. We need the extended family to help out by giving monolingual models of behaviour and a haven from the pressures of bilingual family life. However their understanding is needed, as criticism can be detrimental to the child's progress.

Siblings pose many unanswered questions. Anecdotally we can see that they are very different children, but it could be because they simply need to behave differently or that we as parents have subtly changed the rules of the games. Like enforcing good eating, sleeping and behaviour patterns we tend to have more success with a first-born or only child. More than one child becomes a separate identity and they ultimately make the rules and we cannot interfere with their language choice, even if we would like too.

The bilingual family is not an island and is frequently exposed to strange looks, comments and even criticism in public. The strength to keeping using OPOL in public or with people who may not approve is a test of the family. Much empathy and adapting to each circumstance are needed.

We now take a closer look at the bilingual family and some of the issues that can affect it – from losing a parent to having speech problems.

Case Study 11: Pierre – Following a One-Grandparent-One-Language Approach With Great Success

Pierre is of French origin and lives in Abingdon, near Oxford with his English wife, Norma. He has applied the OPOL approach to helping bring up his grandson, Olivier who is nearly eight, bilingually. Their daughter, Colette, 35, is the mother of Olivier and works in publishing. She was not brought up bilingually because when she was a young child the standard advice was rather different. As Pierre recounts, 'The linguist books all recommended teaching a second language at age five, but by then Colette had started English school and had many English friends, so she wasn't very keen to start French then.' However, Pierre has more than compensated with his grandson.

Pierre came to live in England when he was ten to rejoin his French mother. She was subsequently to remarry his step-father, a Polish refugee. They lived in London where Pierre continued his education at the *Lycee Francais* with a year in Boulogne to conclude his secondary education. Pierre taught French as his profession and since retirement looks after Olivier three days a week when Colette works. Pierre decided to use French with Olivier right from the start and has profitably used their time together to create a unique French environment. When Olivier is with his grandparents he uses French with *grandpere* and English with Granny. Norma enjoys hearing Pierre speak his mother-tongue and frequently invites Olivier's French friends to their home.

As a young child, Pierre took Olivier to local toddler groups, but always spoke French, as he explained, 'I always use French when I am with Olivier, even at the doctor's surgery when I accompany Olivier there.' He adds 'I even managed to contact some other French-speaking mothers locally and we arranged for the little ones to play together whenever possible.' Pierre encouraged Olivier's love of reading through the *Maison Francaise d'Oxford* (a French cultural centre) where he remembers, 'Olivier was a great attraction there and we've read and re-read all the books suitable for his age there!'. They also enjoy singing French songs and watching satellite French television and videos together.

For the last four years, Olivier has been attending the European School in Culham, near Oxford, which is funded by the EEC, but offers places to local children who are bilingual in European languages. The school operates administravely in English, but each child is taught according to his language. There are five main language sections. Olivier is part of the French section and therefore follows a curriculum identical to that in a French school, except he has extra time for study of English, as a second language. He tells me 'I like school a lot, I have lots of French friends there. I will do my *baccalauréat* in French when I am 16!'. Olivier reads and writes in French very well and is just starting to read in English, although the transfer is easy, as he is very familiar with English books.

Colette benefits from hearing more French around her, she has a good knowledge of French and regularly visits friends and family in France. Interestingly Olivier calls her *maman*, not 'mummy', although Colette thinks this is probably reinforced by both Olivier's school and his close French friends. This example of one-language-one-grandparent is an inspiration to anyone who regrets not passing on their language to their children, for various reasons. Although not all children are lucky enough to have such a dedicated teacher/grandfather, and a multilingual school close by, it shows the effect that the extended family can have. The bond between grandfather and grandson is stronger with their shared language and culture.

Case Study 12: Mary – Bilingual Grandmother Helping Her Daughters Bring Up Their Children Bilingually Too

Mary, 54, is American and is married to Hartmut, who is German. They live in Trier, Germany where Hartmut is a university professor and Mary does freelance translation work. They have two daughters, Elisabeth, 31, who is married to an American and lives in England with her two-year-old son, Max, and Jessica, 28, who lives in Trier with German husband and one-year-old son, Felix. Mary and her husband successfully brought up the girls bilingually, even though she says 'There was virtually no literature available thirty years ago on raising children bilingually. Any books that I found concerned, for example, Mexican children going to an American school.' Relying on her instincts she followed the OPOL approach as she remembers 'It just made more sense to me because I wanted to speak my own language and my husband wanted to speak his.' She also wanted the children to have a good relationship with their grandparents, which she supported by spending summer holidays in California every other year. The family spent a year on sabbatical in California when the children were in third and sixth grade, which helped their English enormously, and gave them a cultural insight into America.

After starting Nursery school German became the dominant language for the girls as Mary recounts, 'In general, I spoke English and the girls answered in German (which was the system that Hartmut and I were using too). I never felt that it was really possible to insist that they speak only English with me because I couldn't pretend that I only understood English!'. However, with their monolingual family the children spoke perfect English so Mary wasn't too worried. She adds though, 'Our use of two languages often attracted attention when we were out in public, and occasionally people would even ask us why we were using in two languages? When the girls were pre-teens or early teens they would even tell me that I had to speak English because I couldn't speak German properly!'.

Now within the close family and English-speaking friends living in Germany they have established a code-switching pattern, which they call *Germish.* This is a mix of German and English, as Mary explains, 'It could be described as language-laziness as we tend to use the term (either English or German) which comes to mind first, since we know that the person we are speaking to understands both languages. It's not only laziness though, because not all terms and concepts are easily translated, so in some cases the term in German is more accurate (even if I am speaking English). And sometimes I don't have the proper vocabulary available in English, if I am describing something that I have experienced in Germany.' The family use it to create jokes, puns and even as a secret language! Elisabeth's American husband, Richard, found it quite intimidating at first, but now joins in the game too!

Mary is now busy helping out Jessica, 'I have looked after Felix at least once a week ever since he was born. I only speak English with him, although when other people are around, I might speak German, in order not to be impolite. He already responds properly when I ask him, for example, "Where is your foot?" or "Where is the car?", etc. Jessica is pleased that I am doing this, because she only speaks German to him.' As a wonderful grandmother and role-model Mary is inspiring Max and Felix to enjoy the benefits of bilingualism and soon they will join in with the family language of Germish, making jokes and playing with languages too!

• See also *Case Study 1: Richard and Elisabeth* (Chapter 2) for more on Mary's daughter, Elisabeth.

Case Study 13: Nicola W. – Spanish Language Helps Keep Her Anglo-Chilean Family Heritage Strong

Nicola Wilkinson, 41, British/Chilean is married to Peter, 51, who is British. She works as an international aid worker and Peter is a business advisor. They met in Nairobi in 1987 and now live in Northamptonshire, England with their daughter, Lizzie, who is three. Nicola speaks Spanish, some Portuguese and French, which she puts to practical use, while working on international aid projects in Africa. Wanting to pass on her paternal Chilean language heritage Nicola decided to follow the OPOL approach and bring up Lizzie bilingually from when she was born. The main family langauge is English, and Nicola has spoken to Lizzie since birth in Spanish although is also supporting her English language learning too.

Nicola's father is Chilean and her mother British, giving Nicola a personal insight into being bilingual and bicultural. Her family lived in Ethiopia, Argentina, Ecuador and England with her father's job, and she had little contact with her father's home country, as she says, 'I only travelled first to Chile in 1976, when I was 15 and since then I have spent some eight years in Chile.' While in Chile she learnt Spanish and is now fluent in it, although she says it will never be a first language. She now tries to return once a year for at least four weeks long holiday, visiting friends and her father who has now remarried a Chilean woman and lives there. Lizzie has already been there four times and benefits greatly from the visits, as she attends a Spanish-speaking nursery there and sees the family and close friends with young children. After the trip and back in England, Nicola tells me, Lizzie continues to speak only in Spanish for at least a week after, but otherwise her verbal Spanish is limited still to occasional words.

Within Nicola's family speaking two languages is '. . . highly desirable and valuable, but also something relaxed and enjoyable'. One of her brothers married a Chilean and they now live in England with their two children. When together the family regularly mixes Spanish and English, because they are bilingual and also to ensure that anyone not fluent in Spanish can understand. Nicola also remarks that 'When we are with people who speak no Spanish at all our conversation is in English.'

Lizzie is enjoying beginning to read and write in English, and Nicola hopes to transfer this early interest into Spanish too. However, she's had problems finding books in Spanish and laments the lack of foreign language material in her local libraries. Her local library only stocks ten Spanish books aimed at a particular age and Nicola relies on annual book buying trips. Nicola otherwise translates an English bedtime story into Spanish every other night, but says 'I'm more aware now of the gaps in my Spanish, especially words from children's stories, which take some translation, like *wiggle, splash* and *squelch!*'.

Nicola and Peter are clearly dedicated and committed to their language strategy but acknowledge that Lizzie gains confidence particularly when with Spanish speaking children. On the journey to Chile Lizzie is amazed at the fact that there are other people speaking Spanish and that she can understand it! The family use the annual trips to Chile as a way for Lizzie to be totally 'immersed' in Spanish langauge and Chilean culture, build her own friendships and thus give her the gift of a strong second language linked to a country and her grandfather.

Case Study 14: Hedi – A Hungarian/English Family With Jamaican Roots

Hedi, 36, is Hungarian and is currently training to be an accountant. Her British partner, Paul Morris, 40, is a design engineer. They live in Gateshead, England with their two children, Elvira, four and Aaron, who is 18 months. Hedi came to England in 1991. She met Paul six years ago in Gateshead, and they have always spoken English together, while Hedi now speaks Hungarian to the children. When playing together the children speak about 70% Hungarian and 30% English, although Hedi worries that later the children will speak more and more English. Paul likes the strategy too, saying, 'I am learning words and phrases of Hungarian in the process!'.

Paul comes from a 'big happy' Jamaican family, who immigrated to England in 1959, and subsequently returned to Jamaica in 1991. Hedi says, 'There are few Jamaicans living in our area, so we make sure that the children spend time with their cousins in London, where some of Paul's brothers and his two sisters live. As they have plenty of friends coming to the house my children got used to calling every child they meet in London their cousins, even if they are from Ghana, or England!'. The couple have visited Paul's father in Jamaica and he comes over to England too. He has even spent a week with Hedi's family in Hungary, and the two families found many cultural similarities between them. The couple say: 'We definitely want to take our children to Jamaica, but we shall perhaps wait until they can actually appreciate it a bit more and learn something from it.'

Hedi is very close to her family in Hungary, telling me 'Whenever I had time and money I went home. In fact, in the last ten years I only had two proper holidays, the rest was visiting family. Since the children were born we visit up to four times a year.' Elvira chats to her Hungarian grandmother nearly every day and is very close to her. They usually spend a month in Hungary and Elvira fits in well as Hedi comments, 'When we are on vacation in Hungary no one ever assumes that we live abroad, although my children are darker skinned, because Elvira's Hungarian is often clearer and richer than the local children.'

Aaron is just beginning to be aware of the two languages and Hedi reports, 'He never speaks Hungarian to an English person, but he must have figured out that I speak English, because he often speaks English to me!'. This seems typical of the second child in a bilingual family, as Hedi says that Elvira never did that! Aaron is not as fast in his language acquisition as Elvira was, he started speaking later, but in the last month he has learnt than ever and will soon catch up with Elvira.

This unusual tricultural family manages to keep the relatively minority-language of Hungarian strong, and balance that with a rich source of Jamaican culture. These children are growing up with such a wide range of cultures that they will transfer this openness to their daily life, welcoming new friends from any country as cousins!

Chapter 5

One-Parent-One-Language Families – Expectations and the Reality

This chapter looks at some of the areas which can affect the success and failure of bringing up our children bilingually. Families all over the world, multilingual or monolingual, have to deal with difficult times, be it one parent feeling excluded, separation, divorce or death of one parent and problems with the child's speech or language ability. These can truly test the bilingual family and cause conflict.

In the first section we discuss how the parent's expectation of a perfect family don't match with the reality. The positive or negative beliefs of each parent in their child's potential bilingualism can affect the outcome. We then read some comments from the parents about what they think are the advantages and disadvantages of having bilingual children. I also look at how the gender of the parents can be a factor and the prestige of each parental language in the society where they live.

The second part concentrates on some issues, which not all families will have to deal with, but should be aware of. We look at how a partner can easily feel isolated, linguistically and culturally within his or her own family. We hear some comments from parents about this too. Next we see what might happen in a one-parent family and how families cope with this. Finally we cover speech problems and how they can erode the confidence of the family in supporting bilingualism when under pressure from monolingual speech therapists.

At the end of the chapter there are five case studies describing a parent feeling excluded, life as a single parent, and some speech problems that they have encountered in their family

Part One: An Ideal World vs the Reality of the OPOL Family

Often we have too high expectations about having bilingual children. As we heard in Chapter 3 the cultural balance of the family can lean one way or encompass both parents. One parent will most likely be bilingual from the start, while the other one chooses whether to catch up or not bother learning his or her partner's language. We often read of 'success stories' of young children who are perfectly bilingual or even trilingual with apparently little effort. What is not so well known is the reality of life with two languages, which like bringing up children in general is never smooth. Stages of development produce different problems, there can be problems adjusting to different children and trying to give the same amount of language input to each of them. Children rarely succeed at everything and some simply will not be good at language – their parental ones or ones learnt later at school. Being brought up bilingual does not guarantee anything. Equally parents brought up in a monolingual environment have little idea of what life will be like, they may be shocked to feel excluded when the partner speaks to the child or unable to keep up with the fast progress of the child. They may prefer a mono-lingual/monocultural life secretly and unconsciously pass on this to their children.

The following comparatives show:

(a) an ideal version of bilingual life, which is achieved by some families;
(b) the more typical family, who have compromised and accepted each other's language and culture, and
(c) families who are risking becoming monolingual/monocultural or are strug-gling to and under pressure to give up by families and health professionals.

(a) Perfect World

Both parents support bilingualism
Both parents have a level of fluency in each other's language
Both parents are able to use both languages in public
The children speak both languages at a good level
Both parents enjoy being a bicultural family
Neither parent is isolated or excluded
Father and mother have equal roles in bringing up children

(b) Typical Family

One parent is more positive than the other about bilingualism
One parent is bilingual, the other has some knowledge of partner's language
One parent may be shy or uncomfortable in public using partner's language
The children have one dominant language and there may be some delay or
    minor speech problems
One parent is bicultural while the other one supports and accepts his/her culture
One parent may feel excluded, at times, linguistically or culturally
Mother is more involved in childcare in the first three years, father takes over
    later

(c) Cause for Concern

Neither parent cares about bilingualism
One parent is bilingual, but the other refuses to speak partner's language

One parent insists on translations or only using his/her language at home
Children refuse to speak one language or are having major problems commu-
nicating verbally
One parents dislikes the other's culture
One parent is constantly feeling isolated
One parent may be absent or unwilling to be involved with the upbringing of
the children

These categories are of course not absolute and families may well go through periods when they do have cause for concern as we have done ourselves over the last six years. On the other hand parents who are particularly committed and have succeeded in bringing up their children bilingually and equally keeping both partner's satisfied and involved deserve a pat on the back, as it is certainly no easy task. For the most part we manage perfectly well with the typical family scenario and total commitment and bilingualism from both parents is not essential.

The Parents Beliefs About Bilingualism

Parents of children are often mystified as to why their child doesn't simply 'pick up' the two languages. Some parents are sure that children will acquire languages 'naturally' if they are young enough. So why is it that some parents achieve more success at bilingualism than others do? Research has shown that exposure to two languages, even in a consistent manner does not guarantee active bilingualism. Therefore, we have to look at exactly what messages the parents are giving to their children. Annick De Houwer (1999) looked closely at the role of parental beliefs to discover the link between bilingual development. She found that parents could influence the child's language progress. Annick calls this *impact belief*, which she defines as the belief '. . . that parents can exercise some sort of control over their children's linguistic functioning'. We can see this visually as a continuum:

LOW IMPACT BELIEF ——————————— *HIGH IMPACT BELIEF*
Not interested   Passionately commited

At one end of the spectrum there are some parents who simply do not care about passing on their language; they have a low impact belief. This could be because by marrying a foreigner they have left their culture and language behind and wish to make a fresh start in their second language. They may not care if the child speaks their language or not, since it is not that important to them. Some may feel that nothing they do will affect the child's linguistic outcome anyway and he/she will pick it up anyway regardless of their effort. Others may feel that bilingualism is 'doomed to disaster' and they won't even bother trying.

At the opposite end, those with a high impact belief are parents who are very keen to bring up their children bilingually and these are often those people who discuss, read, and plan their strategies for bilingualism well in advance of the child's arrival even. They highly value bilingualism and it's benefits to both the individual and society. The parents may adopt rigid established methods and ideas, such as starting simultaneous bilingualism from birth for maximum exposure, carefully organising language input or strictly following the one-person-one-language rule. Case studies showing such commitment and strength of character are Ronjat (1913), Leopold (1939–49), Saunders (1982), Taeschner (1983) and Juan-Garau and Perez-Vidal (2001). Ronjat, for example, refused to give the German equivalent of French words, sending Louis off to his mother for help. Saunders persevered in using German in public when his children felt uncomfortable, and Taescher applied the severe *Wie Bitte?* strategy, that we heard about in Chapter 1. Juan-Garau and Perez-Vidal made major efforts to halt the majority-language overtaking the minority-one too. They all achieved success, but one wonders at what cost for the child?

Being too strict can have drastic consequences too. The Ziener family living in Peru refused to let their German/Spanish son speak Spanish until he was three. They forbid his Spanish-speaking grandmother and local children to have contact with him until he spoke a good level of German (Ziener, 1977). Other studies describe parents punishing children for 'wrong' language use, such as one mother who withheld food from her English/Hebrew child when he spoke Hebrew to her rather than English (Fredman, 1995). Although we all have times when we would like to 'control' our children's behaviour, in reality we cannot force them to do anything.

There are also many families who never manage to get started with bilingualism in their family or stop when it gets difficult. The Søndergaard (1981) family tried to bring up their Finnish/Danish son, JH, bilingually in Denmark but failed. Their main reason for stopping was the disapproval of the Danish monolingual family. However, both parents were competent language speakers. They state (1981: 297) that there were two reasons why they wanted to bring up JH bilingually:

(1) He would be able to communicate with monolingual Finnish-speaking members of his family;
(2) as an adult he would have the possibility of living in Finland, and this implies a native-like command of the language (because Finnish is not an Indo-European language the distance between the languages is very great). The father had seen that people who, like himself, had learned Finnish as adults often had a poor command of the language.

Søndergaard appeared to have good reasons, but at the age of three when JH's Danish was 'below average' and he 'did not say anything voluntarily in Finnish' they gave up and concentrated on a Danish monolingual upbringing, reserving

Finnish for holidays and grandparents. Bent does wonder later if he should have kept going longer and persevered more with the Finnish, and ignored his families' comments. His wife appears to have had a rather low impact belief too and quickly dropped Finnish for Danish.

For bilingualism to work the belief in intrinsically wanting your child to be bilingual has to be there. As we saw in the first part on ideal or typical families a common occurrence is a family where one parent, typically the mother, has a high impact belief, and is sure that it will work and is important. However the partner may be not so keen – he or she typically lives in their own country and are not so bothered about it. The high impact parent either has to persuade the other to see the benefits or simply promote bilingualism on her own. If the partner is particularly against bilingualism or disproves of his or her efforts they become a cause for concern.

As the great majority of families in my studies showed; the ones who are committed, have read some books or articles, have supportive family and friends, maybe have joined a minority-language playgroup or found ways for the child to meet other minority-languages speakers are usually more successful. Like all families, the bilingual family will have difficult phrases, such as when the child first talks, the intensive mixing time around age two and three year when the child starts school or when relatives criticise the child's language use. In those times some support is needed to guide, reassure and bolster the parent's belief in bringing up their children bilingually. If not, there is a risk that bilingualism will be demoted and a monolingual or low impact belief will take over. Most importantly, even young children are sensitive and aware as to whether it is important for them to be bilingual and will strive to please their parents.

Advantages and Disadvantages

At the end of the questionnaire I asked parents what were the positive aspects were about being a bilingual family? An extremely high percentage of parents enthusiastically gave their reasons for bringing up children bilingually. The ten most quoted advantages were:

- A better start in life.
- Good job/study prospects for the future.
- More freedom to be mobile and work in several countries.
- An increased tolerance in the world towards other languages and cultures.
- An understanding of other foreigners needs.
- Learning two languages simultaneously from birth is better than later acquisition.
- Good ear for language learning in the future.
- Increased intelligence and meta-awareness.
- Able to have a dual-cultural heritage.
- Able to communicate with other family members.

The parental comments below show us what dreams and aspirations the family has for their children and how strongly they believe they will be successful.

What Are the Advantages and Positive Aspects of Being a Bilingual Family?

'They might learn languages easier later on – but above all I think it's necessary to speak my own languages – to be able to express myself well, when speaking to them.'

'Gives our child a better start to life, is much more interesting, widens all our horizons, allows my husband to improve his Dutch at the same time.'

'Greater tolerance towards minorities and different cultures. Greater freedom in later life to move around Europe. Easier access to jobs. Keeping my culture and understanding of my home country and family.'

'That's a little like asking what the advantages of breathing are! To me, it's the normal state of affairs and I would not have it any other way! If I had to put words to it they would be personal gratification, cultural and linguistic enrichment and a head start in learning and intellectual development.'

'Richer communication and closeness within the immediate family. Deeper understanding between generations (grandparents to grandchildren).'

'We have direct access to a richer cultural heritage. Our daughter is aware of linguistic and cultural diversity, which will hopefully help to foster tolerance and respect.'

'I want to do what's best for my children. I think passing on traditions and culture will widen their horizons and will make them better, all more tolerant people. They will feel at home in at least three cultures.'

'I think it's important for children to learn languages and this is an easy way.'

'I found it very fascinating to witness a simultaneous emergence of two languages.'

'To be more open-minded and I hope it will help them in the future to find a job and to learn other languages. Most important is that they can talk with my family.'

'I believe my children are growing up not only with an ear for languages which might be useful to their later life but also more flexible, accommodating and understanding of other cultures.'

'Belonging to two cultures, feeling comfortable communicating with people from minority-languages/countries especially relatives. Increased confidence generally and at school for children.'

'Bilinguals learn to think differently than monolinguals. They have two ways of articulating things and ways to reach out to a wider audience.'

'There's something very satisfying about knowing another language and having some insight into a different culture. It's fascinating seeing how the children's languages develop and I feel pleased that they can communicate in both easily. It was much harder for me to learn a second language!'

'We feel this is a wonderful gift that we are able to give our child.'

'I could not imagine any other way of life.'

I also asked the parents what the disadvantages and negative aspects were of being a bilingual family. In this instance many families replied that there were 'none' or 'I can't think of any!' which is a sign that all is going very well for them. Others did give some negative aspects, which in general came from the external pressure of society to conform, not from inside the family. The most common complaint was that it was hard work! However this may only apply to one parent, who is in the minority and has to work harder to preserve their language and culture. The ten most frequently mentioned disadvantages were:

- Hard work, determination and effort needed.
- Not being a 'normal' family.
- Child never reaching 'native speaker' level.
- Explaining the family situation to monolinguals.
- Their child being bullied or 'picked on' at school for being different.
- Worries about language development and mixing/code-switching.
- Having to frequently translate or ask for translations.
- Having to invest time to teach child at home to keep both languages strong.
- The extra effort and expense of having materials in both languages and visiting family.
- Potential misunderstandings and chaos of having two languages at home.

Here we can see some of the comments made by the parents regarding some negative aspects:

What Are the Disadvantages of Being a Bilingual Family?

'When my husband doesn't understand – it creates misunderstandings. It's a bit chaotic at times!'

'Keeping on track is a constant struggle – concepts learnt in English at school have to be learnt again in German at home. It's often difficult to behave naturally in social situations too – what feels right can be perceived as wrong. There is sometimes the feeling of not belonging anywhere completely.'

'I fear rejection or ridicule for my daughter in the future. Some people might find we are odd or rude.'

'It is very expensive because we buy lots of Dutch material to have readily available here in Australia, plus travel costs for regular trips to Holland.'

'It's difficult to accept that my children will never be 100% "bilingual". They will need lessons or how to read or write in my language (French).'

'I found it quite hard at the beginning (i.e. when the children were only just speaking) to be the "intermediator". People would ask the children questions and I had to translate for them – it took away the spontaneity of conversation.'

'It's difficult to maintain the level off language skills over time. There are communication problems due to lack of vocabulary in certain topics in one language.'

'I do not always understand what's going on.'

'Not necessarily a disadvantage but does require enormous effort and determination with slow (if ever) reward.'

'Life is expensive having to travel between two countries.'

'The 'local people' may stare at us when I speak my language to my children, making me feel like I am not at home. Sometimes we don't get the same treatment in shops, restaurants etc.'

'I has been a lot of hard work for me to keep it going. It would have been much easier to stick to a majority-language.'

'Maybe I couldn't have made myself understood completely since there are so many things I wouldn't explain through words. Also there was the time when I compared two cultures and disliked one part of one culture which confused me.'

'Children don't want to be different to their peers so negative attitudes can discourage them.'

'Not everyone understands about bringing children up bilingually, and many people are ready to criticise that the children are being confused. I think because we are so open minded, we forget that everyone else isn't.'

'We are not a "normal" family.'

'The children might never have the command of a language that a native speaker of only one language has.'

'It can be quite hard work after the children pass the baby stage and you have to make more of an effort to stick to your language and make sure they are being exposed to a wide range of subjects and vocabulary.'

'Constant worry about the language development.'

'A feeling of guilt and failure if one language is not spoken as well as the other.'

Differences Between Mothers and Fathers

There can be difference between maternal and paternal communication patterns. Naturally, as we heard in Chapter 2, when a new baby arrives there is a strong bond between the mother and child The language heard in those early days by the baby, although not immediately evident, will later appear later as words and sentences. The mother is more in tune with the child and able to second-guess what the child wants or needs. Fathers, on the other hand, can find the early stages frustrating and can hardly wait for a time when they can really talk to their child and have a conversation. Ronjat, Leopold, Saunders and Fantini were observing and compiling studies on their children and probably made more effort than most fathers would. This is not to say that all fathers sit back and do nothing regarding talking to their child, but that they often take more of a background role or are simply not around as much as the mother. Fathers get the upper hand later on when they are able to chat with their child. This could be due to male/female differences in parenting or simply a wish not to interfere with the important bonding of mother and child in the beginning. Fathers tend to really come into there own when the child reaches the age of around three and four years and can then offer a different view of life and language use.

There has been much research done on difference between adult male/female speech forms (see Jennifer Coates, 1988). The main conclusion, although it remains debatable, is that women use more formal, standardised speech. They prefer more indirect commands, use a wider range of vocabulary and use 'prestige' forms in their speech to impress others. Their intonation tends to rise at the end of a sentence, rather like American or Australian accents and they add more 'tag' questions such as 'It's a nice day, isn't it?'. Men are much the opposite, using more swearwords, less prestige language, direct instructions and care less about how they sound to other people. Women pay more attention to politeness and using the appropriate complement to facilitate social integration. We can argue that these traits are linked to traditional roles of housewife mother and working father because men who are at home all day do tend to use 'softer' language while working woman swear more and become more direct. However in many cases the mother is very involved in the early years and her speech patterns would have an effect on the child.

In terms of monolingual speech, mothers are more child-centred, attending to their needs, asking them how they feel or what they want to do. Their language is softer, kinder and uses familiar nicknames like 'Sweetie' or 'Baby'. The fathers have a more challenging language pattern with lots of questions like, 'What did you see?' 'How can we make that work?' which the child can link with practical physical play. The fathers tend to use shorter imperative phrases and expect faster answers too. The mother usually lavishes praise on children when they utter their first word, while men are less encouraging and expect a higher level of conversation. Swain (1992: 28) found that males interrupt more than females and use more 'direct speech' than women, and females use more forms such as 'yeah, mmm, right . . .' in conversation. Consequently the father–daughter speech pattern would be very different from the mother–son one.

In regard to bilingual families Una Cunningham-Andersson (1999: 54) cautions about being the only model of a language. In her case, being the main English-language speaker around her three bilingual English/Swedish boys, they may pick up a rather 'sissified' language, lacking a masculine role-model. Conversely a girl could be rather 'tomboyish' until given appropriate female-modelling. This kind of sophisticated language adaptation is important if the child is to fit in and feel part of the community where the parent originates. This can be compensated by enlisting opposite-sex grandparents, family friends or finding suitable male/female media to show the wider range of accents, tone of voice and appropriate slang and so on. In general it should not be a problem if the child has lots of varied input and children are extremely sensitive to such language use and will learn quickly.

Looking at bilingual families and the parent's role Naomi Goodz (1989: 40) did a study of four English/French children and their parents. She found that not only were fathers less sensitive to language use but they were also '. . . more demanding of their child's linguistic efforts than are mothers'. She also discovered that the fathers 'adhere more strictly to a language separation than do mothers' and are 'less encouraging and supportive and more demanding of their children's early linguistic efforts'. This conclusion is shown in her study by the lower rate of code-switching with fathers than with mothers, thus showing a low paternal toleration for it.

G.J. Harrison and A.B. Piette (1980) made a wider social and psychological investigation into mother/father roles in Welsh/English bilinguals. One conclusion they found was that mothers have a very influential role on the child's bilingualism. They asked mothers what they expected for their child's bilingualism and four-fifths had children with language skills in line with their original intentions. However monolingual (English) husbands who discouraged bilingualism in the family resulted in monolingualism. Harrison and Piette also discovered that mothers in bilingual families are much more tolerant of errors and mixing in a young child than their monolingual counterparts.

This was echoed in a large study also set in Wales. Jean Lyon (1996: 229) looked at bilingual and monolingual English/Welsh families. She found that the wives appear to make great efforts to 'accommodate' their husband's main language. By this they will often learn his language rather than him learning hers. This is born out in my study too with the great majority of English-speaking fathers not speaking their partner's language. Jean goes on to say: 'Men appear to have greater influence on the language used in the home than women.' However the mother does have an important role too as Jean concludes: 'The mother's language is the best predictor of a child's language at age three.'

She also mentions the importance of having a positive attitude to language use, which combined with a bilingual mother, improves the chances of the child becoming bilingual.

Results from my study showed also that the mother has a strong advantage up to age three. As Figures 5.1a and 5.1b show she is the first choice in the beginning and the father second choice, but this shouldn't stop the father giving up hope because the situation changes after age three when school, friends and the country language take over.

As we can see there is little we can do about changing the typical language-gender patterns of our partners but they should at least be taken into account. For example a minority-language mother should make the most of the early years as a way to set-up her languages in the child before age three. Then after that age the father can step in and take over. In that situation the mother's language may become less well-used and she will need to find ways to supplement language use. If it is a minority-language she will need to find male speakers of her language to pass on both sides of the language as early as possible.

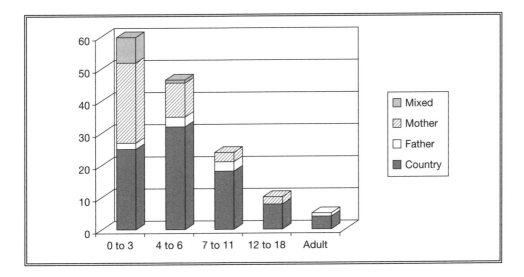

Figure 5.1a Age and first language choice

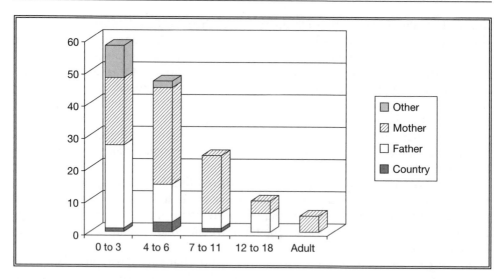

Figure 5.1b Age and second language choice

The Prestige Value of One Language

The OPOL approach is often criticised for being elitist (Romaine, 1995) and only suited exclusively to higher socio-economic class families speaking prestigious languages. This is often confirmed by the combinations of languages seen in case-studies: German/French (Ronjat), English/German (Leopold and Saunders) and Italian/German (Taeschner) to name but a few. More combinations of languages can be seen in Appendix 1: Studies on Bilingual Children.

These families certainly had enough money to pay for au-pairs, extra teaching materials and trips to visit family and friends in the minority-language country. Europeans often prefer the OPOL approach as Henrik Holm (1998) found in an international online survey. Therefore we would expect a high number of double-prestigious families coming from Europe, where combinations such as French/English and German/French are widespread due to close borders and intermarriage. Susanne Döpke (1992a: 1) in her introduction comments that:

> The degree of bilingualism achieved by the 'one-parent-one-language' principle varies considerably and can be disappointing for parents. The very fact those families who follow this principle tend to belong to the higher socio-economic classes and that they raise their children bilingually by choice rather than out of necessity produces very specific problems.

Looking at the occupations of the families in my study the majority were in good economic circumstances, although the parent's job made no difference to the child's level of bilingualism. I had expected children of linguists, interpreters, translators or teachers to have better skills but there was no link.

However, I did find a correlation between the value each language holds within the family. The level of value or prestige a certain language has is always debatable; so the results must be seen with caution. I wanted to know many mothers or fathers were using what might be considered a prestigious language or not. Prestigious languages are well-known and spoken throughout the world – they are highly regarded and have value as aiding job prospects so are often studied as a foreign or second language. The prestigious languages are English, Spanish, French, German and Italian. I coded as non-prestigious all the other languages. Do bear in mind that I had very few Chinese, Arabic or Indian continent speakers in this study, which would have made a difference.

There were only 10% of fathers using a non-prestigious language compared to 20% of the mothers. This would be expected, as there is a majority of English-monolingual fathers with a partner who speaks a non-prestigious language. Mothers are more likely to be bilingual and bicultural, with a prestigious language such as English, German or Spanish as their second language too. The next question is how many of the parents have two prestigious languages and how many form a non-prestigious/prestigious couple? Figure 5.2 gives the percentages of such parents:

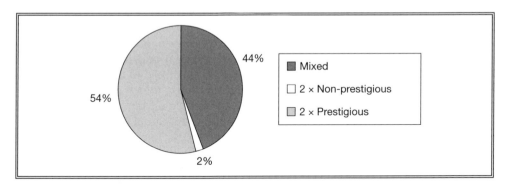

Figure 5.2 Prestigious languages in the family

The families are split in to two halves – those using two prestigious languages (54%) and those with one prestigious and one non-prestigious language. Would such a language combination affect the child's language proficiency? Therefore, Figure 5.3, compares the parents with a mixed language base to those with a double-prestigious one:

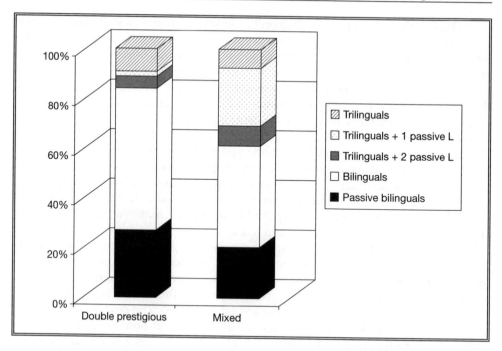

Figure 5.3 Child's language ability depending on prestigious languages

The double-prestigious combination appears to produce more bilingual children. While the mixed family is more likely to have bilingual and trilingual children – nearly 40% of the children are trilingual. This could be linked to the fact that having two prestigious languages already present in the household means that children do not have much need of a third language. The parents may be monolingual or bilingual and be satisfied with passive bilingual or bilingual children. They will already be able to travel, work abroad and have access to a wide-range of information. Whereas, children with one prestigious language would see more value in becoming fully bilingual as the non-prestigious parent would encourage it. These children may also be persuaded to learn a third language for better job prospects and opportunities. This could be a parental second language or one learnt at school. They may have a parent who is trilingual and encouraging about acquiring three languages, and such a role model would inspire language learning too.

We now take a look at some of the more difficult areas which parents may have to deal with along the way and how they cope with such challenges.

Part Two: Testing Times for the Bilingual Family

Within the bilingual family there are good times and bad times. Once the initial thrill of hearing your child say a few words in each language has worn off the reality can be quite daunting. You may suddenly realise that you don't actually understand your child when he or she speaks your partner's language. Or you may feel out of depth when family and friends come to visit when they are chattering away in your partner's languages and you wonder what they are talking about. The sheer hard work of bringing up children is already quite stressful as discussed in Chapters 2 and 3. Sleepless nights and fights over eating and behaviour don't make an ideal scenario for increasing vocabulary skills or language awareness. The effort of being sometimes the sole provider and teacher of a language can leave many parents mentally and physically exhausted. We often find ourselves over-using imperatives such as 'Don't do that!' and 'Stop that now!' simply to get control, rather than talking about things. Older children may expect frequent help with their homework, requiring translation skills and knowledge of another countries' curriculum.

At various stages children may refuse to use your language in public or lean heavily towards the majority-language, making your efforts seem worthless. All the long-term case studies report some problems of a parent feeling disappointed or unable to communicate with their child. Leopold felt like this when he saw Hildegard speaking more and more German in her English-language environment. On top of that there is the external subtle or overt criticism from relatives, friends, teachers and so on to be dealt with. It's hard for the bilingual family members to accept failure too. High standards and ideals at the beginning and seeing it not work out as planned can put strain on the parental partnership. You may blame the other person for allowing the children to mix freely, not making enough effort at separating the languages, not being able to speak your language, not being at home enough or not teaching them to read and write at home . . . whatever, there is always something to criticise.

Looking at some of the problems I have encountered and heard about, they do seem to iron themselves out over time. But some issues need more attention – a partner who is feeling excluded or left out, a one-parent family and speech problems or learning difficulties in children. Although the number of families having problems in my study was fairly low there were some. These areas are frequently discussed in bilingual chat-rooms, through letters to *The Bilingual Family Newsletter* and are also covered in some books for bilingual families. See the information at the end of the book for guidance on books relating to these areas.

Feeling Isolated and Excluded Within the Family

Within the OPOL approach it is quite often the case that one partner does not understand the other's language enough to follow conversations. This may not be apparent in the beginning as couples generally use one language together when they meet. Before having a child one parent may have spoken very little of their language in the home, knowing the other's limited use and not wishing to offend. However, with the new baby it all changes. In the early stages when the child is a baby or not really talking much it is not an issue either. But as the mother or father sits reading a story or having a conversation with the child the other parent may find it difficult to understand. She or he may make more effort to invite friends and family who speak their language and encourage the use of songs, videos and music as aids to language acquisition. It's hard to criticise the partner as they are the bilingual one and the couple certainly wants bilingual children.

Annick De Houwer (1999) looked at the effect attitudes to a partner's language can have. In many families one or both parents are fluent in each other's language with positive attitudes on both sides. They may have learnt their partner's language at school or university or lived in the country. Some use it at work or link the language with prestige or high value. For other families the reverse is the case with one parent having little value put on their language and a partner reluctant to use it. They may simply ask for translations or wait for the people he is talking with to switch into his or her language.

Annick notes the use of language accommodation often seen in bilingual families. A partner tries hard to use the other language for smooth communication. This is easy for bilingual parents, but not for those who don't feel confident speaking a second language. When they do have a go, possibly with mistakes or a bad accent, they are often praised and encouraged by native speakers. Consequently the partner appreciates the benefits of his children being fully bilingual. With encouragement from partner and family this tentative language use can grow and become a strong positive language ability and attitude. Several parents reported how their partner had got better at their language over time. The mothers were Swedish, Catalan, Finnish, Hungarian and Croatian woman married to British nationals, who originally thought they would never master such a complicated language, but after some years found they could speak it and actually enjoyed it! Negative stereotypes of English-speakers being bad at languages are hard to change but with a bit of motivation anyone can speak another language.

In a wider sense it is easier if both partners can speak some of the partner's language to have links with the extended family and friends. This provides a good role model to the child and allows the parent to feel part of the family and talk to friends in the partner's language therefore building up a wider social group. In families where one parent has negative attitudes regarding their partner's languages they are likely to place an unspoken ban on using a certain language in their presence. They would make very little effort to use the language with family members and native speakers. In the long-term it will get worse as the child becomes more fluent and perhaps has friends round to visit or wants to spend time with people speaking that language.

Only 20 parents reported feeling 'left-out' or 'excluded' when their parents spoke their language at home. Many more said that they had made great efforts to learn their partner's language since having children and we could therefore presume that at some stage they had felt linguistically alienated. One family in the study, Erika B., is a German mother married to an Englishman. He says that he feels excluded and doesn't understand it when she speaks German to their daughters. Consequently Erika is obliged to speak German only when he is not around and they all use English when together as a family. Other parents reported feeling 'ashamed' at their lack of language skills.

Another situation that can arise is when a minority-language parent is 'marooned' in majority-language community and has little chance to meet other speakers of his or her language. It could be a family living way from urban areas, perhaps in a village or outlying suburb where there is little chance to meet other foreigners. In cities the concentration of foreigners is much higher and there are more opportunities to go to playgroups and meet other parents. Several parents in my study are in that kind of situation and risk being the only language-model for their child. Another case study, Nicola N., talks about her life in an Austrian village and how her two English/German girls rarely play with other English children. After a while the minority-speaking parent may feel diluted by the majority-language and unable to keep it going; he or she may be using the majority-language with their partner, in the community and when dealing with teachers and school-friends too. They may get tired of always being the 'foreigner' and being different and eventually revert to using the minority-language only in the home where it risks becoming passive for the children.

- See *Case Study 15: Erika B.* and *Case Study 16: Nicola N.* in this chapter.

I asked parents how they felt when their partner used his or her language. Positive reactions formed the majority of the answers with most fathers simply replying 'No problem!'. Fathers seemed to take it for granted that the partner would speak her own language and if they didn't understand everything it was not a big problem for them anyway. Mothers tended to comment on the fact that their partner made little effort to use their language and they would appreciate more of their language being spoken by him. As most fathers spoke English and a high majority of mothers also spoke English as a second language, there were fewer mothers feeling excluded or left out. Some parents mentioned feeling left out or not understanding everything, especially as the language gets more complicated. Others had profited and learnt some of the minority-language as we saw in Chapter 4 on interlanguage use in families.

We saw that very few parents ask for translations, and those that do are monolingual fathers. In a group situation nearly a quarter of parents used only their language, which could be monolingual parents, parents not confident in speaking another language in public or those in a group where the majority simply speak their language, like English. Sixteen per cent of parents speak the group language, showing linguistic competence and a willingness to adapt to the group. These are generally bilingual and trilingual mothers. A good half make an effort to speak their language to their children, either in private or as a translation if necessary which reinforces the OPOL approach in public too.

Finally I asked the parents to comment on how they felt when their partner spoke his or her language:

Fathers: How Do You Feel When Your Partner Uses His or Her Language?

Father: It was very uncomfortable at first, because I don't understand her language (German). Although it's more relaxed now I still feel left out.

Father: Slightly frustrated that I am left out, but happy in the knowledge that my children are exposed to more than one language.

Father: It's no problem with us. I wish she would speak her language with me!

Father: Happy about it. Feel it's of benefit to the children to speak their mother's language and my understanding of her language has improved.

Father: I encourage it. I often remind Helen (my wife) to speak Norwegian to the children.

Father: No problem – I accept that I should be able to speak hers.

Father: Ok. We all understand both languages.

Father: No problem except in stressful situations.

Father: Most of the time, I don't really think about it. At times, it annoys me a bit if there's something I haven't understood and/or if our children are causing trouble at this particular time.

Mothers: How Do You Feel When Your Partner Uses His or Her Language?

Mother: I encourage it – I am concerned when he tries to speak my language (German) with my son!

Mother: It feels natural because I understand everything anyway.

Mother: I would prefer strongly that he learnt my language (Italian), so that in the home we could practice the minority-language.

Mother: I think it's very important, but I also appreciate when he uses my language (French), and so do the children – it's rare though.

Mother: I don't mind as I understand most of the things he says and I want to learn more by listening to them.

Mother: Rationally I understand it's a good thing for my child, but I can't help feeling slightly left out even though I understand the language fairly well.

Mother: I am fine with it but I wish he could understand my language so that it would be easier for me to keep to my language.

Mother: I really enjoy hearing them talk French together, the advantage is that I understand them so I don't feel 'apart', I can follow the conversations. Especially songs, nick-names, etc. are a pleasure to hear, language and 'childhood' things come back more easily to him in his own language.

Mother: I've made a lot of effort to learn his language to a high level myself, to be able to communicate with my spouse's family, so I'm not excluded when he speaks Swedish.

Mother: Sometimes I feel left out because I am just starting to learn his language (Hebrew). I feel even more left out when we are with my husband's family. Even though they can speak English they mostly speak Hebrew to each other.

Mother: Proud that our children are bilingual but also a little ashamed that I don't understand his language at all.

Mother: Fine, although sometimes I have to ask for a translation.

One-Parent Families

Within my whole study there were six one-parent families. Because the study was aimed at families I did not expect to have many one-parent families so these six families give an interesting slant to the study. Especially as they are all trying very hard to still implement the OPOL approach, even when in different countries and lacking support in many cases. One-parent families are more common than in Ronjat's or Leopold's time. Previously the widowed or divorced parent left with the children would simply stop speaking the partner's language and return to his or her country of origin. Nowadays with divorced or separated families it seems more beneficial to keep the language active to facilitate keeping family links and have bilingual children as was planned in the beginning. Widowed families would certainly want to keep the lost partner's language strong because it is the children's heritage and a close bond with the parent. Colin Baker (2000: 13) in his book giving guidance to parents and teachers writes: 'Almost all books and case studies of bilingual children assume a two-parent family. By accident and not by intention, this leads to the assumption that a one-parent family has much less chance, or no chance of raising a child bilingually.'

He proposes that it is certainly possible to achieve bilingualism, by using extra linguistic resources such as the partner's family (if they are willing), a school or location to balance the languages. Separated or divorced parents can profitably use the time spent alone with the father or mother at arranged times, such as weekends or holidays. In fact, some working fathers may spend more time with the child than before in the family environment. He may have a whole weekend or school holidays with the child, thus giving them an intensive language input. Other families may chose a bilingual or second-language school for their child as a way to strengthen the other parent's language, although they would have to be fluent in the father's language to deal with homework etc. One French single mother stayed in England after her separation from the English father, as a way to keep bilingualism strong and allow the child contact with both sides of the family. Conversely, a single English mother, who had a French father, felt confident enough to send him to a French school in England as a way to become bilingual.

Victoria Obied's (2002) study on the sibling factor in language literacy which we heard about in Chapter 4 had a single-parent family who came out as more successful that the other three dual-parent families. The three teenage children had a Croatian/American father and a Scottish mother, who now had a Dutch partner. The family lived in Portugal. The older siblings were the role-model for the others and they had formed a warm bond of shared language use, which was often a mixture of two or more languages. They particularly enjoyed telling stories together and helping each other with words they could not remember. As Victoria says: 'In the absence of interparental conflicts the siblings have a well-established flexible model of language use in the home.'

Can being a bilingual family lead to separation and divorce? The problems I have highlighted regarding isolation and exclusion may be the cause of a break-up in a relationship. A partner who does not accept the other using his or her language could be giving the message that they don't appreciate the person or their language. A lonely and isolated minority-speaking parent might be regretting attaching him or herself to the majority culture and wish they were back home. The extended family may be cold or unfriendly and critical of their strategy. Nevertheless, partnerships and marriages break up for many other complicated reasons of which language and identity are only partly to do with it.

Two of my friends talked frankly to me about the reasons for their partnerships breaking up. Erika J., a Swiss-German speaker met her Australian husband in England. They spoke in English together, and agreed that Erika would bring up their child to speak German. However, it was soon clear that Rob disliked her using German at home and would not make any efforts to learn it. Erika also missed her home country and eventually they separated, although they have stayed in regular contact. Jeanne, a Danish speaker lived in Switzerland with her Swiss husband. She began speaking Danish to her son from birth and soon found the family did not accept it. As her son's German usage began to take over from Danish she decided to return to Denmark alone with the child. Now the child spends time in both countries and attends a bilingual school there.

There is another option for the single parent – using two languages at home. This works well for bilingual parents and those who have older children who have already separated the language and can cope with their mother or father changing languages frequently. Erika J. comments that she likes to talk English (the father's language) and watch videos in English with her son, who is six, as a way to keep his English strong because they live in Switzerland. The child understands clearly the reason why she is using her second language and they can enjoy the time together using another language, which they both speak very well. We can see that the OPOL approach can be adapted to suit different circumstances and even with only one parent the original one-person-one-language formula is still applicable, with enough support.

- See *Case Study 17: Jeanne* and *Case Study 18: Erika J.* at the end of this chapter.

Speech Problems

Many parents' report minor speech problems over time. This can range from Spanish or French speakers not being able to roll their 'r's properly or German-speaking children mixing up their verb endings. English speakers may never get the 'th' in 'there' sound quite right. Many languages have specific sounds not common to other languages, which may take time to be established in the child's repartee. Others have problems with reading and writing in one language or both languages and some children stutter. It is easy to blame bilingualism as the root cause, but we must remember that monolingual children equally have speech problems too. In Marc's class of thirty children four monolinguals are having extra help with speech or reading abilities.

There can also be what is known as cross-linguistic interference between two languages. One parent, Nicola N. noted her four-year-old daughter's English/German speech and how she translates a sentence from German to English literally, saying for example, 'What side are we on' rather than 'What page are we on?' because in German *'seite'* means both 'page' and 'side'. In our family Marc, age three, stuttered to the consternation of his teachers and had problems to say 'y' and 'sp' sounds. He also said *'J'aime toi'* instead of *'Je t'aime'* as a result of the English grammatical form 'I love you' being transferred across into French sentence structure. These have since disappeared. On holiday in France Nina, age three, said to me 'How age has he?' using the French *'Quel age a lui?'* as her reference point.

This kind of language interference is well documented in the case studies on bilingual children (Leopold, Saunders, Fantini and Döpke to name but a few) and is, like mixing, a stage of bilingual development that children take time to learn. These little crossovers can be amusing to close family members and are worth recording for posterity. Gentle correction and more input to the other language(s) are usually the cure. They usually wears off in time too as the child reads and learns more and becomes aware of errors, although if there is too much interference more investigation may be needed as to why the child is doing so. They cause more problems for strict monolinguals such as teachers, in the same way as mixing does.

Li Wei (see Wei *et al.*, 1997), a specialist in Speech Disorders, replies to anxious parents writing into *The Bilingual Family Newsletter* about linguistic problems. He notes that, unfortunately that most speech therapists are trained in monolingual terms and have little experience of bilingual children. He notes that mixing of languages, grammatical 'interference' between the languages, delayed language use and creative sentence structuring are all typical of bilingual children. The areas to look out for and react to are:

> • Inability to produce certain sounds which are common in the speech of similar age children no matter which language you encourage him/her to speak.
> • Inability to understand words which are familiar to children of a similar age.
> • Inability to say words which are common in the vocabulary of children of a similar age.
> • Inability to remember the pronunciation of new words no matter which language you use.
> • Inability to express him/herself in grammatical sentences in either language.

Children, who have a higher vocabulary count in one language and make pronunciation errors in one language, but are fine in the other language, do not have a problem. Children who can express themselves grammatically in one language and occasionally chose the 'wrong' language are also not considered in need of help; they just need more language input in one language. The child may also be going through a language refusal stage or is an emerging bilingual who is struggling to cope with two languages alongside all the emotion and effort of growing up.

This is one area we can't really prepare ourselves for, since speech problems are not really evident until around age two-and-a-half to three. Reading and writing problems or learning difficulties usually come later when the child starts school. Most schools run some kind of test on the child when he or she begins and that is when you usually find out your child has a problem. Doctors and speech therapists often over-react to simply immature language use or minor interference, by recommending dropping the minority-language. George Saunders (1988) recounts that a doctor advised using only English with three-year-old Thomas after a brief 15-minute check-up. One mother, Vilma, a Spanish-speaking mother and her French husband on a year's sabbatical in Canada were warned that 'three languages would be too many' when the child had his 15-month check-up. Letters are frequently sent to *The Bilingual Family Newsletter* asking for advice in how to deal with such monolingual-minded doctors, speech therapists and psychologists. On the positive side more training is being given regarding bilingualism and armed with more information and publications on bilingualism parents can attempt to educate teachers and other health professionals too.

However, some problems are more serious as one letter to *The Bilingual Family Newsletter* revealed. Ann, a Swedish-speaking mother who lives in England with her British husband, was concerned about her eight-year-old daughter's speech. This was particularly evident when Ann spoke to her in Swedish and had to repeat things in English. Ann wondered if she had what is known as a 'semantic-pragmatic' disorder. After further investigation it turned out that the girl has a mild form of Aspergers' Syndrome, which can affect speech. Ann has battled with her local authorities to get a proper assessment of her daughter and extra help with schooling.

• See *Case Study 16: Nicola N., Case Study 19: Ann*, in this chapter and *Case Study 2: Vilma* (Chapter 2).

Summary

This chapter has dealt with several issues relating to bilingual families, which are often ignored. We see how our expectations can be too high and unrealistic or too low and lacking support from one parent. The advantages of a bilingual are numerous and well defined by the families, who are in general extremely motivated and benefiting from the experience. However, it would be naïve to say that it is all good news, there are certainly several disadvantages and these need to be thought about and reacted to as necessary.

Part One looked at gender differences between parents, and how maternal and paternal speech patterns can affect language use. We also saw how more mothers speak a non-prestigious language than fathers do. However, the number of families having with a one non-prestigious language is equal to those with two prestigious languages. The children of families with one non-prestigious language are more likely to become bilingual and trilingual. This could lead to the conclusion that OPOL is an approach highly regarded by Europeans, and it can also be used successfully in a marriage of one prestigious and one non-prestigious language-speaking parent.

Part Two examined the more complex problems of one parent feeling isolated or not part of the family. This is a common issue, probably felt by many parents at some time. It can be remedied with understanding from the whole family. Parents may not realise what living in a bilingual is like, because often they have had no experience themselves. This can lead to problems within the couple.

We see that the one-parent family can still work with just one parent, either through death, separation or divorce, and that OPOL is not restricted to two-parent families as there is plenty of language support available through school, family and location.

Speech problems affect many parents in varying degrees and are often blamed on bilingualism. As we can see a problem is not serious unless both languages are affected and stuttering, interference and mixing can fade out with age. More specialist speech therapists are needed to help and guide bilingual families instead of offering outdated monolingual advice.

In the next chapter we look at the trilingual family and how they deal with three languages and cultures.

Case Study 15: Erika B – Husband Sometimes Feels Excluded in German/English Household

Erika, 40 a translator, is German and married to Clive, 43 who is English and works as a managing director. They live near Bristol, England with their two daughters, Maria, 8 and Anna, 6. Erika has been living in England for 16 years and tells me she feels more at home in England than her native country. Both children were born here and attend local English schools. However, she still has close links with her family, who live near Frankfurt and she regularly visits them for summer holidays and family occasions. Her family also visits her in England and is very supportive of their family's language strategy. Erika says that it takes about a week for the children to readapt to speaking German. They begin with an English accent but are soon speaking like natives and are at more or less at the same level as their German peers.

The family follows the OPOL approach, with English being their language of communication. Clive does not speak much German, so Erika has adapted the OPOL approach over the last seven years to suit her family. She speaks English to her children when her husband is around, so he can be part of the conversation and not feel left out and German in private or when he is in another room. When asked how he felt when Erika spoke, German Clive said: 'I felt very uncomfortable at first, more relaxed now, but because I don't understand German I still feel left out sometimes.' Erika is a naturally sociable person and enjoys her extended family but had to adapt to her English in-laws, who preferred her to speak English to the children when they were around. As an excellent English speaker she doesn't mind but says about family gatherings, 'Sometimes it feels as though we walk on egg-shells!'.

We talked about the children's use of what Erika called 'social switching', when they purposely change languages to suit the situation, probably imitating Erika's, who is a significant bilingual role-model. Erika recounts a story about Maria, age two, 'She was cross with Daddy and surprised us by immediately switching to speaking German in his presence – actively wishing to cut him off from our conversation!'. This tactic continues in the family, and can upset Clive sometimes, and it is Erika's role to smooth out linguistic differences within the family. Maria and Anna are often in contact with monolingual children and were recently made aware of their bilingualism when they met some bilingual German/English children. They remarked afterwards how amazing it was that they could talk both English *and* German to them and the children would understand!

Case Study 16: Nicola N. – English/German Family Living in an Austrian Village

Nicola Nightingale, 35, is British and lives in Thalgau, near Salzburg, Austria with Georg, 35. He works as research assistant and she is currently at home with the children. Nicola studied German at university in England, and met Georg, who is Austrian, in 1987, in a village where she had worked as an au pair in Austria. They married in 1992, and both their children were born in Salzburg. The couple now have two daughters, Katharina, who is four and Anna Sophie, two years old. At home the family uses German, mainly the Austrain dialect and Nicola has a good command of the local dialect too, which she uses in the community. Georg and Nicola have always spoken in German together, ever since they met, and Nicola describes her children as having English as their first language and German second.

Katharina is currently using the dialect at her local Kindergarten, but will move on to learn Standard or High German later in Primary school. Nicola says 'We live in a village and everyone speaks dialect here. The girls are confronted with dialect more than High German. Katharina is aware of the fact that High German is always written in the newspaper or she hears it on the radio or the TV. So much so that when she is pretending to read she speaks High German!'. Katharina clearly categorises the languages too – High German is for anything written (books, newspapers, posters etc.) and Austrian dialect is for her close family and friends. As Nicola reports, 'This past summer we noticed how Katharina started speaking German to all children she met – for her playing with children is always done in German. She doesn't really know any English-speaking children.' The two girls use both languages when playing together usually.

Nicola, having studied languages, is very interested in the girls acquisition of the two languages and notes that Katharina often translates between languages. One such example is Katharina asked her mother 'What side are we on?' in English, instead of 'What page are we on?'. This cross-linguistic kind of interference comes from her German knowledge, where one word, *seite*, means both 'page' and 'side'. Katharina also has some problems with articles and tends to over-use *die*, possibly because it sounds like the English 'the'. She also has some difficulty pronouncing the rolling German R and has been to see a speech therapist.

The family have a sense of being strongly attached to the Austrian village life and equally have an English identity from Nicola and going back to England once a year for a month to visit family and friends. The next step will be to keep the English language strong when school and peer-pressure takes over, as German may become the dominant language, but I am sure they will manage, as Georg is very positive towards using English and they have made a great start.

Case Study 17: Jeanne – A New Life in Denmark for Danish/Swiss Family

Jeanne, 37, is Danish and lives in Copenhagen with her five-year-old son, Jonas. She was married to Hansueli, 41, who is Swiss and works as an optician in Zurich, in the German-speaking part of Switzerland. Jeanne speaks fluent German and English and Hansueli speaks good English. They met while travelling in Australia and for a long time the couple used English as their language of communication. Jeanne studied High German and picked up the Swiss-German dialect from the community when she came to live and work in Zurich. Jeanne and Hansueli often spoke in Swiss dialect, although Hansueli was not very interested in learning Danish, relying on the Danes high level of English when visiting the country. Since moving back to Denmark three years ago, Jeanne has been studying for a Masters degree in Copenhagen.

As a baby and toddler Jonas had regular contact with Hansueli's family and attended Swiss crèches, therefore his dominant language was Swiss-German. However, with Jeanne he spoke some Danish and had exposure to Danish from books and videos at home and from her Danish friends. They also made several trips back to Copenhagen to visit family. When Jeanne separated from Hansueli in 1999 she was concerned about Jonas' reaction to being relocated to Denmark and starting kindergarten there. Jeanne reports that he has progressed very well, quickly becoming fluent in Danish and settling in to his new life. She notices that German is now his weaker language.

After Danish-speaking kindergarten, Jeanne has decided that Jonas will go to a German/Danish bilingual school, as she wants to keep Jonas' German strong, so that he can keep in contact with his family over in Switzerland. Jeanne tells me, 'Children start school very late in Denmark. Jonas will not be starting school until summer 2003, when he is six-and-a-half, and that will only be pre-school. The German School clearly wants the children to start late, as possibly they see a bilingual education as more demanding for the children.' In the meantime, she is encouraging him to read in write in both languages as preparation for school. As she notes 'Jonas has started to write only a little in Danish, but recognises both Danish and German letters and words. He has books and computer games in both languages too.'

I asked Jeanne how Jonas gets to spend time with his father and she explained 'Until Jonas was four we travelled back to Switzerland every two to three months. Now Jonas is five he flies alone at least once a month and spends time with Hansueli's new wife and family. I think I will go back maybe once a year from now on, although I have almost no contact with Hansueli's family. When I go back I visit friends – three out of the five friends I meet up with are mixed-language couples too.' Although separated by distance this family is able to bridge the gap with frequent trips to family in Switzerland. As multilingual role-models Jeanne and Hansueli are making great efforts to give Jonas an opportunity to feel at home in two cultures and languages, giving him a positive bicultural identity. Jonas will also benefit greatly from a bilingual education, where he can use both his languages and gain literacy skills in both Danish and German, and possibly English too in the future.

Case Study 18: Erika J – Return to Switzerland for Swiss/ Australian Family

Erika J, 31, is Swiss and lives in Zurich, in the German speaking part of Switzerland. She has been married to Rob, 38, an Australian teacher working in a Greek bilingual school in London for almost five years. They have one son, Nick, who is now six. The couple met when Erika was studying English in London in 1993. Erika moved to London in 1995 and after Nick was born decided to stay at home with him as a way to increase his Swiss-German input. She came back to Switzerland frequently for long holidays with the family and Nick soon picked up the dialect of Swiss-German, and also some of the standard form or High German.

The couple always spoke English together, as Erika is bilingual. Rob, however, was not very interested in learning German, especially the dialect of Swiss-German. As Erika said the main disadvantage for her is that: 'I can't share certain things with Rob language-wise, and Rob doesn't understand when I speak to Nick in "our" language.' On holiday when they visited family in Switzerland Rob sometimes felt excluded and couldn't join in with family conversations, although the family made efforts to translate for him. When Rob's Australian family visited them in London, Erika remembers that Rob's mother also felt excluded when Erika spoke German to Nick.

Although Erika tried hard to fit in to life in London she missed her country and eventually decided to move back to Zurich in 2000. This was hard for Nick, but he coped very well and adapted to starting school in German and making new friends. He had attended nursery school in England before, but it was not a great success as Erika recounts: 'Nick did not socialize with the other children much. It seemed as if he wanted to but didn't know how. He was then mainly used to speaking English with Rob (an adult) and didn't have much contact with other English-speaking children. I thought it might have been that he didn't have the "same" language as them, even though his English was good.' Erika felt he simply wasn't enjoying school. Back in Switzerland I asked Erika about Nick's progress and she said: 'Nick has settled well in kindergarten and will start primary school later this summer. He speaks a rather funny children's High German, like all the others. He gets it mainly from television.' She tells me that

Nick has begun to read and write phonetically in German and is transferring those skills to English. Erika is considering extra classes to support his English skills.

Now back in Switzerland, Erika has changed her strategy to Minority-Language at Home and speaks English with Nick at home whenever Rob is around, and occasionally when he is not. Nick still switches between the two languages easily. After making great efforts to pass on her Swiss heritage in London she now enjoys sharing English cultural things with Nick, and showing him how he too can be bicultural like her. At home they often watch English videos, read books and Nick chats to his father on the phone almost every day and sees him usually once or twice a month at weekends and in the school holidays. Rob and Erika are still together as a couple although living apart currently. This family has had some language difficulties but seem to have found a solution. Erika is now happy with Nick's enjoyment at school and socialising with his new friends and they are able to keep up the English language at home through frequent contact with Rob.

Case Study 19: Ann – Swedish/English Family Struggling To Get Help With Speech Disorder

Ann, 46, is Swedish and married to David, 46, an IT consultant who is British. They met on a walking holiday in Scotland in 1981. The family now lives in Stockport, England with their two children, Ian, 13, and Helen, 9. The Giles family follows the OPOL approach and uses English as their main language. David has studied Swedish so he has a good understanding of it too. Ann is fluent in English and lists her children as speaking English as their first language and Swedish as their second. The children go to local English schools. Ann also tells me that she is part of a Swedish church, which helps them reinforce Swedish culture and meet other Swedish families socially.

I first heard about Ann through *The Bilingual Family Newsletter*, when she wrote in asking for advice in 2001 because she was concerned about Helen's speech development. Ann wrote that when she spoke Swedish to Helen she often needed to repeat her sentences in English as Helen hadn't understood what she was saying. Ann wrote, 'There appears to be a small gap between her hearing/speaking and her brain – if the message gets across she's fine. When it doesn't she risks people thinking she is stupid, rude, unwilling or inattentive.' Ann explained further, 'After years of knowing there's something not quite right I think that she has what's known as semantic/pragmatic disorder.' This was proving to be quite a social handicap for Helen, especially with strangers or people who didn't know what the problem was.

Since then Ann has seen several speech therapists, who are generally monolingual and test Helen in English. Consequently they have not been much help. Ann has done extensive research herself and a year on from her initial diagnosis she thinks that Helen is mildly affected by Asperger's Syndrome, which is affecting her speech. This condition affects 26–36 per 10,000 children and is related to Autism, a disorder which severely affects speech and social interaction, although in general, children with Asperger's Syndrome do well academically and have good social skills. There are some second cousins in David's family who have been diagnosed as having Asperger's Syndrome and Ann has visited them to see how children behave with this condition. The condition is more prevalent in boys too, as Ann says, 'It is particularly difficult to get girls diagnosed as they hide so much of their problems.' Her aim now is to have Helen properly diagnosed and professionally 'labelled' by a specialist so that her school can provide extra help and support.

This case study shows some of the difficulties of living outside of your home country and the generally monolingual attitudes that prevail in countries like England. Ann goes back to Sweden two or three times a year and although they have very few family members there now both children are able to practice Swedish in the community, meet other children and gain a cultural insight too. Hopefully Ann and David will get a report and a professional label soon, allowing Helen to have support at school. Ann is doing a wonderful job; she is an excellent bilingual role-model and is working hard to research her daughter's condition and find different ways to help Helen.

See also Ann's letter to *The Bilingual Family Newsletter* (2001, Vol. 18, No. 1) on semantic/pragmatic disorder.

Chapter 6

Living With Three or More Languages . . . One-Parent-Two-Languages (or More)

Trilingual and multilingual families are more common than we think; they may live in an area of established multilingualism or have two parents speaking different languages living in a third language country. Some parents use a third language between themselves and others want their child to learn a third language for economic or social reasons.

In Part One I look at what the multilingual family is exactly and hear about the case-studies done in this area. They are not as numerous as those on bilingual families but offer many useful insights into mixing, dominance of one language and input. We also look at what the parents think about their trilingual children and how they cope with three languages at home and being tricultural.

Part Two has a summary of a study I made in 1999 on ten trilingual families. It includes data on the children's language dominance, education and cultural definition. Finally, the five case studies at the end of the chapter show how families adjust and live with three languages on a daily basis.

Part One: Defining Trilingualism and Multilingualism

Trilingualism is generally discussed as another 'type' of bilingualism. Theories and results for studies on bilinguals are often assumed by extension to be applicable to trilinguals. It is often explained as a strange phenomenon of bilingualism, with special cases of brain damaged trilinguals who recover all three languages, or young children who are precociously trilingual.

Hugo Baetens-Beardsmore (1982: 4) suggests:

> There is no evidence to suggest that the fundamental principles affecting language usage are any different whether two, three, or more languages are being used by one and the same speaker, and the major question is whether they differ significantly from cases where only one language is being used.

Academic research into multilingualism is a relatively new field, and encompasses various disciplines such as psycholinguistics, neurolinguistics and sociolinguistics. The links between language and culture, social status, and mental processes, are still being investigated. There is a lack of data specifically comparing monolinguals or bilinguals to trilinguals, and little research on the social or cultural effects of using three languages, or how the family as a whole unit uses three languages. Many bilingual theories simply cannot be transferred to trilinguals. Trilingualism is unusual because the three languages (or cultures) cannot be 'balanced' or equal, as in a bilingual. One (or two) languages are always at risk of becoming under-used or 'passive'.

Around the world many children grow up with three or more languages. This can be linked to where they live or the situation within the family. In Scandinavia, Africa, India, the Middle East and south-east Asia, trilingualism and multilingualism is very common with children learning, for example, a dialect or language from their parents, the dialect or language from neighbouring countries and the country's official language. Some countries, such as Switzerland, Luxembourg, Singapore and Malaysia actively support multilingual policies through education and provide media in the three or more languages used by the population. Regional trilingualism is common in countries such as Africa and India where there is a national language as Hindu, and lingua franca such as English or French and a local language. The languages each have a place in society – a language for trading, reading the newspaper, chatting to friends, etc. In general, one language will be what we might call prestigious, while the others are specific to the region or country. Other families living in border countries such as Luxembourg, learn three languages through school as part of their heritage and for economic reasons.

Being multilingual is seen as normal state of affairs and not something special. In monolingual countries there is often surprise and wonder that children can grow up with three languages and not be confused. However, simply being exposed to two or three languages does not guarantee multilingualism. The inhabitants may have a good level of comprehension, but not all are fluent in all languages, unless it is necessary for social communication, work or tourism. To acquire a language a learner needs to have specific 'input' – that is a good range of verbal examples from different people, alongside media such as books, songs, television, etc. to reinforce the language. This is particularly important in the trilingual family because each parent is responsible for his or her language.

What constitutes a trilingual family? Charlotte Hoffmann (2001: 3) gives a typology of five scenarios:

(i)   Trilingual children who are brought up with two home languages which are different from the one spoken in the community.
(ii) Children who grow up in a bilingual community and whose home language (either that of one or both parents) is different from the community-languages.
(iii) Third language learners, that is, bilinguals who acquire a third language in the school context.
(iv) Bilinguals who have become trilingual through immigration.
(v)   Members of trilingual communities.

Children are able to acquire three languages with the same ease as they pick up one or two. Cognitively they are able to deal with three languages simultaneously, although there may be some delay and passivity in the case of one of the languages in the early stages. Although very few studies have been done on young trilinguals, those that have (see Hoffmann, 1985, Widdicombe, 1997 and Quay, 2001), show the child mixing two, sometimes three languages and learning to code-switch proficiently between the three languages early on. Generally the parents are linguistically competent too and can help with language development at home.

Regarding the trilingual family, one scenario is a couple from two different language backgrounds who then choose to live in a third language country. This can be for work, economic reasons or to be distanced from their own language and culture, such as a French/German family in my study who live in Ireland for his job. A bilingual family may migrate permanently to another country for work or other reasons too. Another scenario is a family where the parents don't speak each other's language and use a third lingua franca as a way to communicate. One such family that I know has a Hungarian father, a Bulgarian mother and they speak English as their lingua franca together. They had previously lived in Australia where they established their English skills. Now they live in the French-speaking part of Switzerland where their ten-year-old daughter attends a local school. Finally, we have bilingual children who learn a third language at school, either by choice or because it is part of the curriculum.

Tracey Tokuhama-Espinosa's (2001) book *Raising Multilingual Children* is aimed at trilingual and multilingual families. She gives numerous examples of successful trilingual families, using two parental languages and a third community one and children learning a third language through schooling. In her case they began as an English/Spanish bilingual family and then when they moved to Switzerland with her diplomat husband, the three children became exposed to both French and German from the community and school. Apart from some minor difficulties in initially adapting to four languages the children appear to be coping well. She advises multilingual families to give language input through schooling and extra-curricular activities and always retain language consistency within the family.

A large-scale study was recently done by Annick De Houwer (2004), on over 18,000 families in the Flanders region of Belgium. This is a predominately Dutch-speaking region and within these families only 2% were trilingual. However, Annick looked in more depth as these 244 trilingual families and realised that only two-fifths of the children were actually using three languages, although they were exposed to three languages at home. She found two important factors: firstly, families whose language combination included Dutch had much less chance with active trilingualism. Annick called this the 'Dutch factor' and speculates that the children either had little reason to use the other languages as their parents could use the country languages or did not have enough exposure to the other languages. Secondly, those families where both parents spoke each other's languages proved very successful at achieving active trilingualism. A combination of no Dutch at home and bilingual parents was the best one. As Annick concludes: '. . . when parents do not speak Dutch at home and/or both speak two languages X and Y there is a three in four chance that they have at least one child who speaks three languages. Parental input patterns, then, certainly seem to affect child language use.'

Nevertheless, Colin Baker (2000) warns that 'stable trilingualism seems less likely than stable bilingualism'. Most researchers cite the eventual dominance of the country language or school language in time and that one language will become passive. As Hoffmann (2001: 5) confirms: 'It is seldom the case that three languages are of equal importance to the individual, and one of them eventually tends to become the least used one.'

Looking on the bright side though, if both parents are fluent in at least two languages and manage to keep the country language at bay within the home they have good chances. Parents giving a strong linguistic role-model and who are very committed to their child's future multilingualism will also have more success too.

Trilingual Family Case Studies

Although not as numerous as bilingual family studies, several important studies have been done, usually on families where each parent speaks a different language and the family live in a third language country, either on a temporary or permanent basis. The main factor seems to be that both parents are bilingual (and often trilingual) and language is clearly related to time or place (for example, school or time spent in a foreign country). Most parents tried to follow the OPOL approach. Arnberg (1987) mentions a tricultural Finnish/Kurdish/Swedish family where the Kurdish father works away from home and Kurdish begins to disappear in time as the school and community-languages take over. Harding and Riley (1986) talk about a trilingual French/German/Portuguese family, who lived in Brazil. Portuguese is his first language but when they return to France the child forgets all his Portuguese and French becomes his dominant language. Longer studies from Hoffmann (1985), Helot (1988), Widdicombe (1997) and Quay (2001) are mentioned below, as are two unusual autobiographical memoirs of a trilingual childhood from Elwert (1959) and Schmidt-Mackay (1977).

Recently Suzanne Quay (2001) investigated the links between input and parental style. She followed the early trilingual development of Freddy, who had an English-speaking mother, a German father and lived in Japan. He began to attend day-care in Japan when he was just one year old and the study covers the period of one year to 21 months. Suzanne found that Freddy's dominant language was Japanese, as this was the one to which he had most exposure on a daily basis and the most useful language. Freddy had a high social sensitivity and guessed that his parents also understood and spoke Japanese well so he used Japanese with them too. Suzanne says that they 'consistently accept utterances in Japanese without indicating non-comprehension'. On top of that the parents insert Japanese words into their speech and sometimes code-switch. As we heard about in Chapters 1 and 4, the parent's attitude and acceptance give implicit dominance to the community-language.

Charlotte Hoffmann (1985) wrote about her two trilingual children, Christina, aged eight and Pascual, five (see also Chapter 4 on siblings). It remains one of the most in-depth and illuminating studies on trilingual children. Charlotte spoke German to the children, her Spanish husband used only Spanish and they lived in England. The family supplemented the parental languages by having Spanish and German au pairs, long holidays in Germany with other families and frequent visitors from both sides of the family so they kept to the 'one person-one language' rule. The children were very different kinds of trilinguals; Christina being a balanced German/Spanish bilingual who added on English slightly later. As Charlotte reports: 'Her first utterances in English were whole sentences; in other words she learnt English "wholistically" and used formulaic expressions.'

After starting school, English became her dominant language, although at the end of the study she is described as being able to read and write in all three languages and use each language appropriately. The younger child, Pascaul, was exposed to all three languages simultaneously. Around aged two he began to talk, often using his 'own language' (neither German, Spanish nor English!) which was difficult for the family to understand. His Spanish was stronger than German, even though as a baby and toddler Christina talked to him in German. Pascaul had a lot of exposure to English through his sister and when he started playschool at age three it became the language of the children for play, etc. Charlotte writes that at aged five he finally mastered German and his Spanish was less fluent although he made grammatical mistakes in both. Like his sister starting school made English his dominant language. Charlotte notes the efforts the family made to give sufficient exposure to each language as she remarks that because Spanish-speakers particularly 'take gregarious pleasure in conversational exchanges, repetition and emphasis' and she wanted to provide the same rich environment in German too. The children have acquired enough German and Spanish for all their everyday needs and have a strong 'emotional interaction' between children and parents.

Christine Helot (1988: 285) looked at two French/Irish families living in Ireland where English and Gaelic is spoken. In Family 1 the children are 13 and 8 years old and in Family 2, nine and seven years old. Both families have French mothers, although in Family 1 both parents spoke French until the older child was three, when the father reverted to English after establishing French. Family 2 is more OPOL orientated, the English language came 'from the street' from age three onwards and from school. Their schooling is different too: Family 1 chose an English school with Irish as a subject. Family 2 chose an Irish-medium primary school. Christine found a strong link with location and that the language changed depending on whether they were in Dublin, where they spoke English, France, where they spoke French on holiday or in Gaeltacht, an Irish-speaking summer-school environment. Although the children frequently answer their French mothers in English when in France they switch to French, especially with monolingual family members. Christine comments on the status of the three languages noting that: '. . . French and English are not in competition with each other, reflecting the positive attitudes towards French shared by the largely English-speaking population. At the same time French being a "foreign" language does not represent a threat to the Irish language.'

Susan Widdicombe (1997) recorded the code-switching of her trilingual English/Italian/French son, Robin, at age five. He was able to use all three languages in one sentence, although this is not a regular occurrence as he usually hears English/Italian at home and French in the school/community. Usually he uses a combination of two languages, with French 'as the most favoured language' for switching. Robin appears to have a competence for all three languages and chooses selectively to code-switch for effect or communication. He often repeats a word in two or three languages, perhaps to clarify parental comprehension or translate. He also changes some verb endings (i.e. *criato* from *crie*) or pronunciation to make them 'fit' the language, which is not correct but very creative! Susan also notes that more switches were made using French, although his parents do not switch or use French at home. However, like Freddy in Suzanne Quay's study, the community-language French has taken over probably because he has a wider vocabulary and range of input and he knows his parents understand it too.

Some examples are:

(Trilingual): 'Mum, DEVO *FARE* BOUCLES D'OREILLES' (. . . have to make [Italian], some earrings [French]).

(Trilingual): 'I can't see you behind this and then *ANCHE* COMME CA I can't see you, you see?' (. . . like [Italian] like this [French]. . .).

(Bilingual): '. . . either you take away that (-) or all my JOUETS PAR TERRE' (. . . toys will fall to the ground [French]).

(Bilingual): 'Papa, quel bambino a CRIATO al cane' (Papa, that little boy shouted (crie in French) at the dog [Italian].

A recent case study on trilingual children was done by Helen Le Merle in 2002 on her two children aged Tania, aged five and Kevin, seven. She recorded some of the trilingual and bilingual mixing her children do. Like Susan Widdicombe most mixing is done using English and French, which are the languages of the community and father. The mother speaks Norwegian, English and French according to the time and subject. Trilingual mixing in one sentence is rare. Here's an example:

Tania: *Kevin, kommer du?* (Kevin, are you coming?)
Kevin: *Ja*, but wait a minute *et je vais venir après. Nå kommer jeg!*
        (Yes, but wait a minute and I'll come afterwards. I'm coming!)

She also reports some interference between the languages as in this example:

Tania: *Kevin har ikke **usé** den grønne farva* (Kevin has not *used* the green crayon).

The language chosen for her sentence is Norwegian, the verb is correctly used in the French past tense, but the choice and pronunciation of the word 'use' comes out of her English memory compartment ('user' in French would mean 'use up', which is not what she meant).

Helen notes that they only mix in the company of people would understand and never mix with a monolingual such as a grandparent or local friend. Another factor could be that Helen, a competent trilingual herself frequently code-switches and mixes, giving the children a role-model of language use best described as *one-parent-three-languages*. She has made efforts to link languages to time and place, for example, speaking English after collecting the children from their English-language school and French in the evening when her husband is around.

Autobiographical Studies

It's unusual to have real stories about childhood experiences of trilingualism as most are by parents about their children. One such autobiography is by Elwert (1959). As an adult he published his story about how he grew up with three languages. He was brought up in Italy, where his English mother spoke English and German and his German father German and Italian. Together the parents spoke German and they spoke English to Elwert. He remembers many examples of one-person-one-language, such as his mother's friends who only spoke English to him and his father's friends who only spoke Italian. At aged eight his parents employed a German nanny, in preparation for the next years move to Germany. Going from a trilingual to a bilingual situation was quite hard and Elwert was teased for being an Italian. From age 9 to 16 he lost contact with Italian and concentrated hard on settling in Germany. From his story, it sounds like his father gave up using Italian with his children temporarily, in an effort to help Elwert and his sister become fluent in German. As an adult, Elwert considers that his identity is linked to each cultural group when he speaks the language, for example, if he is with Germans his 'inner language' is German too. He strongly links each language to a time and a place, rather than to a person.

Ilonka Schmidt-Mackay (1977) also gives a brief insight into the world of a multilingual child. She lived in Serbia with her multilingual parents who spoke Hungarian, German and Serbian. Her father was a Hungarian/German bilingual and the family lived in Serbia. To Ilonka the parents spoke German but she would rather have had them speak Hungarian, their language of parental communication as she remembers: '. . . my father and mother spoke Hungarian among themselves and *that* language seemed infinitely more endearing to me than German'.

Ilonka says that she accepted that Hungarian was their language but adds: 'In a way I felt like an outsider, and at times I was envious of my mother, who seemed to be getting a greater share of my father's love.'

She actually had a very good passive knowledge of it and eventually the father did speak Hungarian to her but only when she was at University. Ilonka describes speaking Hungarian with him as '. . . giving me a feeling of warmth and tenderness which was always lacking in our German relationship'. Ilonka went to a French-speaking kindergarten when she was four-and-a-half and later to a German-language primary school where she learnt Russian from her teacher, a native Russian. Some Romanian language skills were also picked up from her doctor father's patients who as she says '. . . whom I heard chatting in the waiting room'. However, Serbian remained a passive language until Ilonka was nine and began schooling in Serbian and her mother '. . . worked long hours with me to teach me Serbian'. Consequently she spoke German and Serbian (depending on the topic) with her mother, who would reply in either German or Serbian too.

Parent's Viewpoints of Being Part of a Multilingual Family

For the first three years of being a family we were an example of Hoffmann's type (i); an English mother and French father who lived abroad for work reasons in Hungary, Egypt and Switzerland. Our two children were born respectively in Budapest and Zurich. I spoke English at home and Jacques spoke French. We both used limited Hungarian, Arabic and Swiss-German in daily communication in the community, such as shopping or talking to our neighbours. In Switzerland around age two Marc slowly began to talk and communicate not only with his parents but also with the local children in the park and his Swiss childminder. His vocabulary was very low, and limited to *Nie!* (No!), *Tschuss!* (Bye-Bye!) or child-child interactions like 'it's mine!'. He was becoming an emerging trilingual, with English as the dominant language and French and German equally second depending on where we were and the people around him. Back in France on holiday the German would disappear but in Switzerland he found French hard work and used it only if requested. English stayed about the same, except when on holiday in England when it improved.

In our family the difficulty came when Marc was three and ready to start at preschool. The English and French private schools were expensive and a good distance away from where we lived, so it would be hard to meet up with children outside of school. The Swiss school did not begin until aged six and Marc would have to improve his Swiss-German to cope with that, possibly putting pressure on his English/French skills which were already verging on passivity. Consequently, we made a decision to go back to France and England to work, therefore reverting back to a bilingual family. One factor that did contribute to the decision was that my German skills were very low and I struggled to communicate. I was concerned that if Marc began school I would be unable to talk to teachers and understand homework, etc. It was a case of parental attitudes forcing a decision. I also lacked advice about how to bring up children trilingually and had little contact with parents in the same position.

Many questions are directed to *The Bilingual Family Newsletter* regarding trilingualism and multilingualism, especially in last few years as interest in trilingualism has grown. Several parents have shared their success stories and problems too. Jason Campeau, a regular contributor to the newsletter, lives in Canada near a French-speaking region in south-west Ontario. Jason speaks English, his wife is from Belgium and speaks Flemish and the children go to French-speaking school. Jason refers to his three young children as 'trilinguaphones'. They appear to benefit from separate environments for each language so Jason tries to keep language use tied to one person. His role is 'language policeman' in the family. The parents are both fluent bilinguals too and speak other languages. They value each other's languages by support the minority one, which is Flemish, by frequently seeing Belgium relatives and Flemish-speaking friends.

Alathea Andersson is also a regular contributor to *The Bilingual Family Newsletter* and shares her experiences of being herself a German/Welsh/English trilingual married to a Moroccan, who speaks Arabic and French. Their two teenage daughters, Sophia and Maryam, are attending a French and classical Arabic-language school in Morocco, where they live. Morocco is a multilingual society, with French and Arabic and the local Berber language. Many people speak three or more dialects or languages, although they many not be able to write or read them all. Code-switching and mixing are the norm, with language use reflecting the situation and topic. They girls use a mixture of English, French and Arabic with Alathea, who began using English with them when they were small but adapted to school and social needs by encouraging them to switch languages appropriately. As she says: 'I would rather encourage them to express the ideas which are important to them than insist on the use of English at all time.'

Jean-Marc Dewaele, a lecturer in French and bilingualism at the University of London, has recorded his trilingual daughter's speech in an article in *The Bilingual Family Newsletter* (2000, Vol. 17, No. 2). Jean-Marc speaks French, his wife Dutch and they live in London with their daughter, Livia. He describes the pattern of languages within the family and Livia's acquisition process. The parents speak Dutch together and three-year-old Livia also spent time with an Urdu-speaking childminder before starting English nursery school. She copes very well with the four languages, although Urdu has never became gone beyond the one-word stage for her. She had an early awareness of different languages at aged one year and nine months and now corrects her mother's English pronunciation sometimes! As Jean-Marc notes: 'Having been in contact with different languages since her birth, multilingualism is seen by Livia as the norm rather than the exception.'

What Do the Parents Think About Trilingualism?

Within the 2001 study there were 11 trilingual families who were following some kind of OPOL approach. I was not expecting to have so many and it was a bonus to hear about their experiences and compare them to the bilingual families. Seven families were two parents with different languages living in a third language country. Three lived in areas of bilingualism (North Wales, the border of France and Italy, and Singapore), where one parent was bilingual and the other parent had a third language. Two mothers had been brought up bilingual themselves and had confidence that it would work. One Canadian-French/Hungarian family used a third language (English) between the parents. The data from the study also included many children who had picked up a third foreign language from school, and this third language was usually passive or developing over time. In this case I am concentrating only on families who use three languages in the home and community or attend school in the third language.

Looking at their questionnaire replies the parents are usually fluent bilinguals with knowledge of one or more other language. They are making much more efforts to keep all three languages active and have a high awareness of the importance of keeping each language alive. They have no concerns about mixing or code-switching (which they do themselves) and see themselves as tricultural or multicultural.

• See *Case Study 20: Miklos, Case Study 21: Ljlijana, Case Study 22: Lon, Case Study 23: Judith* and *Case Study 2: Helen* at the end of this chapter.

I also include below some of the comments written by the trilingual families in the 1999 study that we will hear more about in Part Two:

Mother: Both children absorb everything, but I believe they are slower at speaking each language properly. There is lots of mixing between the three languages (Spanish mother/English father in France).

Father: Although absolutely confident in all three languages when asked by local people, children and adults alike, to repeat something in English or Polish, they will invariably refuse claiming they "Can't remember . . ." We presume they associate their other languages as something private (for use with Mummy and Daddy) and find speaking English or Polish to German-speakers inappropriate (Polish mother/English father in Germany).

Mother: Our son, Greg, knows that Mummy speaks English, Papa speaks Dutch and Greg speaks German in Zurich, Dutch in Brussels and English in Dublin! (Irish mother/Dutch father in Switzerland).

Mother: We are living in Katmandu where bilingualism isn't anything special, but very natural. Many expatriates are living here and because Katmandu is a very small city we have many connections with other trilingual families . . . it helps us to have a very positive and supportive attitude towards trilingualism. Our children are used to mixing with people and other children who speak different languages (French mother/Dutch father in Nepal).

Parents: We are trilingual and I wouldn't want to miss it for one day. I am so much used to it. It makes me feel rich, proud and versatile and more flexible than others (German mother/French father in France, using English as language of communication).

Mother: I am from a bilingual family myself (Dutch/Italian) so for my family trilingualism was a natural choice. My husband's family was worried three languages were 'too much' and that we should speak English to 'help' the children. Now that they see my eldest speaks three languages well, and her English is above average they are very proud! (Dutch mother/Italian father in England).

Mother: Having grown up bilingual ourselves we decided to have our children educated in English. When we moved to Brazil our children were exposed to English at school and Portuguese in the community, as well as German at home. Both children always insisted that I spoke German to them, as this was the language they were used to me speaking to them. When we moved back to Switzerland we dropped Portuguese, but continued their education in English (German mother/Spanish father in Switzerland – children attend English-language school).

Mother: The father only speaks his language. I speak my language (German) during nine months of the year. The remaining three months I speak father's language (Danish), as the children see (and hear) less of their father than me. This way we try to achieve the best possible balance of language input for the children (German mother/Danish father in England).

Mother: Once Anthony could read and write in German he started going to an English teacher to have private lessons for reading and writing (he didn't want to learn with me!). He can read English well, but tends to spell according to German rules. We never pushed having formal French reading/writing lessons as we thought it might be overloading it a bit, but he picked it up himself and already is doing quite well (English mother/Swiss-French father in German-speaking part of Switzerland).

Mother: We lived in France, Italy and England and therefore German never could be a dominant language. I tried to speak German with my two older children (now age 19 and 12 years old) during the first two years, but the community-language always took over. Although my husband speaks fluent German, finally we came to speak only French at home – a language which had become a constant factor during our 'voyage' through Europe (German mother/French father now living in UK).

Mother: I understand everything and often feel like getting involved in the discussion and when I do so, I would use his language (Hungarian). He right away corrects me and asks me to speak in English with him and French with our daughter. I find it hard to have 'family discussions' (French-Canadian mother/Hungarian father in Hungary using English as parental language).

Part Two: 1999 Survey – Issues Surrounding Multilingual Families

Much research has been done on bilinguals, but relatively little on trilinguals. This is due primarily to the fact that comparative testing or longitudinal studies are difficult to administer with three languages. Additionally, it is also hard to find a sample of trilinguals using the same three languages, at roughly the same competence levels, with similar backgrounds. Individual case studies of trilinguals exist, but they are restricted in number and scope.

In 1999, as part of a Masters in Education degree, I made a study of trilingual families like ours at that time (see also Barron-Hauwaert, 1999, 2000a, 2000b, 2003). We were living in Zurich, in the German-speaking part of Switzerland and so were an English/French/German trilingual family. I had found so little research material on trilingual families I wanted to know more about this unusual situation and if it worked. In fact more and more bilingual families are relocating to a third-language country for various reasons and the numbers of multilingual families increase every year. Twenty-five families were contacted through *The Bilingual Family Newsletter*, adverts in international schools and expatriate publications in Switzerland. I selected ten families who had two separate parental languages and lived in a third language country. Between them they had a total of 14 languages and children aged from 2 to 12. They lived in Belgium, France, Germany, Switzerland, England and Nepal, India. Table 6.1 shows the languages, age, and number of children and country of residence of the families:

Table 6.1 Families with two parental languages, living in a third language country

Family	Mother's language	Father's language	Country/language	Age of Children
1.	German	English	Belgium/French	3 yrs
2.	Spanish	English	Belgium/French	3 yrs
3.	Swiss-German	English	Belgium/French	4 yrs
4.	Catalan/Spanish	English	France/French	3.5 yrs
5.	Bulgarian	Hungarian	Switzerland/French	10 yrs
6.	English	Dutch	Switzerland/German	3.5 yrs
7.	English	Swiss-French	Switzerland/German	10 yrs
8.	Polish	English	Germany/German	8 and 6 yrs
9.	Czech	Italian	England/English	9.5 and 3 yrs
10.	French	Dutch	Nepal/English	2.5 yrs

I sent out a detailed questionnaire, beginning with general questions for both parents and two sections – one for the mother and one for the father regarding maternal and paternal attitudes. The first section verified how long they had lived there and their occupation. I also asked the families to rate each person's language abilities. Details were given on the language of education and how they found information on bilingualism too. The questions for each parent dealt with attitudes to code-switching, what strategy they applied, how they felt about their partner's language, how they passed on their cultural heritage and how the children coped with learning three languages.

Due to the wide age range of the study (from age two to ten years) I had some fluent trilinguals, children who were 'emerging' trilinguals and a few who only had passive knowledge of one language due to lack of exposure or interest in that language. However, it was possible to compare and find some patterns in the families. A summary of the results is shown below:

Results of Trilingual Family Survey 1999

The typical child acquisition pattern is: monolingual output (mother's language) up to age 3.5 years. bilingual (mother's and father's languages) from 3 to 5 years and fully trilingual (mother/father and country language) at around age five or six years.

The country language takes first or third place in the child's language order, depending on age. The parental language was first and most dominant for the younger children (under age six). The country language took over as most dominant for school-age children.

All the children attend schools using the country language although generally parents had no experience of bilingual education.

The parents are bilingual or trilingual too and actively support trilingualism.

Mixing and code-switching is prevalent but is seen as part of the development process of a trilingual.

The one-parent-one-language approach is not suited to trilinguals and an updated approach is needed, one which appreciates that the parents use (minimum) two languages on a daily basis just by living in the third language country.

Most families have passed on two parental cultures alongside the country culture and it is likely that the children will be tricultural.

I will describe in more detail at four areas of the study, which were particularly interesting:

(a) Which language is dominant within the family?
(b) Language use within the home.

(c) Education of the trilingual child.
(d) Living with three cultures.

(a) Dominant Languages Within the Family: Country-Language vs Family-Language

All multilinguals have a language order, with the most fluent one being considered the 'first' language. Bilinguals may have equal usage of each language, but for a trilingual the choice of first, second or third is due to their circumstances, which can change language frequency. For example, the language of the kindergarten or school may become the first language as the child spends a large part of the day there. A summer vacation spent in the country of one parent could upgrade a language from second or third to first. Socialising with friends who speak one of the languages will have an effect too. The trilingual child therefore uses each language to suit the current situation.

I considered the most fluent language of the child to be the dominant language. I found that 50% of the children had the country language as their most dominant language. These children were aged between 6 and 12 years, and also used this language at school. These families I labelled *country-language dominated*. They were long-term residents of the country and usually both parents spoke three languages too. The other children were *family-language dominated* – with a parent's language being their dominant one. This was clearly linked to age, as most of these families had young children under the age of four who spoke the mother's language (probably because they were at home more with her). However, some children aged between four and six years old had the father's language as first. This could be because the child had established the mother's language and was now practicing the father's language. When the parents talked to each other 70% chose to use the father's language. Many fathers spoke an 'international' language such as English, French or German, which tended to overwhelm other languages such as Polish or Dutch where the mother's language would take second or third place (Figure 6.1).

Country-language dominant		*Family-language dominant*
1st *country* language	or	1st *mother's* language
2nd *parental* language	or	2nd *father's* language
3rd *parental* language	or	3rd *country* language

Figure 6.1 Country-language vs family-language dominated children

(b) Language Use Within the Home

Parents bringing up children trilingually usually begin to have problems when the child begins to talk. The child then has to learn that there are three ways of saying every word and that can be overwhelming or frustrating causing delay or refusal to use one language. We heard about this phenomena in Chapter 2 regarding bilingual families too. Families writing in to *The Bilingual Family Newsletter* frequently ask for advice on toddlers or pre-school children growing up with three languages, worrying that they are overloading their child and considering dropping one language.

Although it is now clear that multilingualism does not cause stuttering, dyslexia or a gamut of other speech impairments (Wei *et al.*, 1997), the concern expressed by parents is often validated by their children's slower language development. Around the age of two to three years children begin to have a metalinguistic awareness of the two language systems. However, families and friends often expect a 'double monolingual', or triple in the case of trilinguals, level of vocabulary from a child and are disappointed at the child's low output.

Trilingual children generally used the appropriate language to each parent with consideration for a parent's non-comprehension of say one language. Families can have rather bizarre conversations with at least two languages being used in the same conversation if several members are present and so parental knowledge of each language seems to be important in a trilingual family. Between siblings a mix of parental and country languages were used depending on the situation; a role-play of the mother would be mimicked in her language, vice versa for the father. A role-play involving a local character such as a doctor would be done in the language of the country.

Bearing in mind that the trilingual has potentially three labels for every object, verb, expression etc. some delay in verbal competence is natural as trilingual children decide which language to use with which person. Do trilinguals mix up the three languages in the same sentence? The parents reported lots of mixing but generally only in two languages and closely linked to context and place. Asked whether they minded their children mixing languages the majority of parents in my study ignore it and then simply repeat the right word in context to the child as Table 6.2 shows. This shows that many parents are sympathetic to the child's linguistic trials and can understand what he or she is saying so the child is not frustrated by not being able to communicate.

Table 6.2 Parent's response to use of 'wrong' language

	Mother	*Father*	*Total*
Correct the child	0	0	0
Translate the word for the child	1	1	2
Ignore it, but repeat back in the right language	6	8	14
Ignore it, and continue the conversation	3	1	4

Which language does the trilingual family use with a visitor? This can be a tricky situation with simultaneous translation not at all conducive to natural conversation. As Table 6.2 shows most families chose a lingua franca or common language. A third chose to use the language of the visitor to make them feel at home too. Parents act as strong role models for children and showing they can change languages to suit the situation is a good example for future trilingual children. Support is also important for trilingual families and most families knew at least one other trilingual family in their area. These families gave each other support and recommended books on bilingualism and multilingualism, and *The Bilingual Family Newsletter* as offering helpful advice. Parents are generally very committed at helping their children practice language at home with a most encouraging 90% of the fathers being involved too! The parents used videos, films, books, music and songs in their own respective languages. Some parents also listed day-today habits of watching television in a certain language and playing games together

Table 6.3 Use of language with visitors

	Mother	*Father*	*Total*
Each person speaks his/her own language	2	2	4
One or some people translate	1	0	1
The language of the visitor is used	3	3	6
A language that everyone knows is used	4	5	9

(c) Education of the Trilingual Child

Finding an ideal school is often a difficult issue for families, regardless of their language status. With trilinguals, the problem is complicated further. The choice of educating a child in the mother's, father's or the country language is a difficult one to make. It is restricted by a lack of multilingual schools, or more importantly multilingual teachers and educators. However some schools that emphasize trilingual education do exist.

One such school is the *European School*, which is funded by the European Economic Community for its staff and related employees. Ten European Schools are specifically designed to promote multiculturalism. The largest school in Brussels has eight languages. The school aims to guarantee the development of the child's first language, 'promote European identity' in at least two languages, with compulsory learning of a third language and options regarding a fourth (Beatens-Beardsmore, 1993).

In these schools the child's first language is maintained throughout schooling, although usage may decrease with age in many cases. The compulsory second language (English, German or French) is introduced as a subject at primary age. Classes such as Sports, Music and Art are taught in the second language. This use of language in a 'cognitively undemanding and highly contextualised context' is aimed to create a natural setting, and to aid peer group learning. The third language begins in secondary school, and is also a taught subject before it is a medium. Examinations can be taken in any of the three languages. However, many parents do not have the option of the European Schools. Private, fee-paying, bilingual or international schools do exist across Europe, but for many families the only choice is a monolingual state education in the language of the country where they live.

Interestingly all of the families chose to educate their children in a school using the language of the country, as opposed to choosing a school only teaching in a parental language. Most chose local schools in countries such as Switzerland, Belgium, France and Germany and three families had children at European Schools (schools sponsored by the European Union, which are specifically designed for trilingual children). Parents certainly needed some knowledge of the school language to help with homework and understand the curriculum, since expecting a child to become literate and pass exams in a language not connected to a parent could be difficult for a child.

Looking at the parent's educational background I found that only a few parents had had a bilingual education themselves. A typical family had both parents educated in their first language, with university studies in a second language. I presumed that they chose a local school because they live in countries where there is a good education system or that they wish their children to stay with local peer group rather than be sent to a more exclusive (or expensive) private school. Another factor could be that parents think the child can learn an 'international' parental language such as English or French through the local school. Parents were aware of the gaps in their children's linguistic input and often compensated by being teachers at home too. They all reported extensive use of language aids for regular language practice such as children's books, videos and internet use.

(d) Living with Three Cultures

A trilingual child with both mixed marriage parents and a country language culture seems almost doomed for some anomie or language anxiety. The trilingual child may be caught between three competing languages all exerting powerful cultural ties. Figure 6.2 shows how the families see themselves and their cultural description as we heard about in Chapter 3:

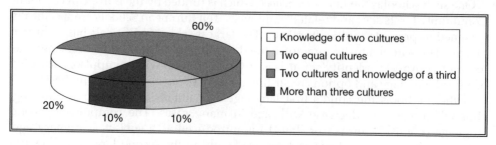

Figure 6.2 Cultural description of the trilingual families

Parents who willingly decide to bring up their children trilingually may take extra care that cultures are passed on carefully and with respect for the other parent and/or country. As we can see 70% of the families see themselves as multicultural. Trilingual families living as expatriates in a foreign country are in the unique position of being able to educate their children triculturally. Unlike trilingual families in Africa and south-east Asia they can travel often, provide extra books and media, and pay for extra private education if necessary. Living away from their home country cultures can focus parents into making more effort to preserve their own cultures, although how the third culture is represented is dependent on length of residence, appreciation of the third culture, and general adaptability in the family.

Regarding the close link of language to culture (see also Chapter 3), all the parents expressed a wish to 'pass on' their culture to their children. One parent described it as: 'The reason of my existence, upbringing and an essential part of myself', while another said: 'It is important for my children's identity.' Parents provided this input with books, films/videos, songs and some special things like nursery rhymes, cooking together or looking at photo albums of the family and home country.

Being tricultural can be difficult for older children or adolescents who want to fit in to their peer group. Therefore the effect of the peer group often brought the culture of the country into the family, whether they liked it or not. As with language use, dominance in one culture may eclipse another at certain times. The child cannot be culturally plural in all three cultures at the same time; likewise he or she cannot speak three languages at the same time. A majority of parents reported that their children were aware of two cultures and knew about a third culture. Trips back to visit friends and family gave children deep cultural knowledge. In general the parents in this study were able to keep up links with their home countries and 60% managed to go back every year, which also helped to establish a concrete cultural and linguistic base for the children.

Conclusions: One-Parent-Two-Languages (or More . . .)

It is evident that trilingual families are a relevant group to study and demand further research. Trilingual families offer an opportunity to study language use and social behaviour one step beyond the context of two languages and bilingualism. The overlapping nature of the languages combined with the changing order of first through to third language gives an insight into how acquisition works and how children evolve linguistically.

All of the parents in this small-scale study are trying to bring up their children trilingually, with varying degrees of success. The parents are all extremely motivated into keeping their languages and cultures alive alongside the country language. However, the families involved in the study are not representative of all trilingual families, as the parents agreed to complete the questionnaire because they are very interested in trilingualism. The study was mainly carried out in Switzerland, a trilingual country, and surrounding European countries where families use mostly European languages, which make them a select group not mirrored in trilingualism on a global scale. Other kinds of trilingual families need to be studied too; families who cannot enjoy the economic and educational opportunities of those in my study, parents using a third language as their language of communication, and families who have permanently emigrated.

The study highlighted the fact that some special guidance is needed too for trilingual families. The OPOL approach was criticised by parents in daily life as each parent speaking their own language is considered strange and unnatural by visitors, especially if they do not understand one of the languages. It is an issue rarely mentioned in advice books for parents and the data suggests that parents prefer a lingua franca to excluding or translating in front of visitors. They are less strict about separating the languages and accept mixing as normal, probably because they frequently mix and code-switch themselves. As children get older the OPOL approach may be frustrating for the trilingual child too; who would rather use a lingua franca than be addressed differently by each person.

Parents often cannot avoid speaking the country language on a daily basis or the other parental language and the situation becomes one-parent-two-languages (or more). It is difficult to even separate the languages as they frequently overlap – trilingualism is much more of a fluid and changeable phenomenon than bilingualism. It seems that trilingual children need more reassurance that each parent understands and speaks a good part of all three languages too as they are expected to do so. Parental efforts to 'keep up' languages are equally important and also the linkage of a language to a culture. It seems that an appropriate role model in the trilingual family is a parent who is linguistically flexible and is able to change languages to suit the current need.

Summary

The world of the trilingual family is similar, yet different to the bilingual family. The languages cannot be equal and have more of a link to a particular place or time, such as school or activities. Parents must work hard too keep all three active and some initial language delay or confusion is to be expected. However, the good news is that the trilingual children are usually very competent and aware of language use and can easily code-switch or use the right language to the appropriate person.

As the case-studies and comments show the families do not consider themselves unusual and are simply living with three languages as a normal way of life. It is most likely outsiders who consider trilingualism too much for a young child to cope with.

There are many different varieties of trilingual families, from those living in third language country, to parents using a third language together. What is common is that the parents generally have a high linguistic level and give a strong role-model to the children that they need to communicate and adapt as necessary. Probably in the future we will see more trilingual children due to the mobility of the international working communities and more advice will be needed for these families.

Case Study 20: Miklos – French-Candian and Hungarian Couple Using English as a Third Language

Miklos, 30, is Hungarian and lives in Budapest with his French-Canadian wife, Marie-Eve, 28. He is a web-publishing consultant and Marie-Eve is an environmental engineer. They met in 1991 as scholarship students at the United World College in British Columbia, Canada. Marie-Eve is from rural Quebec and was brought up in a monolingual French speaking environment. Both parents speak each other's languages and also speak English, which they use together. Their daughter, Delia, is two and they have a new baby, Zalan, born just two months ago in Budapest. In the bilingual family having a new baby means choosing a name that all the family can pronounce, as Miklos says 'We try to choose names where the sounds rules have approximately the same pronunciation of the written name both in French and Hungarian. For example, names including "h", "s", "j" or the Hungarian "sz" were out!'.

I asked Miklos how Delia was progressing and he reported 'Over the last few months Delia has become a little bilingual: she can distinguish between her languages, and knows who speaks which language. Her development in French has been especially rapid in the last two months. Marie-Eve's parents have been with us since Zalan was born, and since they don't understand Hungarian Delia was forced to speak more French. Her French has blossomed – but Hungarian is still her dominant language.' Delia speaks to herself, her dolls and the new baby in Hungarian and has even been teaching her French grandmother a few Hungarian phrases too while she stayed with them! To help keep up her French the family regularly visit their French-Canadian family as Miklos tells me 'Delia has already been to Canada twice so far, and we are planning to go this summer for a month – of which we will spend two weeks in a French-speaking environment.'

Marie-Eve sometimes finds 'family discussions' hard, because she understands everything in Hungarian, and wishes she could speak Hungarian, but Miklos prefers her to speak in English or French, as these are the minority-languages in the household. Sticking to the OPOL approach is sometimes hard outside of the home too, as Marie-Eve says 'I sometimes feel like having a social life of my own with the other moms and speaking Hungarian. It's hard to stick to French with Delia when everybody around me is speaking Hungarian.' Marie-Eve also makes an important point, saying: 'I now realise that much of what I say to her is also meant for other people and I feel like a translator, repeating myself constantly in two languages.'

However, the family considers they have the right balance, with Hungarian from the community and family and French from Marie-Eve and the help of French satellite television and many French friends. Whereas, if they lived in Canada it would be much harder to provide the input for Hungarian in a

French/English environment. They have just renovated an old country house in a village near Budapest and Delia will start going to the local kindergarten in a few years. This young and growing family have made a great start and are aware of the drawbacks of being a bilingual family, but also able to balance the children's language input very well and provide excellent parental role models.

Case Study 21: Ljiljana – Serbian/Arabic Trilingual and Tricultural Family Based in London

Ljiljana, 40, is from Yugoslavia and is married to Abdul, 43, who is from Libya. They live in London, England with their two-year-old daughter, Nadia, and are expecting a second child in September. Abdul has lived in England for 20 years now and works as a graphic designer; Ljiljana is a bilingual secretary for an Arab bank. Ljiljana studied Arabic at university in Belgrade and then worked in Libya for five years, before meeting Abdul in London in 1993. She therefore has a good knowledge of her husband's language and local customs and traditions. Both parents speak fluent English too, although Abdul and Ljiljana use Arabic together. They extended family is very supportive of their trilingual strategy and Ljiljana's sister lives nearby with her son who is 11. They also currently employ a Hungarian au pair, who uses English with the family.

This trilingual language combination was rather confusing in the beginning so Ljiljana wrote to *The Bilingual Family Newsletter* in 2000, when Nadia was 14 months old, asking for some advice. Ljiljana wrote: 'I tried in the beginning to adopt the famous *one-parent-one-language* approach, but found that it does not really work with us.' She went on to explain that in the family Ljiljana often 'spontaneously switches' between Serbian and Arabic when talking to Nadia, as it was often easier for her to join in with her husband speaking Arabic than to exclude him by speaking only Serbian. The reply was not to worry about the switching, as it seemed an appropriate role-model for Nadia in a trilingual situation and that Ljiljana should concentrate on establishing the Serbain first, while she was at home with her and before she started English-speaking schooling.

When I talked to Ljiljana recently she said that Nadia was making great progress in her languages. She explained that her mother lived with them from when Nadia was one year to 18 months, which gave Nadia's Serbian a huge boost. At 18 months she knew about forty Serbian words and it was her dominant language. The Arabic came later, at around age two, and Nadia sometimes uses Serbian words when speaking Arabic, although she is aware of the different languages. The family spent eight months in Arabic-speaking Lebanon in 2000, which also strengthened Nadia's understanding of Arabic. Nadia recently started attending an English-speaking Nursery and she is now amusing Ljiljana by using English phrases picked up there! She copes very well with using all three languages. Ljiljana enjoys reading with Nadia, but lacks appropriate Serbian books so she usually translates English ones, or sometimes reads in Arabic too. Abdul enjoys passing on his cultural heritage through story-telling and listening with Nadia to children's Arabic songs. He often plays the guitar while she sings and dances.

I asked Ljiljana about their plans for the future and she said, 'I would like to teach Nadia Arabic as well as Serbian, but probably with the help of a Saturday school.' She knows many Arabic children who speak mostly English and wants to continue with the good progress they have already made. This trilingual family shows the difficulty of balancing three languages, with the mother taking the responsibility for two of the languages, which as a multilingual herself she is happy to do. This family is more one-parent-two-languages (or more) and has found a way to pass on all three languages effectively. The challenge will be to keep these two languages going against the dominance of English when Nadia starts full-time school.

See also Ljiljana's letter to *The Bilingual Family Newsletter* (2001, Vol. 18, No. 2) on trilingualism.

Case Study 22: Lon – Dutch and Welsh Trilingual Family Living in Bilingual Community of North Wales

Lon Jones-Beenen, 37, and Alun Rhys-Jones, 41, live in Llanfairfechen, North Wales. Alun works as a countryside warden for the local council. They met in 1989 when Lon, who is Dutch, came to finish her studies in English at the University of North Wales. They married in 1994 and subsequently had two children, Iolo, six, and Haf, three who were both born in Bangor. The language between parents is English, although Lon tells me that Alun speaks good Dutch, mainly picked up while on holiday with his Dutch in-laws. Within the family Lon spoke Dutch and Alun spoke Welsh right from the birth of their first child. Lon considers that her children have Dutch as their first language and Welsh as their second. The children began speaking Dutch at first to Alun, but with some persistence and patience they soon switched to Welsh, when they felt confident enough.

Living in North Wales they are part of a Welsh/English speaking community and this is reflected in their daily language use. Both Alun and Lon are fluent in Welsh and English, providing a great role model for their children. The family find living in Bangor an advantage as they can 'get away with using two languages' since using two languages is normal practice for many families. Bilingual schooling is available too, and great progress has been made in the last few decades to foster bilingualism in young children.

When Iolo was three he started a bilingual English/Welsh school. Lon remembers that he hadn't really spoken much English before then, although it could have been because they didn't have a television. However with their second child it is a different story as she has heard much more English, mainly from her big brother! Lon is very keen that Dutch continues to be used, especially in the home and tells me 'We've got some long-suffering friends who are getting quite fluent at Dutch now!'. When Iolo and Haf talk together they generally use Dutch, although more English is beginning to creep in from the effect of school, and playing with other children in English.

Lon visits Holland once or twice a year to meet up with family and Iola and Haf's cousins. She says: 'It's really fantastic to see how the children fit in, the family bond is always there, but the language certainly helps.' At the first Dutch train station Haf is already excitedly telling her Mummy that 'Lots of people speak Dutch here!'. The children are learning fast and Iolo is now able to read in Welsh and English and is transferring his knowledge over to Dutch. For this family living with three languages is so normal that they even have a trilingual cat, who naturally answers to all three languages!

Case Study 23: Judith – Danish/German Trilingual Family Living in England and Rotating Language Use

Judith, 32, is German and her husband, Flemming, 31, is Danish and is an IT administrator. They live near Hull, England and have three children, Jael, their first daughter is five-and-a-half, their son, Timon, is three-and-a-half, and their second daughter, Hadassah, is just 21 months old. Baby number four was born just a month ago! Judith and Flemming are bilingual in Danish and German and also have a good level in English. They met in Poland at a Christian Charity Organisation in 1993, where they both worked and after marrying in 1995 requested to be transferred to England. Nevertheless, they hope one day to return to one of their respective countries, where the children will need good language skills to re-integrate into the demanding schools systems in Germany and Denmark. As English is often taught as a second language in both countries their time here should pay off in the long run.

This family has an unusual approach to language learning, using a truly unique language rotation system. This is how it works – for nine months of the year Judith speaks German, and then for the other three months she speaks Danish, to support the children's learning of Danish. Judith explains, 'When we first met our language was English. During our engagement and first year of marriage we spoke Danish one month and German the next to help each other to be fluent in both languages.' When Jael was born they switched to the current strategy and it seems to work for them. As she says 'It might sound strange to just exchange one language for another, but for us it works very well. The first year I was a much nicer mum speaking Danish to the children, as I simply lacked the vocabulary to tell them off!'. The next Danish phase will start soon, as her mother-in-law comes over to help with the new baby.

Judith taught Jael to read and write six months before she was due to start at her local English primary school, and she is planning to introduce German reading and writing next year for Timon too. It's seems to work well so far, as Judith comments: 'I've discovered that I only need to teach the alphabet and decoding skills once, as a lot is being transferred to the other languages.' She has asked for one afternoon a week off school for German lessons, but so far this has been rejected by the authorities, and she hopes a change of headteacher at the school will help her case.

I wondered if this language strategy causes any confusion or excessive mixing, but Judith says that the children cope very well. Any use of the 'wrong' language is soon translated and repeated back by either Judith or Flemming and it is usually when the child simply doesn't know the equivalent word. The extended family in general are very supportive of their efforts and glad to have a way to communicate with the children. As Judith says, 'Flemming and I are both from large families and we enjoy visiting our brothers and sisters. On the Danish side our children are the only ones so far, but on the German side my parents have got ten grandchildren, the oldest one being six years old!'.

This family certainly have an unusual way of orgainsing languages, but it seems to suit them and their preparation for a future move back to one of their home countries seems a good point to bear in mind for mixed-marriage couples living in a third language country.

See also Judith's letter to *The Bilingual Family Newsletter* (2001, Vol. 18, No. 4) on teaching languages at home.

Case Study 24: Helen – Norwegian/English/French Trilingual Family Now Living in London

Helen and Pascal Le Merle met each other while studying in England. Helen has a Norwegian mother and a British father and was brought up in Norway. Pascal is French, from Brittany and can also speak Breton. They married in Brittany and lived in Paris for a couple of years before starting a family when Pascal began working in Switzerland. Their first child, Tania, was born in Zurich, Switzerland in 1995, and her brother Kevin came along in 1997. Helen would consistently use Norwegian to the children in the home, and Pascal would use French to them. The parents would use French between themselves, as Pascal does not speak enough Norwegian to converse.

When Tania was aged three and Kevin aged one, the family moved back to Paris. Tania was bilingual French/Norwegian at that stage, and Kevin had started actively using some French as well as Norwegian words. Moving back to a French speaking environment and having both parents back at work, however, meant the children had less contact with the Norwegian language. Tania had started French nursery school and Kevin was in a monolingual crèche and the shift in languages was further increased by the fact that both children were now at an age where they would increasingly participate in family discussions, which took place in French only. And Helen found it too complicated to make the children explain in Norwegian what they had been up to all day in their 'French universe', so the family's cultural identity was subtly swerving towards a French family unit with frequent (and much appreciated) contact with the French grandparents.

In 2000, Pascal's work situation took them to London. In order to reinforce the Norwegian language and culture of the family, the children went to the Norwegian School in London for six months. Kevin's refusal to speak Norwegian was quickly overcome, and his sister functioned as his personal interpreter for more complicated negotiations. Simultaneously, the children got a progressive introduction to the English language, which was also reflected in the home, when the family was together as a whole.

Now, two years on, Tania and Kevin have settled into their monolingual English school in London, using Norwegian with Helen for affective purposes (or to exclude others). The main family language remains French, especially on weekends with their father and English between themselves and with both parents. Obviously, the family experiences some pretty intricate challenges to communication at times, but as a whole the family unit has grown closer and more tolerant as a result of the moving around and making contact with various other languages and cultures. The children are almost inseparable and show a particular sense of solidarity when confronted with challenges, both in the home and in the outside world. Helen and Pascal's greatest challenge is the difference in cultural backgrounds and choosing suitable schooling for the children in the long term. But as Helen says 'Happy and confident children find their way in life, whatever the language!'.

See also Helen's article 'Trilingual pre-school children and the parent's role: A case study' in *The Bilingual Family Newsletter* (2002, Vol. 19, No. 4).

Chapter 7

Seven Strategies for Language Use Within the Family

In this chapter we compare the different strategies parents can apply within the bilingual family. Although this book is mainly about the OPOL approach there are some differences within it regarding the balance of majority/minority language within the family. Other parents have chosen different strategies or changed strategy over time, due to their circumstances or success of their children's bilingualism. To help support a fading language the Minority-Language at Home approach might help. Many parents evolve from a strict OPOL approach to a more mixed approach as the children age and become fluent bilinguals. Some parents use the time and place strategy to represent a language, such as school or extra-curricular activities. Finally some parents both speak the same language but want their children to learn a second and often use OPOL as a way to boost a non-native language.

Part One looks at the seven types in detail with comments from parents:

(1) OPOL – ML (majority-language is strongest).
(2) OPOL – mL (support for minority-language).
(3) Minority-Language at Home (mL@H).
(4) Trilingual or multilingual strategy.
(5) Mixed strategy.
(6) Time and Place strategy.
(7) Artificial or 'Non-Native' strategy.

In Part Two we see why some parents have changed strategies and their reasoning for it and read some of the comments parents made on this subject. The chapter ends with six case-studies on families using very different approaches or those who have changed strategies over time.

Part One: The Parents' Options Within the Family

Susanne Döpke (1992a: 12) gives a range of options for families with two or more languages. These can be summarised as:

(1) Parents have different languages and the community-language is the same as one parent. Each parent speaks his/her language to the child.
(2) The parents have different languages, neither of which is a community-language. Each speaks his/her language to the child.
(3) Both parents are native-speakers of the community-language. One parent chooses to speak another language to the child.
(4) Both parents are native-speakers of the same minority-language. One parent chooses to use the community-language to the child.

Within each pattern Susanne gives three additional options for the couple:

(a) The parents speak the community-language together.
(b) The parents speak the minority-language together.
(c) Each parent speaks the language they speak with the child when addressing each other.

She says the (b) alternatives '... guarantee a more extensive and more diversified exposure to the minority-language'. However, in reality most families use the community-language (a) together and the (c) option is rarely chosen.

The choice of language between parents could be an influential factor in the child's eventual language dominance. Books for parents often recommend increasing minority-language use in the home (see Arnberg, 1987, Baker, 2000). Children hearing their parents using a minority-language together would hear more and it would add value to that language. In fact the main factor is the location of the family not whether or not they use the minority-language. Figure 7.1 identifies the difference of a mother or father living in their country.

For the father, living in his country and speaking his (the majority) language to his partner 77% of the children will have it as their L1. When they speak the minority mother's language together 23% will have that as their L1, generally the young children. However in this scenario, using the father's language as the parental language, the mother has a high chance of being the L2 as the results indicate. This is a typical scenario as 80% of the mothers are using a minority-language and living in their partner's country.

On the other hand mothers in their own country have a much higher rate of dominance, with a couple using the mother's language together 94% of the children have that language as their L1. The father only gains a small percentage. Like the mother in the previous scenario he has a very good chance of being the L2.

One study done in America looked at the difference a family strategy could make. Maria Jesús Pérez-Bazán (2002) compared six families with young pre-school children using either a OPOL approach or a Minority-Language at Home one. Four families were Spanish and English combinations, with one English-Spanish/Indonesian and Spanish/Arabic family. Most parents had immigrated to the US.

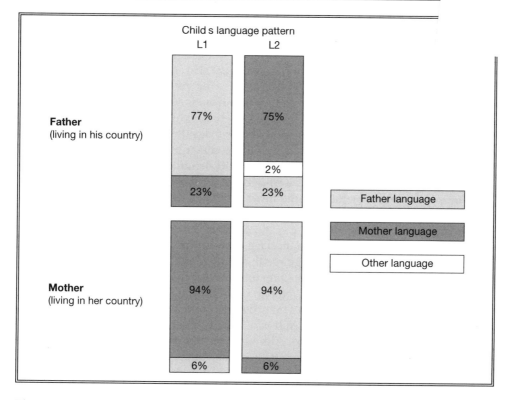

Figure 7.1 Difference of living in mother's or father's country

Four out of her six families were OPOL, but with varying degrees of language competence in the minority-language, although nine were described as being 'Superior' or 'Native' level. Maria found that one factor was the input in the home. All the children, regardless of strategy, could speak English (the language of the community) well. The Spanish-speaking mothers had the most competent bilingual children, but to really develop the language actively the children needed father's who also spoke Spanish (or the minority-language) at home. This reinforcement certainly helped the minority-language and did not affect the majority one at all, but depended on the majority-language speaking parent's commitment and ability.

In the next two sections we see the difference in using the majority and minority-language together.

(1) OPOL – ML (Majority-Language Strongest)

In this context we have a family whose only source of the minority-language is from one parent. I have called this OPOL – Majority-Language Strongest (OPOL –

ML). The parents use the majority-language (usually the country language) together, which they have usually done since they met. In addition since they live in the country where the majority-language is spoken the children will most likely attend school and have local friends round to play. As we have seen there is a high proportion of families following this pattern, typically with the mother having the minority-language. As Jean Lyon remarked the mother has an advantage in the early years, as her language is often the first choice of the child, while still attached and dependent on his or her mother for emotional and physical bonding. The language of the father tends to be the overall language of the home and if the parents are not using the minority-language together then his majority-language will slowly take over.

We have varying levels of partner tolerance of the minority-language; ranging from those who will not tolerate the other language being used in their company to those who simply ignore and accept it. Their excuse may be that the language is 'too difficult' or that they are too old to start learning languages or that it is pointless to learn a less well-used language, as we heard in Chapter 5. Nevertheless, often parents know more of a language than they think. The majority are male and would not own up to actually speaking another language, due to bad experiences of learning languages at school or embarrassment at being made to look foolish in front of family and friends – but they happily live with their Swedish, French, Japanese or German wives. The result is often a partner who in spirit is supportive to the partner's minority-language. Although the main language in the household is the majority one he or she likes to hear the other one and tries out the odd phrases when people visit and even surprises himself by understanding conversations. This still gives the children reassurance that it is positive to speak both languages and they are more willingly to become bilingual.

• See *Case Study 13: Nicola W.* and *Case Study 14: Hedi* (Chapter 4) and *Case Study 16: Nicola N.* (Chapter 5).

OPOL – ML (Majority-Language Strongest)

Father: When the family is together we speak English, alone I speak English, and alone my wife speaks German (German mother/English father in UK) *OPOL (minority L – mother)*.

Mother: I speak my husbands language when the children are around him (German mother/English father in Germany) *OPOL (minority L – mother)*.

Father: I use Swedish only when I talk to our child, for the rest the communication within the family is in Dutch (Majority-Language). Our child uses about a quarter Swedish and three-quarters Dutch when he talks to me, (not mixed). When we spend more time together it's reversed, three-quarters Swedish, and a quarter Dutch (Dutch mother/Swedish father in Netherlands) *OPOL (minority L – father).*

Mother: I speak Norwegian to my children and English to my husband (Norwegian mother/English father in UK) *OPOL (minority L – mother).*

Parents: French is used between the parents. French is used between the father and children. Mother speaks English to the children, who reply in French, i.e. OPOL as far as the children are concerned (English/French mother/French father in France) *OPOL (minority L – mother).*

Mother: I speak mostly my language to our children, but speak in Spanish to them for the benefit of other people, such as other member of my husband's family, or Spanish friends or where necessary in shops etc. My husband speaks only in his language to our children even when other English speaking people are present (Scottish mother/Spanish father in Spain) *OPOL (minority L – mother).*

Mother: Primarily I speak my 'second' language to my daughter. My husband speaks his first language. However I am also adopting a teaching role for reading, writing and speech skills also in English (my husband's language) so I use both without very strict demarcation rules (English/Chilean mother using OPOL approach to pass on Spanish to her daughter) *OPOL (to pass on second language, minority L – mother).*

(2) OPOL – mL (Minority-Language Supported By the Other Parent)

Another side of the OPOL approach has the parents using the minority-language together. This is OPOL – Minority-Language Supported (OPOL – mL). The distinction between this and the previous section may seem arbitrary but it creates a different role-mode for the children. To see parents conversing day after day in a language gives reinforcement and prestige. Bear in mind the parent doesn't have to use his or her second language with the children; that would be going a step further into another strategy which I will discuss next called mL@H. We can see this strategy best employed in the home of Ronjat, where he spoke German to his wife. This was probably a significant factor in the ensuing balanced bilingualism of their son, Louis.

Most typically examples of this language pattern in my study were British or American wives who were living abroad in Germany, Japan, Finland to name but a few. Their husbands were bilingual; often they had met in an English-speaking country, had lived or worked in an English-speaking environment before. One such example is of an Englishwoman, Jane, married to a Finn and living in Finland.

They use English as their language of communication, which balances well with the external input of Finnish from the community and school. Other examples are English-speaking wives living in Japan, whose husband's job may involve working with English so they use English at home as a way to counter-act the dominant community-language. This pattern demands a conscious appreciation of the partner's language and culture and a strong wish to share it. It can also be a step-ping-stone to changing over to a full Minority-Language at Home approach if both parents feel the child is not getting enough exposure.

Several families in the study reported changing from an OPOL – ML (majority-language strongest) to OPOL – mL (minority-language supported). Moving house and seeing the partner's language decrease in use or realising the over-dominance of school and peer-group on the minority-language may prompt this change. Vilma and Martine, both fluent in their husband's language and seeing that he needed some support began speaking his language as a way to increase the minority-language.

• See *Case Study 2: Vilma* and *Case Study 4: Martine* (Chapter 1) and *Case Study 8: Jane* and *Case Study 10: Louise* (Chapter 3).

OPOL – mL (Supporting Minority-Language By Using It as Parental Language)

Parents: We speak our own languages to the children but use English (my language) between ourselves (English mother/Finnish father in Finland) *OPOL father supporting mother.*

Mother: I speak French to my husband when the children are around, and English to him when we are alone (French mother/English father in UK) *OPOL father supporting mother.*

Mother: We don't use strict OPOL though that's our goal for now. I throw in Italian when it's appropriate or when in certain mixed language company (American mother/Italian father in USA) *OPOL mother supporting father.*

Parents: We have always used OPOL with the children. For the first six years we lived in Germany and Switzerland, so my husband and I spoke English to expose the children to more English. Now in the US, my husband and I have been speaking German together for more German exposure (German mother/English father in USA). *Both parents supporting each other.*

Father: We spoke French to each other until two years ago, then switched to English to improve the children's level of English as it was the weaker of the three languages (French mother/English father in Spain) *OPOL father supporting mother.*

(3) Minority-Language at Home (mL@H)

mL@H (Minority-Language at Home) is a relatively new snappy term for families who have decided to use just one language at home. On the bilingual families' web-lists and forums that I visit it is often shown as a description of strategy. For example there will be a comment or question posted by someone, who will write at the end, *Maria, mL Spanish, ML English, mL@H*. We then know that in their family Spanish is the minority-language (i.e. less frequently used) and they follow the Minority-Language at Home strategy. It can be employed temporarily as a way to establish one language in the early years or used as a way to protect a language when living away from the country. There are two kinds of mL@H families:

Firstly, mL@H (bilingual parent) is a mixed-language couple where the parents speak *different* languages. However one parent willingly uses his or her second language at home or with the family to support the other partner's minority-language. He or she would have to be a fluent bilingual, be able to deal with the day-to-day discourse of family life like helping children with schoolwork etc. One parent would need to have a very positive attitude towards his or her partner's language and culture. On a positive note this supports languages that may fade away and become only passive knowledge for the child, who is living in a majority-language country. This keeps the language regularly used and it evolves with the family. Seeing a parent using two languages is a great role-model too for the child, who is expected to do the same. This approach, if started from birth, can also postpone the child's exposure to the majority-language because in the first three years the child's world is mainly home-based or linked directly to the parent's choices of activities, etc.

One of the most in-depth studies in this area was that done by Alvino Fantini (1985). Alvin and his Spanish-speaking wife lived in America and decided to use on Spanish at home to support Mario's acquisition of the language. One important point to note is that Fantini was bilingual and spoke Spanish to his wife, alongside French, Italian and Portuguese. He loved the Latin culture and was keen to pass that on to his children. His wife, Carla, was also multilingual and knew English, French, Italian and Portuguese.

One German/English couple in my study, Gisela and Larry, started their family life together in the German-speaking part of Switzerland. When they moved to America after six years they found that German was fast declining. Therefore Larry began speaking German to his wife and children as a way to support this important family language and he was able to effortlessly communicate with his wife in German in a supportive way.

- See *Case Study 25: Gisela and Larry* in this chapter.

Secondly, mL@H (same languages) is a family with two monolingual parents, who live in another country where they use a second language. A Serbian living in Paris, Pavlovitch (1920) did an early study on using the minority-language at home. He and his Serbian wife brought up their son, Dusan, with Serbian at home with the parents and French from outside and from a daily visit from a French-speaker, who was a friend of the family. However, we only see the results for the first two years and have no knowledge of whether the Serbian was maintained or lost when Dusan began school and found a wider circle of friends

Families may have lived there a long time, moved after their children had already learnt how to talk or are just in the country temporarily on a work contract or diplomatic mission. Like mL@H (bilingual parent) this strategy is done to counter-balance the effects of the communities majority-language by using the majority-language at home. Probably one or both of the parents would use the majority-language in varying degrees in the community depending on their needs and abilities. As long as the code-switching is linked to clear boundaries (i.e. talking to people on the phone, conversing in shops, restaurants, etc.) and the minority-language is actively used at home, it should not stop acquisition. Ingrid's family has two German parents but the father uses English with his daughter to help her acquire the language as early as possible. Another English-speaking family in Australia, Paul and Jozette, have Dutch roots and wanted to pass these on to their daughter so they cultivate the use of Dutch at home to help bring up their children bilingually.

- See *Case Study 26: Ingrid* and *Case Study 27: Paul and Jozette* in this chapter.

---

mL@H

Mother: Until the age of three we all spoke my language (English), but since my daughter started German kindergarten, we have each spoken our own language to her, when she's alone with one parent. As a family of three we usually speak English, but my daughter and husband may make side comments to each other in German (American mother/German father in Germany).

Parents: We lived in the USA on a transfer for several years, and the older two kids were born there. Knowing we were coming back to Japan afterwards, we concentrated on English and spoke English together. We switched to two languages upon our return to Japan (New Zealand mother/Japanese father in Japan).

Parents: We mainly used the OPOL approach, except that my husband spoke Finnish when the children were young (Finnish mother/English father in UK).

---

(4) Trilingual Strategy

This strategy has several scenarios as we saw in Chapter 6. One is that a mixed-lingual couple move to a third language country, where they use the OPOL approach + a third community-language. The varying levels of input in each language will depend greatly on circumstances and external language input such as an au-pair or frequent visits back to the parental language countries. As I mentioned in Chapter 6, Charlotte Hoffmann (1985) observed her two trilingual children, aged seven and five (German/Spanish/English). Charlotte certainly made efforts to give enough input to each language using Spanish and German au-pairs to counter-balance the effect of potentially passive parental languages. They left the acquisition of English to the community, school and local friends, postponing it as long as possible. As we see that Christina, the older daughter spoke German to her brother until the age of three when he started pre-school. The household would have been more OPOL until school age when English became more dominant for the children.

Families can have temporary postings abroad and so the emphasis will be on keeping alive the two parental languages. Judith, who is German, lives in England with her Danish husband. They plan to return to one of their respective countries eventually so to compensate they use Danish for three months of the year and German for the other nine. In other families they may be permanently based in the third-language country and decide that it can have more dominance, perhaps allowing the children to use it at home and attend school etc in that language. This is like a Dutch woman, Lon, married to an Englishman and living in a Welsh-speaking community in North Wales. Another variation on the trilingual strategy can be that one parent is bilingual or from a bicultural background and wishes to pass on those two languages simultaneously, alongside the partner's language. Helen, who is bilingual Norwegian/English and married to a Frenchman, wanted to keep her two languages strong as she was brought up with those languages and it is part of her heritage. In this case they are living in England which means that one of the family languages comes from the community.

• See also *Case Study 21: Ljlijana, Case Study 22: Lon, Case Study 23: Judith* and *Case Study 24: Helen* (Chapter 6).

Another scenario is that the couple speaks a different language but between themselves they use a third language to communicate. This would be OPOL and third language for parental communication. The third language tends to be an inter-national language such as English, Spanish, French or German. The couple may have met in country speaking one of those languages, whilst travelling or gained a good level in the third language by studying it. An example is Miklos' family, he is Hungarian and she is French-Canadian and they use English as their way to communicate together. Caroline is Dutch and speaks English with her Arabic-speaking husband, and spent the first four years of family life in Japan, where they were following a more OPOL approach + a third community-language strategy. This requires two bilingual parents, with a good understanding of the third language. It also requires a sensitivity to language content as since neither of them are speaking their own language misunderstandings can occur. Sometimes couples start out using the third language as the lingua franca but hope that one day a parental language will take over and the third language will fade away. This depends on the willingness of the parent to acquire a second or third language to a high standard as an adult.

- See *Case Study 9: Caroline* (Chapter 3) and *Case Study 20: Miklos* (Chapter 5).

Trilingual or Multilingual Language Use Patterns

Father: I speak my own language to our children (French). My partner speaks hers to them (German). My partner and I mostly speak a third one when talking to one another (English), though we sometimes use French in this case (German mother/French father in France) *OPOL and third parental language and mixed parental language use.*

Mother: If you choose to speak all three languages in the home I believe it is important to create a separation between each language, according to activity, place or time, while maintaining a smooth transition when changing from one language to another (Norwegian/English mother and French father in UK) *OPOL and third parental language and mixed parental language use.*

Parents: We each speak our own language with the kids. Among ourselves, we use a third language (English (French-Canadian mother/Hungarian father in Hungary) *OPOL and third parental language.*

Father: I speak only Russian with the child, my wife speaks only Greek with the child, my wife and I speak only English between us, the little monkey repeats whatever she likes! But she generally discriminates with whom what language to use (Greek mother/Russian father in Israel) *OPOL and third parental language and fourth community-language.*

---

(5) Mixed Strategy

The Mixed strategy is under-reported in academic research because it is often dismissed as a symptom of confused and impure language use. But in reality is exists in many families; these families usually live in an area of bilingualism, such as Alsace (German and French) and Brittany (Breton and French) in France. In Europe alone the Nordic countries, Luxembourg, Switzerland, Belgium, the Catalan and Galician regions of Spain and most border areas of Europe would have such families. Mixed language use is widely used around the world as simply the most effective way of communicating. Continents such as Africa, India and Asia encompass many languages will have large numbers of children growing up with one or two parental languages (or dialects) and then being taught in another one and we heard in Chapter 6.

For example, some children in Egypt are taught in English or French because their parents believe this will equip them better for future job prospects. Alongside that they learn Standard Arabic, which is used formally, particularly for religion. In the family they will speak Colloquial Egyptian, a type of Arabic with some differences in vocabulary and accent. Languages or dialects are mixed and code-switched regularly as all participants in conversation can follow all the languages. Far Eastern countries such as Singapore and Malaysia where trilingualism is common also have a more relaxed and open attitude to children and adults switching and combining languages. The Hispanic communities in America also frequently code-switch and mix as an internal language. The children, without any effort, usually learn to speak two or three languages. Nevertheless there are clear social boundaries to language use linked to place and person. A certain language will be used in a shop, one with a teacher, one for reading a newspaper and another with a grandparent. The child has to learn quickly when and where to use the right language.

Abdelali Bentahila and Eirlys Davies (1994: 114) criticise the 'exceptional bilingualism' recounted in studies such as Leopold and Saunders. They say it is strange to attempt to raise a child bilingually in a monolingual country. Regarding the use of the OPOL approach they say this is not a universal feature of bilingualism because: '... large numbers of bilingual children live in communities where people use both languages interchangeably'. Their study of Arabic-French bilinguals and the differences in code-switching through the generations in Morocco proves that mixing is the social norm. Although as they comment: '... the patterns of language use and dominance can differ from one section of the community to another'.

Very few long-term studies have been done in this area apart from one large sociolinguistic study done in Alsace by Andree Tabouret-Keller (1962), which gives us several examples of child switching in direct relation to the French/Alsation dialect German community where she lives. The family was working class, which is unusual as they generally choose middle-class educated families for studies. Nevertheless the child followed the parent's role model of mixed languages and was educated in French. Andree reports by age two she had a much larger French vocabulary than German and about 60% of her sentences were mixed. She also became aware of the distinction between the two languages much later than the average bilingual child did. However we have no data on her later in childhood, when she most likely used her code-switching skills socially in the community as an accepted way of communicating.

Mixing often attracts criticism for being the result of slack or lazy language parenting by strictly practising OPOL parents. They cannot see a pattern to the child's language input and link mixed language from parents with inevitable mixing in children. However it is important to distinguish between young children mixing by default and the older child's and adult specific and rule-governed code-switching (see also Chapter 1 on mixing and Chapter 3 on older children's code-switching). As we saw in these chapters families often find themselves mixing more and more as they tire of OPOL and all members of the family can understand each other. OPOL can evolve into mixing and it is not a sign of failure, simply a different approach.

In my study, I did not attract many families who could be described as using a mixed strategy, as I specifically requested those using the OPOL method. However, there were one or two families who had become disillusioned with the OPOL method and looked for a better way. One such family was Diane, a French mother and English father living in England. Their children attended French school and Diane had a lot of support for her language. She found, eventually, after trying the OPOL approach that the children were no worse when she mixed according to topic. Diane found it more realistic to chat about the day at school in French or for the whole family to change languages in the company of French speakers. Another family ran a hotel near the border of France and Italy. The locals are used to switching between the two languages, for tourism and communication. The Dutch mother, Jose, recounts how the bilingual parents use French and/or Italian depending on the setting and other people. Their children are being brought up to use all three languages interchangeably as their parents do.

Nicola W. remembers her childhood with an English mother and Chilean father:

> I was brought up bilingually and my side of the family interchanges English/ Spanish all the time. When we're together we try to ensure anyone who doesn't speak Spanish can understand enough so sometimes we translate. If we are with family/friends who speak no Spanish, I continue to speak Spanish to my daughter but may also do a summary style translation for others to under- stand the nature of our conversation. For my family speaking another language is considered highly desirable and valuable but also something relaxed and enjoyable.

Mixing even has a name in mother and daughter Mary and Elisabeth's reper- toire. Their blend of German and English became known as *Germish*. The children are now adults and have their own families but still enjoy the private language and the jokes it provides through code-switching.

• See *Case Study 1: Richard and Elisabeth* (Chapter 2), *Case Studies 12: Mary and 13: Nicola W.* (Chapter 4) and *Case Studies 28: Jose and 29: Diane* in this chapter.

Mixed Parental Language Use

Father: When talking with our daughter I speak only English, and my wife speaks only Japanese to our daughter. However, my wife and I use both languages when talking to one another. We tend to favor English; however, we use both. Our daughter, however, is 100% consistent: only Japanese with mom and only English with dad (Japanese mother/English father in Japan).

Mother: We both MOSTLY speak only our native language to the kids, but there's some mixing from time to time. Parents speak both languages to each other (New Zealand mother/Japanese father in Japan).

Mother: At first we used the OPOL strategy for our first child. Then with the second child we realised that me and the children are actually using whichever language is best for the topic and situation, and it fluctuates (French mother/English father in UK).

Mother: I would say that now that I tend to speak more Spanish to the children in front of other family members and other people in the street than when my first child was very little (Scottish mother/Spanish father in Spain).

Mother: The strategy has become more lax over the years. For example when we talk about school it's quicker and easier to use English. Also I am sometimes unaware of which language I am using. I have to make more of mental effort to use Swedish than I used to (Swedish mother/English father in UK).

(6) Time and Place Strategy

This method is quite rare in bilingual families. Time and Place uses external places or certain regular activities or rituals as a way to acquire, practise and use a language. It exists either as a compromise situation or as a way to inject more of a minority-language into the household. Some of the families that are in contact with the bilingual families websites often describe how they speak one language at the weekends or one language around the dinner table or one language on alternate days. Recently it was reported on a bilingual website about an English/Japanese family with a new baby who are unsure whether to go for the OPOL approach or not because the husband doesn't speak much English and would feel excluded. One respondent replied that they could try a 'softened' OPOL approach using OPOL in the week and all speaking the majority-language (Japanese) together at the weekends. Obviously the whole family needs to go along with it and support it. This kind of strategy needs strict control and organisation and risks the children refusing to do the activity or use the language on demand unless they can see a point to it.

However the strategy can be effectively used on holiday with children; out of their normal routines and daily lives children are more willing to accept a language change. Typically parents drop OPOL – ML to either an OPOL – mL, Mixed or mL@H strategy temporarily to increase usage. Or one partner could try out using the other one's language for a change with no pressure on the children to change. It could be useful as a step towards changing the parental language of communication in the family. Families staying with monolingual relatives or friends may wish to speak the language of the hosts rather keep on practising OPOL, as we heard in Chapter 5.

One such family living in England reports using the father's language, Swedish, while on holiday as a way to feel at home there and increase the children's appreciation of it by seeing their mother use it too. Another mother, Judith, uses one language for three months of the year to concentrate on her husband's language and the other nine are reserved for her language. This requires great dedication and prior agreement with all the family and children.

• See *Case Study 23: Judith* (Chapter 6).

The Caldras and Caron-Caldras family (2000) also employed such a strategy to great effect in their family's language use. Stephen is American and his wife a Canadian French speaker and they use a MLaH approach but in a very defined way so as to encourage the use of French in the family. The family live in Louisiana, America where their ten-year-old twin daughters attend French school. This has greatly improved their use of French at home and the parents encourage use of French particularly around the dinner table. However their older son, John, 12, goes to a monolingual English school and does not speak much French. Luckily the family decamp to Quebec every summer, spending about two and half months there. The children attend a French-language day camp and have the opportunity to meet lots of other children. Here we see a marked increase in John's French linked to the location and activities, which he enjoys. Some mealtimes the whole family speaks nothing but French showing that reserving a time and place for a language can work.

Tracey Tokuhama-Espinosa (2001: 57) and her family follow a rather unusual strategy. After spending time in Ecuador, where her husband is from and America, Tracey's home country, the family and their three children now live in Switzerland (see also Chapter 4 on siblings). They practice OPOL to give the children English and Spanish, alongside an education in German and French from the community and various activities. Tracey says: 'Since arriving in Geneva, we have added the use of "Place" to define the boundaries of French. My daughter takes ballet and music classes in French after school and she associates those places with that language.'

The children are happy to switch languages according to activity and it seems to be working although some families might consider it too much linguistic jumping around and prefer to stick to three languages at this stage leaving a fourth for school later on. This concept can be very helpful to parents wanting to give more exposure to a minority-language, particularly for younger children who enjoy activities and social events. The disadvantage is that this kind of 'organised OPOL' needs sufficient time and income to keep it going and when the child grows out of it or gets bored with a certain activity a new one is needed to replace it quickly.

> **Time and Place Strategy**
>
> **Mother**: The father only speaks his language. I speak my language during nine months of the year. The remaining three months I speak Father's language, as the children see (and hear) less of their father than me. This way we try to achieve the best possible balance of language input for the children (German mother/Danish father in UK) *Time and Place strategy and OPOL and third community-language.*
>
> **Mother**: He speaks Swedish to our child. When we are in Sweden on holiday we all speak Swedish (English mother/Swedish father in UK) *OPOL and Time and Place strategy.*
>
> **Parents**: When our child was age 4 the mother spoke mainly English (her second language) in order to improve language skills before starting school, but she reverted after one year (Swedish mother/English father in UK).

(7) The 'Artificial' or 'Non-Native' Strategy

The Artificial or Non-Native strategy is one chosen by two native speakers of the country language who want their child to speak a second language. Many parents in this situation wait until their child is old enough for foreign language lessons or see if they could employ a nanny or au pair from that country. They might even move the family to the country either temporarily or permanently. Committed families choose to bring up children bilingually by introducing two languages from birth and at home in the same way that two parents with different languages do. Usually parents have a reason for the child learning another language, be it for future employment, cultural reasons or maybe a relative who was from that country or spoke the language. Whatever the reasons it needs one fluent bilingual parent who takes on the role of an OPOL parent, in that he or she speaks only that language to the children. He or she also needs to enjoy the culture and include some of that interest in the learning process, through music, films, books and meeting people from that country. Another great aid is to have an opportunity to visit the country for at some point in the child's development process.

George Saunders (1988) a German language teacher in Australia wrote how his three children learnt German primarily from him. His book *Bilingual Children: From Birth to Teens* describes his application of OPOL parenting to non-native language acquisition from birth through to teenagers (see also Chapters 2 and 4). His wife, Wendy, always spoke in English they used English together although she had a good knowledge of German too. He describes the acquisition process and their ups and downs combined with the different levels of German reached by each child. When the family had a chance to spend a sabbatical year in Germany they found the children had a good passive knowledge and could actively use German where appropriate with the locals. The secret of Saunders' success was probably his consistency in always speaking German and his enthusiasm for the language. This led the children to learn more vocabulary and grammar and to constantly aim high. They obviously enjoyed their linguistic link with their father and the 'secret' language aspect too. Saunders and his wife also were extremely motivated to continue, even in the face of criticism from health professionals and teachers.

I have two examples in my study. One is Reva, an American mother who studied Spanish to a high level and wished to raise her children bilingually in English and Spanish. Although her husband does not speak much Spanish he is committed and appreciates her interest in the Hispanic culture and language. Although she finds it hard she has found a Spanish-speaking playgroup for her young pre-school children and is based in California where she has an opportunity to meet Spanish-speakers. Another is an American who wished to bring up his son to speak Swedish. He started when the boy was 16 months and has limited time, as he is only able to teach him on weekends and evenings.

• See *Case Study 30: Reva* in this chapter.

Artificial or Non-Native

Father: I started speaking Swedish to Sam when he was 16 months old. Prior to this, we both only spoke English (American parents bringing up child to speak Swedish in US).

Mother: We used the OPOL approach from when April was born, but I spoke German to my husband. I started to speak English to him to support April's English when she was about two-and-half years old (German parents bringing up child to speak English in the Netherlands).

Part Two: Changing Strategies To Suit the Circumstances

Many families change or adapt their initial strategies over time because of changes in circumstances, unrealistic expectations, a change in parenting attitudes or a wish to increase or decrease use of one language in the family. Some families may start with OPOL and realise that the minority-language is slipping away and then convert into mL@H. A parent may feel excluded within the OPOL approach and ask the other parent to speak more of the majority-language when he or she is around. Or a parent who is already using the minority-language with his or her partner may decide they are confident and fluent enough to use it with their children as well.

One family who did this purposely was the Caron-Caldas family, who I mentioned in Part One. They employed a mix of OPOL, mL@H and Time and

Place strategy with their teenage children. The couple started with OPOL and then decided after 18 months that the English-speaking father would use French with his wife and children. Leopold asked his wife to change languages periodically to support his daughter's language use since she could speak both languages. When they spent time in Germany he asked her to change to speaking English, so Hildegard would not lose her English. He also proposed that she spoke German in America but she refused saying she did not feel confident enough in her abilities. They compromised in the end by Leopold speaking German to her, and his wife answering back in English.

The Tokuhama-Espinosa (2001: 169) family has used two different bilingual strategies and one trilingual strategy as the mother, Tracey, explains in her book *Raising Multilingual Children*. The Ecuadorian Spanish-speaking father and American mother began successfully using an OPOL approach when their first and second children were born in Quito, Ecuador. Three years later Christian, a diplomat, was then sent to America for two years and the family decided to follow a mL@H strategy because Tracey speaks fluent Spanish. They wanted to preserve the Spanish in the face of the majority English language input all around them and keep it strong for when they returned to Quito. This was difficult for Tracey as she remembers in a diary extract: 'I am the one who has to switch and begin speaking to my children in Spanish now, something I consciously fought not to do the whole time I was in Ecuador.'

Their three-year-old daughter, Natalie, coped and settled in well. Unfortunately for the younger child, Gabriel, then only 13 months, this was not a success. He barely talked and relied on his sister to translate or speak for him. As Tracey comments it was probably hard for him to see his mother suddenly speaking his father's language and seeing his father using English at work and chatting to neighbours and locals in his mother's language.

After two years the family moved to Geneva, in the French-speaking part of Switzerland where they once again changed languages strategies. They returned to their previous OPOL approach, of Spanish/English at home. As I mentioned in the section on in Part One the family also follow a Time and Place strategy for the third and fourth languages, the children go to a German school and French is in the community and extra-curricular activities such as ballet classes after school. Tracey recommends being consistent and sticking to your own language even though you think you are helping the child, particularly at a young age.

Una Cunningham-Andersson (1999: 39) points out that many parents start using the mL@H approach when the children start pre-school or to make making local friends to counteract the strength of the community-language. However, the children may still use the majority-language to the parents, even though they could use the minority-language. But as Una comments:

> While this may be disturbing for the parents and seem to upset the minority-language only policy that the parents are trying to implement, there is probably little that can be done about it. The relationship between siblings is private and really nothing to do with the parents.

In our family too changes have been made, mainly due to moving house and jobs. We began with a trilingual strategy of English/French and a third community-language of Hungarian, Arabic and then Swiss-German. We followed the OPOL approach as best we could. Then when Marc was three and Nina one we moved back to France where we became OPOL – mL, because Jacques continued to speak English with me at home and supported my language. A year later we moved to England for work and changed to an OPOL – ML approach as English took over. At this stage more mixing is prevalent in the family and we could probably change to me speaking French to Jacques. However, I prefer to stay with English (which we have used together for over 12 years), but when we are on holiday in France or with French friends, I use the Time and Place strategy and speak French to everyone.

The Parent's Choice of Strategy

I first asked the parents in the study what kind of strategy they used at home. As I expected the majority of respondents to the questionnaire were using OPOL; the difference was whether the parents used the minority or majority-language between themselves creating extra support or restricting the minority use to only one parent (usually the mother). Most families had an OPOL – ML approach. But their comments showed that they supported the minority-language and although the couple may not actually speak the language together they respect it. Some families had a combination of OPOL and Mixed too, with one parent followed the OPOL approach while the other followed the Mixed approach with the child.

A high number families mixed both languages as their way of communicating between parents, probably due to the bilingual abilities of many parents who have studied languages or lived in the country for a long time. The 11 trilingual families had an OPOL approach with a third language, either between themselves as a language of communication or the language of the community. A few families started with a mL@H approach, mainly to support the mother's minority-language and later changed to an OPOL one later when the languages were established. Time and Place was also used by a small group of families as a way of separating clearly language boundaries, but remains a supplementary approach.

The main factor in choice of strategy seems to be age. OPOL is seen as more applicable to younger children and we see a gradual decline in OPOL and an increase in mixing languages in the home with age as seen in Figure 7.2.

This could be a choice of the child, who is now bilingual and able to switch easily from language to language. The parents may feel they have successfully established the two languages and can relax somewhat on language enforcement. Does mixing more in the family affect the child's language ability? The graph on the facing page, Figure 7.3, compares the child's language proficiency to proportionally to the strategy used at home.

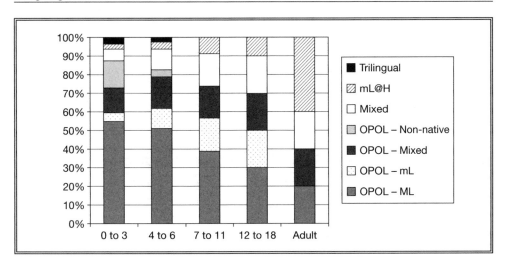

Figure 7.2 Strategy depending on age of child

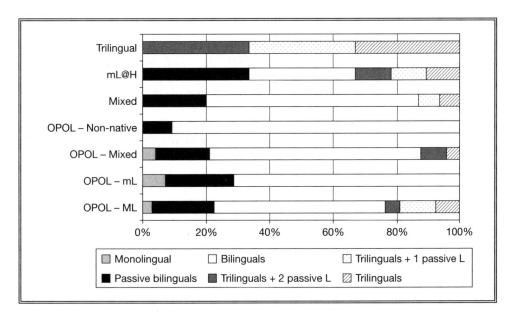

Figure 7.3 Children's proficiency compared to parental strategy

This graph indicates very little difference too between families who mix and those who follow OPOL exclusively as Bain and Yu (1980) concluded in their study. The three strategies that have most monolinguals are the OPOL approaches, with similar levels of passive bilingualism. It is impossible to say which strategy is best, since all strategies are dependent on many other factors such as age, school, attitudes and the location of family. However, we should not rule out mixing as a negative approach, and perhaps it's more natural structure is more suited to bilingual children who themselves regularly switch, even when talking to their parents. More research needs to done on these strategies and the effect of sticking to one or changing over time.

The Parent's Comments Regarding Changing Strategies

I asked parents in my study if they had changed strategies since the birth of their children and if so why? The majority of families had kept the same strategy from birth onwards, however 26 mothers and 17 fathers noted some change in their strategy over time. They can be divided into three groups:

(a) Changed strategies since moving countries, which meant that one of the parental languages had changed emphasis. Some parents changed the language they spoke to their children but the most likely scenario was that the parental language of communication changed to support the minority-language in the new country.
(b) The parents had relaxed their implementation of the OPOL approach and had reverted to previous social mixing patterns or using both languages at home depending on the topic or situation rather than strict separation. These were usually families who had older children and they were less worried about the effect of mixing on them.
(c) A third group had chosen to tighten up their language use at home. Some were making more effort to have their child not mix or use the other language with them. Others were trying to reduce the effect of the dominant country language.

(a) Moved Countries and Changed Strategies . . .

Parents: Maintaining strategies has been difficult. Moving from French-speaking Luxembourg to the UK shifted to a focus in the home from French to English (French mother/English father in UK).

Mother: I spoke only Norwegian during Tania's first three years and Kevin's first year. Then we moved to France and French became more dominant for a year or so (Norwegian/English mother/French father currently in UK).

Parents: We moved from the UK to Holland two years ago. By then English was a more active language in our family than it is now. We do not use English to our son now (French mother/Dutch father in the Netherlands).

Father: While I have always kept to speaking English, my wife has used more or less English according to circumstances. There have been occasions when our child was receiving very little English input. Or on the other hand when we lived in England he had lots (Japanese mother/English father in Japan).

(b) More Mixing in the Family . . .

Mother: Our approach is less rigorous over time (Swedish mother/English father in UK).

Mother: Our strategy loosened slightly since the girls started Nursery school. English seems to be faster and more straightforward to use. It needs more and more effort to stick to German only (German mother/Scottish father in UK).

Mother: With time there became more mixing of languages as my husband's Croatian improved (Croatian mother/English father in UK).

Mother: Now that both boys are fluent in Finnish I do speak English with them when English speakers are present (Finnish mother/English father in UK).

Father: Because of our son attending a German language school we speak a lot of German too, which is my second language (Finnish mother and American/Austrian father in Austria).

(c) Tighter Controls Over Language Use

Mother: I am stricter about speaking French between father and mother in front of children to reinforce input of French (French mother/English father in UK).

Mother: I try to use English more consistently despite the environment. When I noticed one or both children's Japanese is out pacing their English (Japanese mother/English father in Japan).

Parents: We changed from Dutch to French when we talk to each other. We decided to do this when our son started talking – otherwise it would be an 'overkill' of Dutch (home, nanny, family, shops etc. etc.) Try to balance a bit by letting him hear more French at home (Dutch mother/French father in the Netherlands).

Mother: Since Caspar has started speaking properly I am trying to always address him in German and I do always speak German to my baby daughter (German mother/English father in UK).

> **Mother**: Since the birth of my second child I have been more determined to stick to my language when I address my children. I did use a lot of English with my first child and mixed the two a lot (Italian mother/English father in Singapore).
>
> **Father**: I used to speak French to Emily for the first year after she was born, but I switched back to my native English as I did not feel comfortable (French mother/English father in UK).
>
> **Mother**: I kept the same strategy, but my daughter (aged four) insists that I speak English with her! This demand is recent, just in the last six months (Catalan mother/English father in UK).

Summary

As we can see there are several strategies to follow. In general most parents choose one that is suitable and stick with it, although it may be adapted along the way. No one strategy guarantees successful bilingualism and the strategies depend very much on other factors such as the motivation of the parents and the language of school and friendships. The two OPOL approaches: OPOL – ML and OPOL – mL certainly both work and have their own advantages and disadvantages. Parents preferring using the country language together will be more integrated in their community and more able to cope with the school and homework. Parents using the minority-language together will support it more, which can be important with a rarer language that lacks input. Both approaches demand one bilingual parent, but usually those in OPOL – mL families are both bilingual.

The decision to follow a mL@H approach is a protective one and can be very effective, but it needs full co-operation of all the family and strict boundaries of language use inside and outside the home. This is more applicable to younger children as a way to boost early appreciation of one language before the community/school language takes over.

Trilingual families are faced with the decision of which language to support, and being a bilingual couple they can alternate, but need to keep some language boundaries, especially with younger children. A mixed approach is probably better in the long run for trilingual families.

Mixed language use seems to be suitable for older children, able to keep up with rapid switches. The parental language of communication is hard to change from using a majority to minority-language too. So if it is not possible to communicate fully in the minority-language then a more mixed approach may be more suitable.

Finally, the strategies of Time and Place and Non-Native are more unusual. Time and Place can supplement other strategies effectively, but cannot work alone, or the language acquisition will be more like a foreign language and children can be confused by frequent changes of language. The Non-Native approach is a challenge and requires a great love of a language to work. It will never be the child's first language, but can be successfully taught as a second one.

I conclude the book in Chapter 8, with a brief summary of the main points and recommendations for the future.

Case Study 25: Gisela and Larry – From Switzerland To America With Support For the Minority-Language

Gisela, 39, is German and lives in St Joseph, Missouri in America with Larry, 42 who is American. Larry is a scientist and Gisela is currently at home with their two children, Lukas, who is nine and Selina, seven. The couple met in 1987 in Munich, Germany, where they both worked at a research centre. Both Larry and Gisela speak each other's language and have knowledge of French too. The family has lived in Germany, where Lukas and Selina were born. They have a strong connection to Germany and feel very much at home there. In Germany they made a decision to speak English together and at home, to support that language.

In 1995 Larry was posted to Lausanne, Switzerland and the children were exposed to French, as Gisela remembers, 'At first Lukas, who was four, refused to go to preschool. Once he went he did not try to speak any French for one year. Then he suddenly he became fluent!'. There is often a difference between siblings in a bilingual family as Gisela adds: 'When Selina was two she went to a pre-school for a few hours per week. She didn't mind the French language and imitated it immediately!'.

Since moving back to America in 1998 they have changed strategies and speak German at home to increase the children's German exposure. As Larry says, 'Now I speak only German to my wife and I speak German to the kids when we are together with my wife.' This is a combination of OPOL and mL@H designed to really help the children and balance out the input of a parental language vs the community one. It can be a bit tricky at times as Gisela relates, 'A year ago we insisted *German only* at the dinner table and they are still adjusting. We did it because they would only talk to Daddy at the dinner table because they preferred to speak English and we wanted them to practice their German more.'

Gisela remarks on how people view their bilingual family: 'Everybody thinks it is a great opportunity to be bilingual automatically, and they think it is easy, although it is not always!'. Gisela actively promotes her language and culture, telling me: 'Last year I taught German once a week on a volunteer basis in Lukas's Third Grade class. This year I have shared German books in Selina's First Grade class and the teacher reads the English translation. I have also shared different German traditions and crafts with several classes.'

Lukas and Selina are just starting to read and write in German, now they have established reading in English. They usually visit family in Germany for three weeks every year and usually do a lot of German work at home during the three-month summer vacation. The high cost of importing German books and videos can be expensive too, but Gisela says the cheap internet and telephone lines keep the children in touch with her family too. The changing strategies in this family seem to work and help build on the minority-language, which in their case, depends on where they live. Gisela's involvement at school is great, not only as a excellent role model for her children but also to widen the horizons of many other monolingual children in St Joseph.

Case Study 26: Ingrid – German-Speaking Parents in the Netherlands Using English At Home

Ingrid, 38, and Manfred, 38, are German and live in the Netherlands. They come from the same place – Vreden in Germany and lived there until 1989. Manfred is a Project Leader and Ingrid is currently at home with the children. They have two children, April, four-and-a-half and Zander, who is 18 months old. They follow a combination of mL@H approach and OPOL, since Manfred decided to speak English with the children. The family lived in England for eight years, until 1997, before they came to live in the Netherlands and the children were born there. The couple are fluent in English and also speak Dutch in the community. Manfred usually speaks English to Ingrid while she uses a mix of English and German depending on the circumstances. Ingrid and the children speak German together.

Ingrid tells me that when April was born she spoke German to Manfred. However, when April was two-and-a-half years old she changed and began to speak English to Manfred to support use of English at home. As a pre-schooler April had a wide range of activities often linked to a language – she went to German Toddler groups and has some German friends. She attended an English speaking Nursery with several English friends, and she also had contact with Dutch speakers through crèche and her local friends. Ingrid thought German was her dominant language. Now she has started school and Ingrid comments: 'We chose an English-language school, because before English used to be her third language and was only spoken to Papa at home. Now English has become her first language, German her second and Dutch her third.'

The family are based in the north, near to the German border and as Ingrid tells me, 'We go to visit our families quite regularly, every four to six weeks. Our home town of Vreden is only two hours drive away. Both my parents and Manfred's mother are dead so we mainly visit Manfred's father. We also visit

Manfred's two sisters and my brother and two sisters. All but one have older kids between the ages of ten and thirty-two!'. They often go on camping holidays too with German friends and families in the summer, giving them more input in German.

When I asked Manfred about this unusual situation and how it could benefit the children he said: 'Apart from the advantages I hope this will give my children, it gives us the flexibility to relocate. It also gives me a sense of achievement to hear my daughter speak several languages.' For the family the three cultures are fairly similar and they see themselves more as Europeans, and speaking three such useful languages will undoubtedly help the children in the future and we will probably see them in the European Parliament one day!

Case Study 27: Paul and Jozette – Dutch Heritage in Australia Supported with *Minority-Language at Home* Strategy

Paul, 32, is Australian and lives in Melbourne with Jozette, 32, who is Dutch, and who came to live in Australia when she was 12. Paul is a research scientist and Jozette works as a midwife. They met in 1987, while taking Dutch exams at the same time. Paul was born in Australia and comes from a Dutch family who still speak Dutch at home. His parents were born in Indonesia, and at age 13, his father went to the Netherlands for schooling. His mother moved to Australia when she was seven, after her father died in the war and her mother married an Englishman. Paul's mother studied languages and studied in the Netherlands, where she met and married Paul's father and they later returned to Australia. Paul and Jozette now have a son, Tom, who is 29 months old and they have a new baby, Tess, born three months ago.

At home Paul and Jozette speak Dutch to each other, while to Tom, Paul speaks only English and Jozette speaks only Dutch. They were very keen to adopt this mix of OPOL and mL@H given that both sets of grandparents also speak Dutch to the children, and are very positive and Paul says 'My mother is a language teacher and would be disappointed if we did not raise our children bilingually!'. Paul speaks fluent Dutch, too, and I asked him how he learnt it, he replied: 'At home my parents always spoke Dutch to my brother and me, and we all continue to speak Dutch to each other. While my spoken Dutch was quite good, my reading and writing were not as well developed when I was younger, and later I had help from my mother, who is a teacher of Dutch. We were also fortunate enough to make several trips to the Netherlands. This helped me to place the language in context. I recall thinking when I was very young that my parents had made up this language to speak to us!'.

I asked how Tom's languages were developing and Paul replied that he has an equal knowledge of Dutch and English, although more English from the community. Paul also remarked 'What is interesting is that Tom keeps the languages completely separate. He will say a Dutch word to Jozette, and switch to the correct English word as soon as he looks at me. I can also ask him for the word that Jozette says, and he will give me the correct Dutch word. I am also able to teach him a new Dutch word by putting it into the context of 'When Papa says . . ., Mama says . . .'.

Jozette is keen to pass on her cultural heritage of growing up as a child in the Netherlands with all the related songs, games and traditions that she remembers. Although the family currently does not have the opportunity to visit the Netherlands they are able to keep the Dutch language and culture alive within their family circle.

Case Study 28: Jose – A Mixed Language Approach in a Bilingual Community in Italy

Corrado, 35, and his Dutch wife, Jose, 36, run a hotel in the bilingual resort of Courmayer, in Italy, which is close to the French and Swiss borders. The couple met in France, and their children were born there too. Corrado is Italian, he also speaks very good French, which he learnt at school, and English and Spanish. Jose has lived in France for 12 years and Italy for seven years, giving her excellent linguistic skills too. They have two children, Dennis, five, and Mara, who is three-and-a-half. The children speak Italian as their first language and Dutch second. They are also learning some French at school, where there is a bilingual policy to promote French in the region. Recently Jose organised an International Day at the children's school, with foreign parents talking to the children in their native languages, showing maps and pictures and tasting typical food from the country

The couple use French and Italian when speaking together, and Jose will switch to Italian especially if other Italian-speakers are present. They follow the OPOL approach while talking to the children. When Dennis and Mara are together they sometimes switch from Dutch to Italian. As they are living in a bilingual community where switching is normal and accepted this is understandable. They are also following the pattern of their parents who switch languages too, as a way to communicate easily with each other and their hotel guests.

The respective grandparents are not quite so understanding and Jose reports that they can often feel excluded, but as she says: 'They accept and understand that it is important for the children.' Jose considers her cultural heritage very important, and retains close links with Holland. They have a Dutch au-pair, as they both work in the hotel and this helps the children speak and hear more Dutch at home. Jose goes back twice a year with the children to visit close family and friends too.

Jose and Corrado make great role-models, as they use their wide range of languages to look after their guests, showing their children clearly how languages can work for them. As Jose says: 'It is very useful in this business to be multi-lingual and it is good to know different cultures. Because you will know what people like for their breakfast, what kind of restaurant they will prefer, what they will like to visit, etc.' In this multilingual and multicultural family Dennis and Mara will grow up with a sensitivity to language and culture, which will certainly help them in their future.

Case Study 29: Diane – A More Relaxed OPOL Approach in French/English Family

Diane, 37, is French and married to Alistair, 38, who is British. They live in London, England with their three children, Sebastian, seven, Eléonor, five-and-a-half and Cassian who is three-and-a-half. Alistair is an owner/manager and Diane is a part-time translator and also runs a website for bilingual families. The couple only speak English together but the children are balanced bilinguals. The two eldest children go to a small part-private/part-subsidised French school in London and Cassian goes to an English-speaking nursery. Diane says that because they are based in England indefinitely they appreciate the French school as a way to counter-balance the English monolingual environment.

Both parents have always been committed to bilingualism. Diane says, 'In my case, being a French national married to an Englishman and living in London, family bilingualism was the obvious choice! My family and friends quite rightly would have never understood if I had chosen to bring up my three children entirely in English!'. The children can communicate just as well with their British monolingual cousins and their French monolingual ones and they feel equally at ease sharing in a traditional Christmas with their maternal grand-parents in Provence or celebrating, for example, Guy Fawkes Night with their paternal grandparents in Jersey. As Diane remarks, 'They navigate between the two cultures and the two languages with native fluency.' Sebastian never mixes the languages, while Eléonor and Cassian went through phases of mixing languages all the time but their syntax and accent are faultless. None of them has ever confused the languages or addressed an adult in the wrong language. The chil-dren are curious about other languages and cultures too and have recently asked to learn Spanish.

As a family they never stuck to strict rules like the one-parent-one-language approach. Diane explains that she tends to speak French mostly to the children and Alistair speaks English to them, but they switch between codes and use what feels most natural at the time or on a given subject. Diane says, 'If I pick up my eldest from his French school and he wants to relate his day in English, we have a chat in English. Having said that, we try not to switch codes within the same sentence and if a mistake needs addressing, I repeat the correct form as a question rather than point out the error and they correct themselves spontaneously.' The family does have one rule though, which is to have lots of language input such as French tapes in the car, English videos and inviting friends of various nationalities round to play. With the children growing up and starting school, the family has found out that biliteracy is now the next challenge and again time, effort and resources have been mobilised to tackle it! 'It's been a constant learning curve but I think this poses the biggest challenge.'

This bilingual family has the benefit of a French school as a linguistic, cultural support and source of peer-group friends. Although not strictly following OPOL they have a balance of language and dedicated parents who support each other. Diane concludes: 'Each family member needs to invest time and effort to keep the second language alive in a monolingual environment. It is a pleasure to see your children grow up multicultural and experience a richer and more stimulating world.'

See also Diane's website: www.juniorlinguist.com

Case Study 30: Reva – American Mother Using the OPOL Approach To Bring Up Children Bilingually

Reva, 38, and her husband David, 37, are both American and live in Milpitas, California. David is a senior buyer and Reva works part-time as a Spanish teacher. They have two children, Noah, three-and-a-half, and Hannah, nearly two. Reva decided to bring up her children bilingually using a *non-native* language and therefore she speaks only Spanish to her children. I asked Reva why and she told me: 'Over the years as I became more and more competent in Spanish, from living in Mexico, earning my college degree in Spanish and talking to native speakers here in California. I began to think that it would be a great gift to pass on to my children. I think that there are many benefits to speaking more than one language and knowing Spanish here in California is extremely beneficial. I also just love speaking the language and being around the culture and thought that it would be great to share this with my children.'

Reva explained that in the beginning it was quite difficult as she remembers, 'I had planned to speak Spanish to Noah from birth but I struggled with it during the first year. It felt very awkward to me to speak my non-native Spanish to him. During the first year I went back and forth between languages and spoke to him in Spanish at times and in English at times. When Noah was one year old, I made a commitment to myself to speak only Spanish to him. Within a short period of time it began to feel very natural to me and I have continued to speak exclusively in Spanish to him ever since then. I have always spoken exclusively Spanish to Hannah. Now it would feel very awkward to me to speak English to the children.' Noah is fluent in Spanish, and Hannah is doing well, with Noah as a strong role-model, although the children do speak English together too.

Reva puts a lot of effort into her OPOL strategy, using Hispanic music, books and videos to inspire them. She meets up with Spanish friends for extra input and participates with international online discussion groups for advice and contact with other bilingual families. I asked Reva if she knew any families in the same situation and she said: 'I had never met anyone following the same non-native approach as me until about one month ago when I joined a Spanish speaking playgroup. The overwhelmingly majority are native Spanish speakers but there are two other moms that are doing non-native OPOL Spanish. It has been great to meet them and talk to them about their experiences.' Reva is proud that her children actually speak Spanish to her, as she has heard of children of native Spanish speakers who refuse to speak Spanish to their parents because of the English dominance.

David is very positive towards Spanish too, as Reva tells me, 'He understands everything that the kids and I are talking about in conversations and is able to participate in English. He speaks English so that his bad accent will not contaminate their Spanish. The children and I never have to stop and interpret for him.' Reva is certainly dedicated and enthusiastic in her language strategy, which is accepted by the family and will help the children in the future, living in California and giving them more opportunities to travel and experience the enjoyment Reva has in Hispanic culture and language.

Chapter 8

The One-Parent-One-Language Approach in the Twenty-First Century

In this chapter I give a summary of all the important issues raised throughout the book and ten ways to implement OPOL successfully in your household. OPOL certainly has a continuing role, but adjustments may need to be made along the way as children age, develop cognitively, acquire two or more cultures. Alongside this, almost without us knowing, parents change too and their needs require attention too and updating of strategies if necessary.

From Grammont and OPOL - 100 Years On

Society has changed from a predominately monolingual way of thinking at the beginning of the twentieth Century, especially in government and education, to a more multilingual and global approach in the world in the present day. Bilinguals and multilinguals now exist in all countries and continents and are valued as people who can communicate and help trade and diplomacy. A command of two languages, whether they are two well-known ones such as English and Spanish or two lesser-used ones such as Danish and Polish, still gives a wider range of opportunities for a bilingual person. Grammont's legacy was to give us an awareness of the possible success of bilingualism; although it has often struggled against monolingualism to assert itself bilingualism has now proven to be an advantage. Grammont and Ronjat promoted the bilingual family and the concept of one person-one language strategy. Further studies by Leopold, Saunders, Fantini, Taescher and others confirmed the potential in the child and later studies on bilingual children laid the foundations for more study and interest in how children acquire two languages. The research done in the last hundred years would certainly delight and amuse Grammont and in many ways show that his intuitions were right.

Allow Some Mixing at Young Age and Encourage Later Code-Switching

As I mentioned in Chapter 1 the issue of using OPOL as a way to prevent mixing is simply not possible. Children will mix as they learn regardless of the strategy.

Although we see in general more mixing in families using a mixed approach themselves, it is not such a bad thing if done appropriately. In societies where mixing is common a child will be better equipped to be a member of that community if he/she follows the norms. Young children's mixing is quite normal and should be seen as amusing, creative and as a preparation for grown-up code-switching. Since bilingual children cannot avoid switching from one parental language to another just to talk to their parents at the dinner table, it should be seen as an essential skill. The most important thing to watch is whether children can use language appropriately, that is, using just one language with a monolingual grandparent or at a monolingual school. The awareness of where and when to switch is important knowledge and is something the parents can role-model.

Consistent OPOL in the Early Years

The data in Chapter 2 does seem to support the theory, which many parents consider to be common sense, that young children need a consistent OPOL approach while older ones do not. He or she grows quickly from a silent baby absorbing languages to a small child testing out the effect of language use in the family and the wider world. As the child is coping with acquiring two languages he/she does appear to make sense to be as consistent as possible if circumstances allow them. Introducing stable language-linked people who can bring a language to life and show the child a good reason for using it are worth cultivating. We must remember the magical age of three, when the child has managed to get through all the stress and difficulties of the Terrible Twos, both linguistically and emotionally and emerges as a bilingual child.

However, all this good work can be undone by the arrival of siblings or changes in countries and even parental language choice. Children do adapt although they may exhibit some language delay or reluctance to speak one language while changes are going on. Consistency gives the child a framework although no parent can fully pass on a language and culture single-handedly. Simply only using your language will not guarantee bilingualism; a wide range of people, information and media is needed for that. The parent is the starting point and the child's best reference point about what is right or wrong to say or do within a language and culture.

The Possible Effects of School and Peer Pressure on Language Use

As Chapter 3 describes the pressure of school and how its workload and peer pressure can shift from a more-or-less balanced bilingual child to one speaking only the majority-language. Parents often lose their control over children's language use, opinions and friendships when they start school. They may feel more pressure themselves to conform and fit in with other parents, thus prefer using the majority-language rather than standing out from the crowd. Children playing or visiting the home may provoke requests that a parent does not speak the minority-language too. At this stage the minority-language needs help and active use, either in holidays or outside school. One parent will need to work on balancing the skills to compensate for the speed the children are progressing cognitively in the school-language. This can cause problems for parents and even children, who are conversationally good at the language but lack the academic skills. It is the most crucial time for language loss and needs attention to keep the minority-language alive and well.

Extended Family Involvement and Gaining Their Support

The role of the family cannot be underestimated as we saw in Chapter 4. The influence of grandparents, aunts, uncles, cousins and close family friends is essential. Their involvement and positive support can inspire a child to actually use a language and keep going, as they grow older. The monolingual environment they provide can work to the child's benefit and this allows the child to see a different way of life and language use.

On the other hand, we often hear of negative family reactions – unwillingness to allow the minority-language to be spoken, misunderstandings and a dislike of language mixing and code-switching. The key is to explain the situation clearly to everyone and show him or her what they can do. One good thing about bilingual children is that progress is often fast and the extended family can feel a warm glow of pride by helping the child say something, by singing a song or by having a long conversation with them.

Trilingual and Multilingual Families

The addition of a third or fourth language in a bilingual family is not as common as two languages but it is a growing group of families. We see in Chapter 5 the various kinds of families and how OPOL can be used as a base. The juggling of language and cultural input remain the same as the bilingual family and like bilingual family they need to carefully consider the schooling, ask the extended family to help and monitor languages which are becoming too dominant or under-used.

Parents as Role Models

The parent's attitudes and beliefs in the concept of bilingualism can greatly affect the future bilingualism of a child. Those who do not fully accept it or feel threatened by it will pass these thoughts onto a child. Parents who are essentially monolingual will have a different relationship with a child than those who are bilingual. Chapter 6 also looked at some of the difficult issues which can arise when living in a bilingual family, such as one parent feeling isolated, family separation or speech problems in a child. These problems can be overcome but the family may find it hard to keep going with their original plans for bilingualism and then it is truly tested. As the comments from parents show there are many advantages and disadvantages for bilingualism, which need to be balanced. A child may achieve your dreams but equally there may be times when it all seems too much. Often strangers think it is so easy to bring up your children bilingually but the reality is often more complicated with periods of success and times when the child cannot or will not speak one of the languages.

Choose a Strategy to Support the Minority-Language

In Chapter 7 we see a summary of several different language strategies – OPOL, mL@H, Trilingual, Time and Place, and Mixed. These strategies are not legally binding and can be adapted to suit any family. The key issue is to find out which strategy is best for your family. The first thing to consider is the bilingualism level of the parents and whether one of them is bilingual. If so then the next step is to decide the language of communication between the parents. The data suggests that this is extremely important as it can give extra input to a minority-language or conversely strengthen the effect of the majority-language for the child. The fine-tuning of the OPOL approach can be done in stages but is dependent on factors such as location, the period of time one is intending to live in a place/country and on the kind of schooling. Many parents did change or adapt their strategy to changing circumstances, and as long as there is some consistency in the early years and explanation to older children, it should work.

Parents, who both can and want to speak the minority-language in a majority-language country, are better off choosing a mL@H option. The trilingual strategies and mixed strategies generally apply to parents who are both bilingual and passing on a model of their own language use that includes switching languages regularly. Parents wanting to reinforce or maintain a language many consider Time and Place or use it to add on a third language to a bilingual child.

OPOL for the Twenty-First Century

We need to consider how the OPOL approach can be improved and be made more applicable to the twenty-first century. Life has changed greatly as families live apart and have less contact with each other. Women are working as many hours as men now and children live much more pressured and organised lives than before. Women in the Western world now have children later in life, and having extended families to help out with childcare is often not an option for many of them. Although in an ideal world the minority-language grandparents and cousins would help with the child's language learning, we consider this a bonus now not a normal state of affairs. The minority-language working woman cannot pass on her language adequately if she is absent most of the day and like the working father, she needs to organise some other language input such as a nanny, an au pair or a school using her language.

Children may be an only child, or have less brothers and sisters these days, as birth rates plummet due to economic reasons, birth control and improved health conditions. The dynamics of a small family of one or two children compared to a large one with three or more children will be different. It would be more parent-child centred than child-child centred and this can affect language use too. Typically with a large family the children decide which language to use together so having fewer children means parents can control their language more. Children's lives now are full of planned activities, extra-curriculum sports, dancing, singing and music classes, organised trips out and so on. They have more pressure to achieve at school and keep up with their peer-group. This can sometimes put bilingual language learning into the uncomfortable role of another thing to be learnt or a parental achievement issue. Grammont initially wanted a 'natural' way of learning languages at home, out of the classroom. Nevertheless, children certainly need some 'tuition' in at least one language and if it is kept fun they can enjoy being taught by a parent or not even realise it is teaching! Parents wanting children who are bilingual and biliterate need to commit themselves to years of extra study for a good level of writing and reading skills. One positive thing that has happened is that in the twentieth century we have improved global communication and can utilise the telephone, internet, photos and cheap air-travel to allow us to keep in touch with family members who are at a distance.

The OPOL Approach For the Twenty-First Century: Ten Key Points to Think About

(1) It should ideally used with young children up to the age of three as consistently as possible.

(2) The father's language use may be delayed, due to lack of input and the child's natural closeness to mother but can come into it's own around age three and four.

(3) When school starts OPOL may need to be modified to take account of homework/friends/peer group pressure. Parents can be less strict on language use, accept situational switching and translate if necessary but the minority-language should be of importance too and integrated alongside work/experiences done in the majority-language.

(4) OPOL parents also need to provide a one-person-one-culture environment once language acquisition is steady so a bicultural child who will feel at home in either country or culture.

(5) The extended family and closely linked people such as nannies and au-pairs and friends also play a role as one-person-one-language role models. They should be encouraged to play a role, which will benefit them in the long run too when the child has a reason to communicate with them.

(6) Parents need some knowledge of the other parent's language and should ideally be supportive and enjoy hearing their partner use their language.

(7) Parents will need to commit to helping their children to become literate in both languages and allocate time for informal and formal language teaching at home.

(8) Siblings will create their own language environment, independently of the parents and cannot be forced to use a certain language together. They can increase use of either majority or minority-language use in the home, depending on circumstances.

(9) OPOL families ideally need to use the minority-language between parents to balance out the strength of the community or majority-language. Therefore the best option is OPOL – mL – an OPOL approach supported by majority-language parent.

(10) A minority-speaking mother living in a majority-speaking country has more chance of keeping the two languages strong as long as she doesn't revert to the majority-language when school/peer pressure starts.

I hope these recommendations help bilingual families. As a final word I would like to remind families that a positive attitude, parents who can either speak or appreciate each other's languages and enjoy being bilingual and bicultural will have more chances of success. Families over the years will have many challenges and testing times. Even the best planning cannot prevent external factors such a family criticisms or children refusing to speak a language at some stage. However, when you hear your children chatting happily with monolinguals or switching effortlessly from language to language you know are on the right path and can relax and enjoy being a unique bilingual family. I would like to leave you with this quote from a trilingual Polish/English family living in Germany.

Perhaps the most important aspect of bringing up children bilingually is the personal connection it provides between parent and child. What a marvellous feeling of 'close-bonding' one experiences daily. This is something monolinguals would rarely experience. When collecting your child from Kindergarten in front of his peers and teachers suddenly bursting forth in your language telling you all his news or even asking 'What's for dinner?', often leaving confused looks all around! That's when you experience a feeling of being really close to your child because it's just for you. When visiting close family and seeing the children chatting happily with the family there is a great sense of satisfaction, because you realise that this was in fact the only way to raise the children and what a gift the children have!

Appendix 1: Studies on Bilingual Children

With reference to McLaughlin (1978: 87), Taeschner (1983: 7), Hoffmann (1995: 50–2). Note that some of these studies took more specific time periods than others. The authors' original notation has been used in the table.

Author	Year	Languages	Time	Children
Ronjat	1913	French/German	First 5 yrs	1
Pavlovitch	1020	French/Serbian	First 2 yrs	1
Hoyer and Hoyer	1924	Russian/German	First year	1
Smith	1935	English/Chinese	First 4 yrs	8
Emrich	1938	German/Bulgarian	First 3 yrs	1
Leopold	1939–49	German/English	First 2 yrs and 2–12 yrs	1
Burling	1959	Garo/English	1; 4–2; 10	1
Imedadze	1960, 1967	Russian/Georgian	0; 11–3.0	1
Tabouret-Keller	1962	French/Alsatian	1; 8–2; 11	1
Raffler-Engal	1965	English/Italian	First 4 yrs	1
Murrel	1966	Swedish/Finnish/English	2; 0–2; 8	1
Ruke-Dravina	1967	Swedish/Latvian	First 6 yrs	2
Mikes	1967	Hungarian/Serbo-Croatian	First 6 yrs	3
Oksaar	1970	Swedish/Estonian	0; 2–3.0	1
Swain	1972	English/French	2; 4–4.0	1
Volterra and Taeschner	1975	German/Italian	1–3 yrs	2
Bergman	1976	English/Spanish	10 mths–2 yrs	1
Calasso and Garau	1976	English/Italian	First 5 yrs	1
Bizarri	1977	English/Italian	First 3.5 yrs	2

Author	Year	Languages	Time	Children
Oksaar	1977	Swedish/Estonian/ German	1–4 yrs	1
De Matteis	1978	German/Dutch/ Italian	1–2/6–7/ 7–8/8–9 yrs	4
Itoh and Hatch	1978	Japanese/English	2; 6–3; 1	1
Celce-Murcia	1978	French/English	2.4	1
Redlinger and Park	1980	German/Spanish German/English German/French	2–3 yrs 5–8 mths 5–8 mths	4
Cunze	1980	German/Italian	First 5.5 yrs	1
Arnberg	1981	English/Swedish	First 5 yrs	4
Vihman	1985	Estonian/English	1; 1–2; 10	1
Saunders	1982, 1988	German/English	First 13 yrs	3
Taeschner	1983	German/Italian	First 8 yrs	2
Meisal	1984, 1987	German/French	1; 0–4; 0	2
Vila	1984	Catalan/Spanish	1; 2–3; 2	3
Fantini	1985	Spanish/English	First 11 yrs	1
Hoffmann	1985	German/Spanish/ English	First 8 yrs	2
Levy	1985	Hebrew/English	1.7 onwards	1
Deucher and Quay	1989	Spanish/English	1.7–2.3 yrs	1
Goodz	1989	French/English	1.2–4.9	4
De Houwer	1990	English/Dutch	2.7–3.4 yrs	1
Schlyter	1990	German/French	1.11–3.5/2.4– 3.4/1.10–3.5	3
Dopke	1992	German/English	2; 4/2; 8 (6 mths recordings)	6
Meisal and Muller	1992	German/French	1.6–5.0/1.5– 4.3/1.5–4.0	3
Lanza	1992	Norwegian/English	2; 0–2; 7	1
Stavans	1992	Hebrew/Spanish/ English	2; 6–3; 9/ 5.5–6; 8	2
Helot	1988	English/French/ Irish	?	2
Nicoladis and Genesee	1989	French/English	2; 0–3; 6	15

Author	Year	Languages	Time	Children
Widdecombe	1999	English/Italian/French	4; 4–4; 5	1
Mishima	1999	English/Japanese	1; 10–2.2	1
Caldas and Caron-Caldas	2000	French/English	7–10 yrs (twins) and 9–12 yrs	3
Jisa	2000	English/French	2.3–2.5/3.6–3.8	2
Juan-Garau and Perez-Vidal	2000, 2001	Catalan/English	1; 3–4; 2	1
Nicoladis and Secco	2000	Brazilian/English	1.0–1.6	1
Yip and Matthews	2000	Cantonese/English	1–6 yrs	1
Shi	2001	Chinese/Japanese/English	?	1
Quay	2001	English/German/Japanese	0; 11–1; 9	1

Appendix 2: The 2001 OPOL Questionaire

Section A: General Family Background – To Be Filled in By Both Parents Together

(1) Where do you currently live?

(2) What is your current job or occupation?

(3) How long have you lived in your current country of residence? *(Please circle one).*
1–3 years   4–9 years   10 or more years.

(4) How long do you intend to stay in this country?   *(Please circle one).*
1–3 years   4–9 years   10 or more years.

(5) Which languages are used in the family?

		LANGUAGE In order of proficiency	SKILLS (E.g. Speaking, Reading, Writing & Listening)	WHERE LEARNT? (E.g. Home, School, Communitie or Other)
Father	1st			
Nationality	2nd			
	3rd			
Mother	1st			
Nationality	2nd			
	3rd			
Child 1	1st			
	2nd			
	3rd			
Child 2	1st			
	2nd			
	3rd			
Child 3	1st			
	2nd			
	3rd			

What languages are used by family members?

Mother to Father.
Father to Mother.
Mother to child/ren.
Father to child/ren.
Child to child/ren.
Child/ren to both parents.

If you use different languages for each child please give details:

(7) What was/is the language of instruction at school?

	PRESCHOOL (under 5)	PRIMARY (6–11)	SECONDARY (12–16)	COLLEGE (if applicable)	UNIVERSITY (if applicable)
Father					
Mother					
Child 1					
Child 2					
Child 3					

(8) How many other bilingual families do you meet regularly (i.e. once or twice a month). *(Please circle one).*
    None   1–5   6–10   More than 10.

(9) If you need advice on bilingualism where would you look? *(Please circle all those that apply).*
    Books for bilingual families.
    Internet and websites.
    The Bilingual Family Newsletter.
    Local support groups in first language.
    Family and friends.
    Other bilingual families.
    Other.

Section B: Being a Bilingual Family – Mother and Father to Complete Separately

(1) What kind of language strategy do you use in your family? *(Please circle one).*
    I speak only my language, my partner only speaks his/hers.
    We mostly speak my language.
    We mostly speak my partner's language.

We speak another language.
We mix languages and use whichever language is appropriate.
We have no strategy.
Other.

(2) When did you start this strategy? *(Please tick as appropriate)*.

	Child 1	*Child 2*	*Child 3*
In the first year after birth			
Preschool age (2–5 yrs)			
Primary School age (6–11 yrs)			
Secondary School age (11+)			

(3) Has your strategy changed? Yes *(Please give details)* No.

(4) How do feel when your partners speaks his/her language to your children?

(5) What do you do when you are with family and friends who are speaking your partner's language? *(Please circle one)*.
I continue to speak my language to everyone.
I continue to speak my language only to my children.
I speak the language of the group to everyone.
I speak the language of the group to my children.
I ask my partner to translate.
Other.

(6) How do the grandparents (if applicable) feel about your language strategy? *(Please circle one)*.
They are supportive and encouraging.
They accept our language strategy.
They ignore my partners language.
They are not supportive of our language strategy.
Please give more details about your extended family attitudes towards your bilingual children.

(7) How do you feel if your child mixes his or her languages? *(Please give details)*.

(8) How do you define yourself culturally?
A family with one culture.
A family with a deeper knowledge of one culture than another.
A family with two cultures, both fairly well developed.
A family with two cultures and knowledge of a third.
A family with more than three cultures.
Other.

(9) Is it important for you to pass on your culture? *(Please give details)*.

(10) In what ways do you pass on the culture of your country? *(Please circle all those that apply).*
Trips to visit family and friends.
Reading books.
Watching videos/films.
Singing songs/listening to music.
Family history (i.e. photograph albums).
Other.

(11) How do your children react to living with two cultures?

(12) For you, what are the advantages and positive aspects of being a bilingual family?

(13) For you, what are the disadvantages and negative aspects for of being a bilingual family?

(14) What have you read or heard about the one-parent-one-language (OPOL) approach?

Appendix 3: Parent's Nationalities and Country of Residence

Parents nationalities	Father	Mother	Total
British	41	11	52
French	10	8	18
American	8	9	17
German	5	10	15
Dutch	3	10	13
Swedish	2	6	8
Finnish	2	5	7
Japanese	2	5	7
Italian	3	3	6
Australian	2	1	3
Austrian	2	1	3
Danish	2	1	3
Greek	1	2	3
Hungarian	2	1	3
Canadian		3	3
Spanish	1	1	2
New Zealander	1	1	2
Israeli	2		2
Argentinian		1	1
Brazilian		1	1
Chinese		1	1
Croatian		1	1
Norwegian		1	1
Russian		1	1

Parents nationalities	Father	Mother	Total
Welsh	1		1
Costa Rican		1	1
Peruvian	1		1
American/Austrian	1		1
American/British		2	2
American/Canadian	1		1
American/German		1	1
American/Irish		1	1
American/Italian		1	1
British/Chilean		1	1
British/Norwegian		1	1
British/Yugoslavian		1	1
TOTAL	**93**	**93**	**186**

Country of residence			
UK	36	Wales	2
US	9	Greece	1
Netherlands	7	Hungary	1
France	6	Ireland	1
Germany	6	Israel	1
Japan	5	Italy	1
Austria	3	Scotland	1
Belgium	3	Singapore	1
Finland	3	Hong Kong	1
Australia	2	New Zealand	1
Spain	2	**TOTAL**	**93**

Appendix 4: Case Study Families List

Case study	Chapter	Title
1	Chapter 2	Richard and Elisabeth – A bilingual upbringing for Max's mother and strong family support
2	Chapter 2	Vilma – Keeping Spanish and French strong whilst on sabbatical in Canada
3	Chapter 2	Janet – Helped found the ImF group for bilingual families in Germany
4	Chapter 2	Martine and Nicolas – Changed from using Dutch together to support French learning
5	Chapter 2	Izumi – Japanese/English family keeping Japanese culture alive in London
6	Chapter 3	Cornelia – Increasing German input by their choice of school
7	Chapter 3	Christine – Scottish-Spanish blend of cultures in the Galician region of Spain
8	Chapter 3	Jane – Englishwoman settled with her Finnish family and local community
9	Chapter 3	Caroline – Mix of Dutch and Arabic cultures in Qatar
10	Chapter 3	Louise – The New Zealand connection is 'cool' for kids in Japan
11	Chapter 4	Pierre – Following a 'one grandparent-one language' approach with great success
12	Chapter 4	Mary – Bilingual grandmother helping her daughters bring up their children bilingually too

Case study	Chapter	Title
13	Chapter 4	Nicola W – Spanish language helps keep her Anglo-Chilean family heritage strong
14	Chapter 4	Hedi – A Hungarian/English family with Jamaican roots
15	Chapter 5	Erika B – Husband sometimes feels excluded in German/English household
16	Chapter 5	Nicola N – English/German family living in an Austrian village
17	Chapter 5	Jeanne – A new life in Denmark for Danish/Swiss one parent family
18	Chapter 5	Erika J – Return to Switzerland for Swiss/Australian family
19	Chapter 5	Ann – Swedish/English family struggling to get help with speech disorder
20	Chapter 6	Miklos – French-Canadian and Hungarian couple using English as a third language
21	Chapter 6	Ljiljana – Serbian/Arabic trilingual and tricultural family based in London
22	Chapter 6	Lon – Dutch and Welsh trilingual family living in bilingual community of North Wales
23	Chapter 6	Judith – Danish/German trilingual family living in England and rotating language use
24	Chapter 6	Helen – Norwegian/English/French trilingual family now living in London
25	Chapter 7	Gisela and Larry – From Switzerland to America with support for the minority-language
26	Chapter 7	Ingrid – German-speaking parents in the Netherlands using English at home
27	Chapter 7	Paul and Jozette – Dutch heritage in Australia supported with mL@H strategy
28	Chapter 7	Jose – a mixed language approach in a bilingual community in Italy
29	Chapter 7	Diane – a more relaxed OPOL approach in French/English family
30	Chapter 7	Reva – American mother using the OPOL approach to bring up children bilingually

Sources of Information for Bilingual Families

Internet

info@multilingual-matters.com	Request a copy of *The Bilingual Family Newsletter*
www.multilingual-matters.com	Books on bilingualism and multilingualism
www.interculturalpress.com	Cross-cultural books
biling-fam@nethelp.no	Internet list to meet other bilingual families online
biling-fam-digest-subscribe@nethelp.no	Digest version of above internet list
http://www.nethelp.no/cindy/ biling-fam.html	Information put together from biling-fam site
http://www.bilingual-supplies.co.uk	Range of different language books, etc. for children
www.bookswithoutborders.com	Range of different language books, etc. for children
www.multilingualbooks.com	Range of different language books, etc. for children
www.bilingualbooks.com	Range of different language books, etc. for children
http://www.edu.bham.ac.uk/ bilingualism/database/ctlfam.htm	Database from University of Birmingham, UK
http://www.babyparenting.about. com/cs/childbilingualism/	References on articles/books on bilingualism
http://www.linguistlist.org	Updates on conferences
http://www.multi-faceta.com	References and updates
http://www.juniorlinguist.com	Reviews and information
http://www.kagawa-jc.ac.jp/~steve_ mc/jaltbsig	Link to Japanese bilingual family support group
www.mehrsprachige-Familien.de	Link to German bilingual family support group

Books

L. Arnberg (1987) *Raising Children Bilingually: The Pre-school Years*	Multilingual Matters
C. Baker (2000) *A Parents and Teachers Guide to Bilingualism*	Multilingual Matters
A.-M. de Meija (2002) *Power, Prestige and Bilingualism*	Multilingual Matters
M. Yamamoto (2001) *Language Use in Interlingual Families*	Multilingual Matters

E. De Jong (1986) *The Bilingual Experience* — Cambridge University Press

J. Hamers and M. Blanc (2000) *Bilinguality and Bilingualism* — Cambridge University Press

E. Harding and P.Riley (1996) *The Bilingual Family – A Guidebook for Parents* — Cambridge University Press

U. Cunningham-Andersson (1999) *Growing Up With Two Languages* — Routledge

S. Döpke (1992) *One Parent, One Language. An Interactional Approach* — John Benjamins

C. Hoffmann (1991) *An Introduction to Bilingualism* — Longman Linguistics

S. Romaine (1995) *Bilingualism* — Blackwell

D. Romano (2001) *Intercultural Marriage* — Intercultural Press

T. Tokuhama-Espinosa (2001) *Raising Multilingual Children* — Bergin and Garvey

L. Wei (2000) *The Bilingualism Reader* — Routledge

Journals

Applied Linguistics — Codeswitching, applied linguistics

Bilingualism – Language and Cognition — Applied linguistics

International Journal of Bilingual Education and Bilingualism — Bilingual Education

International Journal Of Bilingualism — Sociolinguistics and applied linguistics

International Journal of the Sociology of Language — Sociolinguistics, multilingualism

Journal of Child Language — Child related language issues

Journal of Language and Social Psychology — Sociology

Journal of Multilingual and Multicultural Development — Language contact and bilingualism

Journal of Pragmatics — Codeswitching, applied linguistics

Language in Society — Sociolinguistics

Language Learning — Language learning and policy

Multilingua — Bilingualism and referential meaning

Glossary

anomie: A state of mind when a person feels he/she does not belong in a culture or feels distanced and unable to participate.

Artificial or Non-Native strategy: Parents of the same language and culture who decide to bring up their children from birth using another language. Can be one parent or both.

assimilation: Process often seen in governments and in education to strongly influence bilinguals to use only the majority-language of the country or school for political unity and a national identity.

bicultural: Person who engages equally with two cultures.

bilingual: Person who speaks and understands two languages. They may well be able to read and write in both languages too, but this is not always the case.

Bilingual–Monolingual Interaction Strategy: The way we react to children's mixing. Either a bilingual one, i.e. we mix back or accept mixing in the child, or a monolingual one where we request only one language or pretend to not understand the other language. (See Elizabeth Lanza, 1997a.)

biliterate: Person who reads and writes in both languages.

code-switching: When bilinguals change language within the same sentence, either by inserting words from the other language or switching mid-sentence. It is grammatically correct in both languages and is used between two or more bilinguals who understand both languages. Code-switching can be influenced by the topic of conversation and shared experiences of the bilinguals.

code-mixing: See **mixing**.

country-language dominated: Bi/trilingual child who speaks the country or majority-language as their first language.

cultural acquisition: Process of learning about another culture, from a parent or a country.

cultural description: Description of a family as monocultural, bicultural etc. reflecting their balance of cultures.

cultural understanding: Empathy towards another person's cultural background.

cross-linguistic interference: When the two languages affect each other grammatically. Often seen in children when they transfer the grammar of one language across to another inadvertently. May only be on a temporary basis.

211

double identity: State when person feels he/she has two identities linked to two languages or cultures. See also **bicultural**.

family-language dominated: Bi/trilingual child who speaks a parental or minority-language as their first language.

False Monolingual strategy: Technique used by bilingual parents when their child is not speaking enough of their language. They pretend they don't understand the other language and push child to answer only in their language.

gender stability: Stage when the children understand the concept of gender so they behave in perceived gender-specific ways.

immersion: Intense period time spent using another language, either in a school or with family and friends. Sometimes used to top-up second language skills.

high impact beliefs: Theory that parents convinced that bilingualism will succeed have more chances for success. (See Annick de Houwer, 1999.)

interaction: The day to day communication between people.

L1: First language.

L2: Second language.

L3: Third language.

language accommodation: Person using their second or third language with a guest, neighbour or for business to aid communication.

language acquisition: Refers to how children informally 'acquire' or learn a language from their surroundings and input in their early pre-school years.

Language Acquisition Device: A theoretical brain process devised by Chomsky that allows children brains to acquire a high level of language skills in a short time. Also known as LAD.

language bath: Time spent in a country immersed in a language and culture usually with family or friends.

language differentiation: The stage when a child realises it has two languages in its range and begins to separate them mentally and verbally.

language order: The person' s strongest and most fluent language is listed as first, followed by second, third, etc.

language refusal: Refusal or resistance to use a certain language. Often found in young children and adolescents who will not use one language for various reasons such as power control, peer group influence or lack of knowledge.

language shift: The process of languages changing dominance over time. It can be within the family where the mother's language may be overshadowed by the father or in a country where political or sociological change elevates one language more than another.

lingua franca: Common language, such as English, used by two people with different languages for communication.

low impact beliefs: Theory that parents not convinced that bilingualism will work have less chance of success. (See Annick de Houwer, 1999.)

majority-language: A language with relatively higher prestige and power. Also used in this book to refer to the language used by the parent living in his or her country who is supported by the community in language input.

metalinguistic skills: An increased awareness of the overall form and structure of language, which can help with decoding skills such as reading and writing.

minority-language: A lower status language. Also used in this book to refer to the language spoken by the parent living outside their country/language area who lacks community support.

Minority-Language at Home: Both parents choose to speak the minority-language together and to their children at home. Also known as **mL@H.**

mixing: A term used by some authors to refer to young children who mix two languages, either by inserting words from the other language or switching languages mid-sentence. Children can use it as a way to communicate with other bilinguals, or they may use words that they do not yet know the equivalent for. See also **code-switching**.

Mixed strategy: Bilingual parents mix both languages together when conversing. Mixing is linked to topic or situation.

monocultural: Person who has one culture linked to their language.

monolingual: Person able to speak and understand one language. They can usually read and write in this language, but not always.

motherese/fatherese: The simplified version of speech that parents use when talking to a baby or young children. (See Snow & Ferguson, 1977.)

multilingual: Person who speaks three or more languages.

Non-Native strategy: See **Artificial strategy**.

One-Person-One-Language/One-Parent-One-Language: Grammont's term for the method of bringing up children bilingually where each person or parent only speaks their language to the child, ensuring pure language input and a strong parent-child bond. Also known as OPOL.

One-Parent-Two-Languages (or more): An extension of one-person-one-language/one-parent-one-language: for bi/trilingual parents who usually speak two languages to their children.

OPOL – ML: Strategy where the parents use the majority-language or country language between themselves.

OPOL – mL: Strategy where the parents use the minority-language of one parent living away from their country between themselves.

parental beliefs: Theory that parent's positive or negative attitudes towards being a bilingual family can affect the child's success or failure in being bilingual. (See Annick de Houwer, 1999)

parental strategies: The decision made by parents as to how they will bring up their children. See also **One-Person-One-Language, Minority-Language at Home, Artificial strategies**, etc.

passive bilingual: Person who has knowledge of two languages but only uses one. This may be because one or two languages are not developed or lack practice or opportunity to use.

prestigious languages: Those given high-status in society and often taught as a second language in schools.

sequential bilinguals: Children learning a second language later, after one language is already established.

simultaneous bilinguals: Children brought up with two languages from birth or from a very early age.

situational code-switching: Term for code-switching instigated by the context or place of the conversation with certain people. The context triggers the bilingual to use both languages.

Time and Place strategy: Language learning and practice linked to a certain place, such as a holiday home, or a time, like an extra-curricular class or using a certain language at the dinner table.

tricultural: Person who identifies with three cultures.

trilingual: Person who speaks three languages.

Trilingual/Multilingual strategy: Child is brought up simultaneously with three languages from parents living in a third language country, using a third language together or living in a trilingual region.

une personne; une langue: Grammont's original term for one-person-one-language.

References

Arnberg, L. (1987) *Raising Children Bilingually: The Pre-School Years*. Clevedon: Multilingual Matters.

Baker, C. (2000) *A Parents' and Teachers' Guide to Bilingualism* (2nd edn). Clevedon: Multilingual Matters.

Baetens-Beardsmore, H. (1982) *Bilingualism: Basic Principles*. Clevedon: Multilingual Matters.

Bain, B. and Yu, A. (1980) Cognitive consequences of raising children bilingually: One parent, one language. *Canadian Journal of Psychology* 34 (4), 304–13.

Barron-Hauwaert, S. (1999) Trilingualism – issues surrounding trilingual families. Unpublished MEd dissertation, University of Sheffield, UK.

Barron-Hauwaert, S. (2000a) Trilingual families – living with three languages. *The Bilingual Family Newsletter*, 17 (1). Clevedon: Multilingual Matters.

Barron-Hauwaert, S. (2000b) Issues surrounding trilingual families – children with simultaneous exposure to three languages. Paper presented at Innsbruck Conference on Trilingualism and Third Language Acquisition. Available at http://www.ualberta.ca/~german/ejournal/barron.htm

Barron-Hauwaert, S. (2002) The one-parent – one-language approach and its role in the bilingual family. Paper presented at Vigo Symposium on Bilingualism.

Barron-Hauwaert, S. (2003) Trilingualism – a study of children growing up with three languages. In T. Tokuhama-Espinosa (ed.) *The Multilingual Mind* (pp. 129–50). Westport, CT: Praeger.

Bentahila, A. and Davies, E. (1994) Two languages, three varieties: code-switching patterns of bilingual children. In G. Extra and L. Verhoeven (eds) *The Cross-Linguistic Study of Bilingual Development* (pp. 113–23). Netherlands: Royal Netherlands Academy of Arts & Sciences Press.

Brewer, S. (2001) *A Child's World*. London: Headline.

Bilingual Family Newsletter, The (1997–2003) Vols 14–20, Nos. 1–4. Clevedon: Multilingual Matters.

Caldas, S.J. and Caron-Caldas, S. (2000) The influence of family, school and community on bilingual preference: Results from a Louisiana/Quebec case study. *Applied Psycholinguistics* 21, 365–81.

Child, I.L. (1943) *Italian or American? The Second Generation in Conflict*. Russell and Russell: New York.

Chomsky, N. (1964) *Current Issues in Linguistic Theory*. The Hague: Mouton.

Coates, J. (1988) *Women, Men and Language: A Sociolinguistic Account of Sex Differences* (2nd edn, 1993). London: Longman.

Crystal, D. (1987) *Child Language, Learning and Linguistics*. London: Edward Arnold.

Cunningham-Andersson, U. and Andersson, S. (1999) *Growing Up With Two Languages: A Practical Guide*. London: Routledge.

De Houwer, A. (1990) *The Acquisition of Two Languages from Birth: A Case Study*. Cambridge: Cambridge University Press.

De Houwer, A. (1995) Bilingual language acquisition. In P. Fletcher and B. MacWhinney (eds) *The Handbook of Child Language* (pp. 220–50). London: Blackwell.

De Houwer, A. (1999) Environmental factors in early bilingual development: The role of parental beliefs and attitudes. In G. Extra and L. Verhoeven (eds) *Bilingualism and Migration*. New York: Mouton de Gruyter.

De Houwer, A. (2004) Trilingual input and children's language use in Flanders. In C. Hoffmann (ed.) *Trilingualism in Family, School and Community* (pp. 118–38). Clevedon: Multilingual Matters.

Dehaene-Lambertz, G. and Houston, D. (1997) Faster orientation latencies toward native language in two-month old infants. *Language and Speech* 41 (1), 21–43.

Doyle, A., Champagne, M. and Segalowitz, N. (1977) Some issues in the assessment of linguistic consequences of early bilingualism. *Working Papers on Bilingualism* 14, 21–30.

Döpke, S. (1992a) *One Parent, One Language. An Interactional Approach*. Amsterdam: John Benjamins.

Döpke, S. (1992b) A bilingual child's struggle to comply with the 'one-parent-one-language' rule. *Journal of Multilingual and Multicultural Development* 13 (6), 467–85.

Ellis, R. (1995) *The Study of Second Language Acquisition*. Oxford: Oxford University Press.

Elwert, W.T. (1959) *Das Zweisprachige Individuum: Ein Selbstzeugnis*. Weisbaden: Franz Steiner Verlag.

Fantini, A.E. (1985) *Language Acquisition of a Bilingual Child*. Clevedon: Multilingual Matters.

Foley, J.A. (1998) Code-switching and learning among young children in Singapore. *International Journal of the Sociology of Language* 130, 129–50.

Fredman, M. (1995) Maintaining English as the home language in pre-school bilingual children in Israel. Paper presented at the *International Symposium on Communication Disorders in Bilingual Populations*, Haifa, Israel, 1–4 August.

Genesee, F. (1989) Early bilingual language development: one language or two? *Journal of Child Language* 16, 161–79.

Goodz, N.S. (1989) Parental language mixing in bilingual families. *Infant Mental Health Journal* 10, 25–44.

Grammont, M. (1902) *Observations sur le langage des enfants*. Paris: Mélanges Meillet.

Hamers, J. and Blanc, M.H.A. (2000) *Bilinguality and Bilingualism* (2nd edn). Oxford: Blackwell.

Harding, E. and Riley, P. (1986) *The Bilingual Family – A Handbook for Parents*. Cambridge: Cambridge University Press.

Harrison, G.J. and Piette, A.B. (1980) Young bilingual children's language selection. *Journal of Multicultural Development* 1 (3), 217–30.

Helot, C. (1988) Bringing up children in English, French and Irish: Two case studies. *Language, Culture and Curriculum* 1 (3), 281–7.

Hoffmann, C. (1985) Language acquisition in two trilingual children. *Journal of Multilingual and Multicultural Development* 6 (6), 479–95.

Hoffmann, C. (2001) Towards a description of trilingual competence. *International Journal of Bilingualism* 5 (1), 1–17.

Holm, H. (1998) Henrik's research. Online paper published in conjunction with the *biling.fam* site. Available at www.nethelp.no/cindy/biling-fam.html

Jisa, H. (2000) Language mixing in the weaker language. *Journal of Pragmatics* 32, 1363–86.

Juan-Garau, M. and Perez-Vidal, C. (2001) Mixing and pragmatic parental strategies in early bilingual acquisition. *Journal of Child Language* 28, 59–86.

Kenner, C. (2002) 'My sister, my teacher': Strategies used by bilingual siblings as mother-tongue literacy teachers. Paper presented at the *Second University of Vigo International Symposium on Bilingualism*, Vigo, Spain, 2002.

Lanza, E. (1992) Can bilingual two-year-olds code-switch? *Journal of Child Language* 19, 633–58.

Lanza, E. (1997a) *Language Mixing in Infant Bilingualism: A Sociolinguistic Perspective*. Oxford: Oxford University Press.

Lanza, E. (1997b) Language contact in bilingual two-year-olds and code-switching: language encounters of a different kind? *International Journal of Bilingualism* 1, 135–62.

Lambert, W.E. Giles, H. and Picard, O. (1975) Language attitudes in a French-American community. *International Journal of the Sociology of Language* 4, 127–52.

Lenneburg, E.H. (1967) *Biological Foundations of Language*. New York: Wiley.

Leopold, W.F. (1939, 1947, 1949a, 1949b) *Speech Development of a Bilingual Child: A Linguists Record* (in four parts). Evaston: Northwestern Press.

Lyon, J. (1996) *Becoming Bilingual*. Clevedon: Multilingual Matters.

McLaughlin, B. (1978) *Second-language Acquisition in Childhood*. Hillsdale, NJ: Lawrence Erlbaum Associates.

Meisel, J. (1989) Early differentiation of languages in bilingual children. In K. Hystenstam and L. Obler *Bilingualism Across the Lifespan. Aspects of Acquisition, Maturity and Loss* (pp. 13–40). Cambridge: Cambridge University Press.

Meisel, J. (1994) Code-switching in young bilingual children. *SLIA* 16, 413–39.

Mishima, S. (1999) The role of parental input and discourse strategies in the early language mixing of a bilingual child. *Multilingua* 14 (4), 317–42.

Moon, C., Panneton-Cooper, R. and Fifer, W.P. (1993) Two-day-olds prefer their native language. *Infant Behavior and Development* 16, 495–500.

Nicoladis, E. (1998) First clues to the existence of two input languages: Pragmatic and lexical differentation in a bilingual child. *Bilingualism: Language and Cognition* 1, 105–16.

Nicoladis, E. and Genesee, F. (1998) Parental discourse and code-mixing in bilingual children. *International Journal of Bilingualism* 2, 85–99.

Obied, V. (2002) Sibling relationships in the development of biliteracy and emergence of a bicultural identity. Paper presented at the *Second University of Vigo International Symposium on Bilingualism*, Vigo, Spain, 2002.

Omark, D.R. and Erikson, J.G. (eds) (1983) *The Bilingual Exceptional Child*. San Diego, CA: College Hill Press.

Paradis, J. (2001) Do bilingual two-year-olds have separate phonological systems? *The International Journal of Bilingualism* 5 (1), 19–38.

Pavlovitch, M. (1920) *Le langue enfantin: Acquisition du serbe et du francais par un enfante serbe*. Paris: Champion.

Pearson, B.Z., Fernandez, S.C., Lewedeg, V. and Oller, D.K. (1997) The relation of input factors to lexical learning by bilingual infants. *Applied Psycholinguistics* 18, 41–58.

Pérez-Bazán, M.J. (2002) Family matters: Determiners of language choice in early bilingual development. Paper presented at the *Second University of Vigo International Symposium on Bilingualism*, Vigo, Spain, 2002.

Pfaff, C. (1998) Changing patterns of language mixing in a bilingual child. In G. Extra and L. Verhoeven (eds) *Bilingualism and Migration*. New York: Mouton de Gruyter.

Quay, S. (2001) Managing linguistic boundaries in early trilingual development. In J. Cenoz and F. Genesee (eds) *Trends in Bilingual Acquisition* (pp. 149–200). Amsterdam: John Benjamins.

Ramjoue, B. (1980) *Guidelines for Children's Bilingualism*. Paris: Association of American Wives of Europeans.

Romaine, S. (1995) *Bilingualism* (2nd edn). Oxford: Blackwell.

Romaine, S. (2000) *Language in Society*. Cambridge: Cambridge University Press.

Romano, D. (2001) *Intercultural Marriage: Promises and Pitfalls* (2nd edn). London: Nicholas Brearly/Intercultural Press.

Ronjat, J. (1913) *Le developpment du langage observe chez un enfant bilingue*. Paris: Champion.

Saunders, G. (1982) Infant bilingualism: A look at some doubts and objections. *Journal of Multilingual and Multicultural Development* 3 (4), 277–92.

Saunders, G. (1988) *Bilingual Children: From Birth to Teens*. Clevedon: Multilingual Matters.

Schmidt-Mackay, I. (1977) Language strategies of the bilingual family. In W.F. Mackay and T. Andersson (eds) *Bilingualism in Early Childhood*. Rowley, MA: Newbury House.

Singleton, D. (2001) Age and second language acquisition. *Annual Review of Applied Linguistics* 21, 77–89.

Søndergaard, B. (1981) The decline and fall of an individual bilingualism. *Journal of Multilingual and Multicultural Development* 2 (4), 297–302.

Swain, J. (1992) *Girls, Boys & Language*. Oxford: Blackwell.

Taeschner, T. (1983) *The Sun is Feminine: A Study on Language Acquisition in Childhood*. Berlin: Springer Verlag.

Tokuhama-Espinosa, T. (2001) *Raising Multilingual Children: Foreign Language Acquisition and Children*. Westport, CT: Bergin & Garvey.

Wei, L. (ed.) (2000) *The Bilingualism Reader*. London: Routledge.

Wei, L., Miller, N. and Dodd, B. (1997) Distinguishing communicative differrence from language disorder in bilingual children. *The Bilingual Family Newsletter* 14 (1), 3–4. Clevedon: Multilingual Matters.

Widdicombe, S. (1997) Code-switching, coining and interference in trilingual first language acquisition: A case study. Unpublished MSc dissertation, University of Aston.

Werker, J.F. (1997) Exploring developmental changes in cross-language speech perception. In L. Gleitman and M. Liberman (eds) *An Invitation to Cognitive Science, Vol. 1, Language*. Cambridge, MA: The MIT Press.

Ziener, E. (1977) Experiences in the bilingual education of a child of pre-school age. *IRAL* 15, 143–8.

Index

Anomie 66, 67, 154
Arnberg, Leonore 5, 6, 141
Artificial Strategy 177, 178
Assimilation 49

Baker, Colin 6, 12, 38, 49, 84, 127, 141
Bicultural identity 66-68
Bilingual schooling 48, 49
Bilingual–Monolingual Interaction strategy 14

Code-switching 10-14, 17, 36, 93, 143, 147, 150, 170, 173, 174, 192-194
Cousins 85, 97-99, 100, 194, 195
Cultural heritage 59, 65, 113, 150,

De Houwer, Annick 31, 111, 124, 140
Döpke, Susanne 7, 38, 78, 96, 120, 163, 164

Exclusion 128
Extended family 4, 87-89, 103, 124, 128, 194, 196

False Monolingual 36-38
Fatherese 25, 26
Foreign language classes 53, 54

Gender differences 54-57, 70
Grammont, Maurice 1-4, 5, 10, 192, 196
Grandparents 70, 83-86, 88, 90, 114, 118, 194, 195

Hoffmann, Charlotte 28, 32, 40, 56, 85, 92, 139-142, 145, 171
Homework 52, 53, 70, 94, 123, 128, 145, 154, 196

Impact beliefs 111, 112
Isolation 66, 128

Language accomodation 123

Language acquisistion 24
Language differentation 31
Language refusal 33, 34
Leopold, Werner 2-6, 12, 36, 58, 78, 85, 92, 112, 117, 120, 123, 127, 129, 173, 179, 192

Maternal/paternal differences 117-120
Minority Language at Home 38, 58, 164, 165, 168, 169
Mixed strategy 96, 172-174, 180, 184, 193, 195
Mixing 10, 11, 13, 14, 17, 18, 31, 36, 86, 95, 96, 103, 172-174, 180, 193
Monolingual schooling 48-51, 70, 193
Motherese 25, 26

Non-Native strategy 177, 178, 181, 185,

One-culture-one-language 59
One-parent families 94, 127
One-parent-one-language approach 1-4, 7, 10, 13, 29, 38, 52, 112, 120, 129, 144, 150, 196
OPOL-ML strategy 165, 167

Parental beliefs 112
Parent–child conversations 77
Passive bilingualism 3, 25, 27, 34-36, 39, 57, 83, 96-99, 122, 125, 139, 141, 145, 147, 150, 169, 171, 178, 181, 182
Prestige value 120

Romaine, Suzanne 5, 6, 11, 48, 55, 120
Ronjat, Jules 1, 2, 3

Saunders, George 6, 7, 35, 36, 56, 58, 78, 92, 93, 112, 117, 120, 129, 130, 173, 177, 178, 192
Siblings 6, 12, 70, 92-97, 103, 128, 142, 152, 193, 197
Speech problems 50, 51, 85, 103, 123, 129-131, 194

Stages of development 30, 31

Taeschner, Traute 6, 17, 33, 36, 37, 40, 85, 112, 120,
Time and Place strategy 144, 175-177, 179, 180, 195
Tokuhama-Espinosa, Tracey 56, 93, 140, 176, 179,

Trilingual strategy 170-172, 179, 180, 181, 194
Trilingualism 28, 32, 35, 40, 56, 60, 70, 83, 85, 92, 98, 109, 122, 125, 132, 138-148, 149-156, 170, 171, 194
The 1999 Trilingualism Survey 149-156

Visitors 15, 27, 34, 35, 60, 99-102